DOUBLE TAKE

THE STORY OF THE ELGIN AND WINTER GARDEN THEATRES

HILARY RUSSELL

Design and Production: Andy Tong
Printing and Binding: Gagné Printing Ltd., Louiseville, Quebec, Canada

The publisher wishes to acknowledge the generous and ongoing assistance and ongoing support of **The Canada Council, The Book Publishing Industry Development Programme** of the **Department of Communications,** and **The Ontario Arts Council.**

Care has been taken to trace the ownership of copyright material used in the text (including the illustrations). The author and publisher welcome any information enabling them to rectify any reference or credit in subsequent editions.

J. Kirk Howard, Publisher

Canadian Cataloguing in Publication Data

Russell, Hilary.
   Double take : the story of the Elgin and Winter Garden theatres

Co-published by Ontario Heritage Foundation.
Includes bibliographical references.
ISBN 1-55002-057-9 (bound). - ISBN 1-55002-056-0 (pbk.)
1. Elgin Theatre (Toronto, Ont.) - History. 2. Winter Garden Theatre (Toronto, Ont.) - History. 3. Theatres - Ontario - Toronto - Conservation and restoration. I. Ontario Heritage Foundation. II. Title.

PN2306.T62E57 1989   792'.09713'541   C89-095247-7

Dundurn Press Limited
2181 Queen Street East, Suite 301
Toronto, Canada

The publication of *DOUBLE TAKE* was made possible through the support and resources of The Canadian Parks Service of Environment Canada, and the Ontario Heritage Foundation, an agency of the Ministry of Culture and Communications.

Illustration Credits

*Architects' and Builders' Magazine:*39(right)
*Architecture and Building:*29; 45(lower left and right); 47(upper right); 49.
Archives of Ontario:16(middle left, S312); 16 (lower right, S17268); 20 (L1307); 22(middle right, S15338).
Archives of the Theatre Historical Society of America: 42 (left and lower right); 67(right); 92(right); 123(left); 137(left).
Aylett, Charles (courtesy Royal Alexandra Theatre):27(right).
Bennie, Elsie, Collection:115(right).
Bernstein, Jules, Collection:121(left).
Birkmire, *The Planning and Construction of American Theatres:*39(upper and lower left).
Blakely, Clealon:83(upper left and right).
Brockman, Lance:91(lower middle).
Brown, Abbey, Collection (courtesy Andrew Johnson):90-91.
C.B.C. Collection, MISA, National Archives:143(right).
Canadian Parks Service:9(lower); 12(lower right); 72; 73(lower left); 77(lower left and right); 81; 87; 88(left); 94-95; 98; 110; 129.
City of Toronto Archives:16(upper left, SC608-21, lower left, SC267-42); 17 (James 10,009); 19(upper left, James 320); 56(SC488-1097); 132-33(SC488-1098).
Collections of the Municipal Archives of the City of New York: 45(middle left).
Construction: 4-5; 8(lower); 19(middle and right); 22(upper left); 23(upper left, lower left, upper right, lower right); 35(lower right); 53(upper and middle left); 58; 60; 61(lower left); 62; 66(right); 67(left); 68(upper right, lower left); 78(lower left); 86.
*Detroit Saturday Night:*53(lower right).
Drawing and Archives Collection of the Avery Architectural & Fine Arts Library: 40(upper left); 45(upper left); 135(upper).
Kobal Collection: 133(lower); 135(lower).
Library of Congress:34(right).
O.H.F. (Ontario Heritage Foundation), Janis Barlow:36(right); 37; 40(right); 41(middle and lower).
O.H.F., Gary Beechey:8(right); 9(upper left); 10; 11; 15; 54; 69; 73(right); 76; 77(upper left); 84(upper); 90; 91(upper middle and right, lower left); 97(lower left and right); 145; 146; 147; 148; 149; 150; 151.
O.H.F., Elgin and Winter Garden Collection: 57(right); 59; 61(upper left and lower right); 59; 61(upper left and lower right); 63; 65; 68(upper left); 134(upper left and lower right); 138(right); 141; 142; 143(left).
O.H.F., David Hannivan and Company: 12(upper right and left); 14.
O.H.F., Carol Priamo: 64; 78-79; 83(lower right).
O.H.F., Rick Upton:9(upper right).
Metropolitan Toronto Library Board:22(upper right, T12711, lower); 115(left, collection of Kay Slack Lane).
Museum of Modern Art/Film Stills Archive:131; 134(upper right); 136; 140.
National Archives of Canada:57(left, C-16934).
National Library of Canada, Music Division:127(left, NL16540).
National Vaudeville Artists' Yearbook: 23(lower middle); 43; 96(upper left); 105(right); 111(upper middle and lower right).
New York Public Library, Performing Arts Research Center, Billy Rose Theatre Collection:30; 31; 40(lower left); 93; 96(lower left): 96-7; 101(upper left and right); 102; 103; 104(right); 105(left); 109; 111(upper and lower left).
New York Public Library, Picture Collection:25(left).
Munsey's Magazine: 25(right).
Queen's University Archives, Strathy Smith Collection:122(left); 123(right); 124; 125; 126(upper right); 130; 137(upper and lower right); 138(left); 139.
Rambusch, Catha Grace, Collection: 50.
Scott, Douglas, Collection: 128.
Shubert Archive:27(left); 122(right).
Sprachman, Mandel, Collection:53(lower left); 66(left); 80.
Stewart, William, from *London Illustrated News,* Nov. 1954:127(right).
Theatre Collection, Museum of the City of New York: 34(upper and lower left); 35(upper and lower left); 36(left); 38; 41(upper); 47(lower left and right); 48; 84(lower); 88-89; 92(left); 96-7; 100.
Toronto Sun, Canada Wide Feature Services:126(lower left).
*Toronto Telegram:*117; 126.
Toronto Transit Commission Archives:121(right).
Weber and Fields: A Pictorial Souvenir, 1901: 101(lower left).
Wurlitzer Catalogue: 42(upper right).

CONTENTS

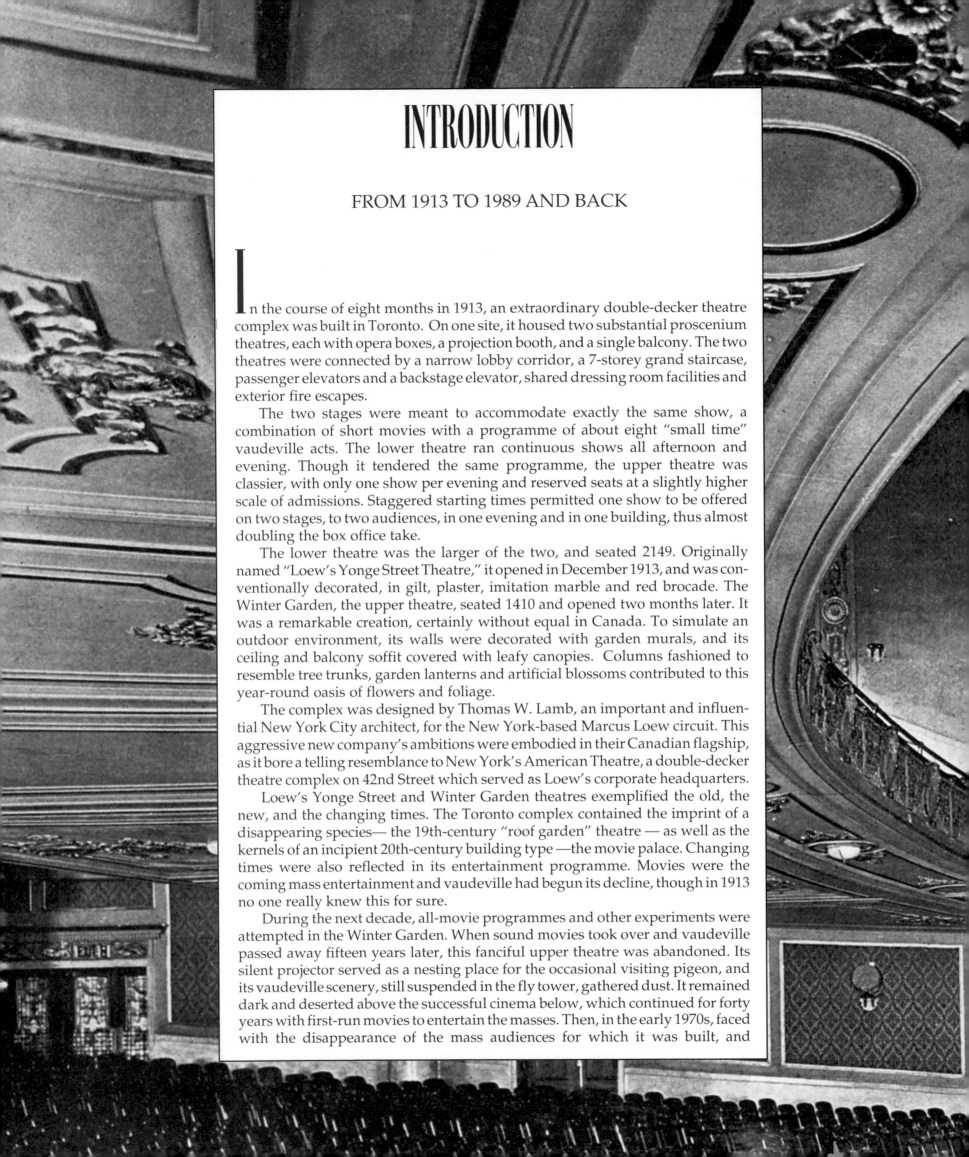

INTRODUCTION

FROM 1913 TO 1989 AND BACK

In the course of eight months in 1913, an extraordinary double-decker theatre complex was built in Toronto. On one site, it housed two substantial proscenium theatres, each with opera boxes, a projection booth, and a single balcony. The two theatres were connected by a narrow lobby corridor, a 7-storey grand staircase, passenger elevators and a backstage elevator, shared dressing room facilities and exterior fire escapes.

The two stages were meant to accommodate exactly the same show, a combination of short movies with a programme of about eight "small time" vaudeville acts. The lower theatre ran continuous shows all afternoon and evening. Though it tendered the same programme, the upper theatre was classier, with only one show per evening and reserved seats at a slightly higher scale of admissions. Staggered starting times permitted one show to be offered on two stages, to two audiences, in one evening and in one building, thus almost doubling the box office take.

The lower theatre was the larger of the two, and seated 2149. Originally named "Loew's Yonge Street Theatre," it opened in December 1913, and was conventionally decorated, in gilt, plaster, imitation marble and red brocade. The Winter Garden, the upper theatre, seated 1410 and opened two months later. It was a remarkable creation, certainly without equal in Canada. To simulate an outdoor environment, its walls were decorated with garden murals, and its ceiling and balcony soffit covered with leafy canopies. Columns fashioned to resemble tree trunks, garden lanterns and artificial blossoms contributed to this year-round oasis of flowers and foliage.

The complex was designed by Thomas W. Lamb, an important and influential New York City architect, for the New York-based Marcus Loew circuit. This aggressive new company's ambitions were embodied in their Canadian flagship, as it bore a telling resemblance to New York's American Theatre, a double-decker theatre complex on 42nd Street which served as Loew's corporate headquarters.

Loew's Yonge Street and Winter Garden theatres exemplified the old, the new, and the changing times. The Toronto complex contained the imprint of a disappearing species— the 19th-century "roof garden" theatre — as well as the kernels of an incipient 20th-century building type —the movie palace. Changing times were also reflected in its entertainment programme. Movies were the coming mass entertainment and vaudeville had begun its decline, though in 1913 no one really knew this for sure.

During the next decade, all-movie programmes and other experiments were attempted in the Winter Garden. When sound movies took over and vaudeville passed away fifteen years later, this fanciful upper theatre was abandoned. Its silent projector served as a nesting place for the occasional visiting pigeon, and its vaudeville scenery, still suspended in the fly tower, gathered dust. It remained dark and deserted above the successful cinema below, which continued for forty years with first-run movies to entertain the masses. Then, in the early 1970s, faced with the disappearance of the mass audiences for which it was built, and

increasingly specialized movies and movie audiences, along with the sharply declining appeal of attending a big, downtown movie house, the lower theatre became a venue for violent and semi-pornographic movies.

When property values in the downtown core began to escalate, it seemed only a matter of time before the wrecker's ball would deprive the world of one of its few remaining double-decker theatres, whose fantastically decorated and almost forgotten roof theatre was miraculously intact, a unique time-capsule of the vaudeville period. Happily, the Government of Ontario did not allow this to happen. It bought the theatres in order to restore them to life, to provide much needed mid-size performance spaces in Toronto, and to boost indigenous commercial theatre and theatrical talent.

In 1989, Toronto boasts a theatre complex even more extraordinary than the one built in 1913. The born again Elgin and Winter Garden theatres are better than ever. Two peerless historic theatres are carefully and lovingly restored to their original gilded and leafy glory, and their stages are alive again. The theatres once again exemplify the old, the new, and changing times. The extraordinary legacy from a bygone era has not been compromised, though it has been adapted for new uses and changing demands of theatre patrons, performers, and producers. The historic theatres are as modern, comfortable, and practical as possible, and they seem destined for stardom as modern performance spaces.

New cascading lobbies and ample 8-storey backstage additions afford the lounge, administration, rehearsal, assembly, service and storage spaces required in a commercially viable theatre building. These additions have been designed by architect Mandel Sprachman with the least possible disruption of the integrity and spirit of the historic building. This heritage is evoked in splendid original vaudeville drops, flats and curtains which adorn the new lobbies.

The restoration pays homage to the uniqueness of the complex in the Canadian architectural and cultural landscape; and to the decorative craftsmanship and ingenuity of the period. It entailed the replication and restoration of metres of relief and running plaster ornament, and all the gilded and marbleized surfaces of the lower theatre, lobby, and foyers, together with the Winter Garden's real beech branches, artificial blossoms, and garden lanterns. Fragile and soiled murals and vaudeville scenery, stunningly rendered in water-soluble scenic paint, have been cleaned and preserved for future generations.

Plaster decorations and features which had been sacrificed to later movie theatre improvements have been carefully restored. The lower theatre's boxes, proscenium arch and columns, sidewall decorations and balcony front ornament, all destroyed in 1960, have been replicated. Moulds were also made from sculpted clay models which reproduced vanished features: the acanthus leaf decoration of the proscenium arch, the gigantic plaster cartouche which had surmounted it, and the ornamental panels which had decorated the balcony and box fronts. A sculptor worked on site from surviving drawings and photographs of the lower theatre to recreate accurately these missing components. Profiles were cut and made to measure for the repair of plaster panels. Latex was brushed over surviving relief ornaments, producing new moulds to reproduce missing and damaged elements.

The restoration project enabled a band of talented young Canadians to become skilled craftsmen, trained in ancient decorating techniques. They repaired scagliola (plasterwork imitating marble) and replicated by hand painting over a thousand square metres of marbleized surfaces which had been stained, scratched or irretrievably damaged by rough sanding and overpainting. The restoration crew regilded by hand to original splendour the lobby, foyers and lower auditorium, patting on one quarter of a million [130 mm square] sheets of gossamer metal leaf, a quantity normally sufficient for all gilding projects in Canada for sixteen years. These featherweight sheets were applied, one at a time

Previous pages: The lower auditorium (originally "Loew's Yonge Street Theatre"), Thomas W. Lamb, architect. The original gilding, wall fabric, and imitation marble (or scagliola) wainscoting and columns seen in this photograph disappeared during subsequent renovations, as did the sidewall cornices and the large lattice ornaments above, the proscenium columns, proscenium arch, opera boxes, balcony front ornament, and the opalescent glass doors at the rear of the auditorium.

and overlapping, to a sticky sized and shellacked surface. Excess leaf was gently brushed off by hand, producing sparkling showers of "skewings". The shiny silver coating was then stained gold, and a final patina glaze applied. These surfaces will never tarnish and darken, unlike those treated with artificial gold leaf.

The restoration of the Winter Garden's unusual decorations posed singular conundrums. How were layers of soot and dust to be removed from the Winter Garden's water-soluble murals without ruining their painted florals, woodland creatures and garden walls? How could real beech leaves be enduringly preserved without excessive cost, and where and under what conditions might approximately 5,000 beech branches be harvested? More importantly, could these new leafy canopies now obtain building code approval?

Solutions found by restoration consultants David and Patti Hannivan mirrored the economy and ingenuity of 1913 concepts. They used an inexpensive and resourceful method of removing dirt and soot on the murals: all-purpose flour was mixed with water to yield small balls of bread dough. These balls were kneaded to just the right (non-sticky) consistency and rolled gently across painted surfaces. The bread dough picked up layers of surface dirt and soot, but almost magically left water-soluble decorations and wall finishes behind. Three hundred kilos of flour restored original brilliance to all painted wall surfaces and theatrical scenery, which were then sprayed with a protective waterproof sealant.

Some severely damaged areas of murals and scenery were repainted to blend imperceptibly with original decorations. Mural decorations directly above radiators required repainting because layers of soot and dirt had been baked on and could not be removed. Some mural areas had suffered water damage. In these areas, the most challenging task facing the restoration crew was to paint intricate florals and other details freely and quickly, capturing the verve and freshness of the original decorations, and to adjust to the varied styles of about four different muralists who had painted the Winter Garden's walls in 1914.

When the restoration project began, the Winter Garden's real beech branches and artificial leaves and blossoms were substantially intact on a wire grid suspended from the ceiling and balcony soffit. Originally covered with two shades of plum and green fireproof paint, the leaves and branches had become coated with soot deposited by decades of coal-burning boilers. The leaves, together with accompanying artificial blossoms of cotton, were deteriorated and brittle beyond repair.

Novel experiments and solutions permitted this integral aspect of the Winter Garden's magic to be recaptured. Few historic restoration teams in the world have required assistance from a Ministry of Natural Resources to find woodcutters and beech trees, and have travelled to various woodlots, armed with hand saws.

The woodcutters had to be willing to cut when trees were in full leaf and full of sap. Beech trees had to be found within an hour's drive of Toronto so that the branches could reach the preservation plant in Toronto before the leaves started to dry. This was no easy task, as the North American Beech is not abundant within this perimeter. Adding to timing complications of traffic jams and mud roads, the mission was also affected by the ravages of acid rain and an infestation of tent caterpillars, along with a sustained drought and heat wave in Ontario during the summer of 1988. Unhealthy, brown, and chewed leaves were obviously unsuitable candidates for preservation. These factors meant that a mature tree yielded only an average of 65 to 75 leafy branches of appropriate size and quality to decorate the Winter Garden.

Right: The lower auditorium (now the Elgin Theatre), photographed near the end of the renovation and restoration process in 1989. Damaged and vanished elements have been repaired and replaced, and its surfaces were still being painstakingly regilded and glazed by hand.

Left: The Winter Garden auditorium, photographed in 1914. Closed to the public since 1928, the Winter Garden remained miraculously untouched by progress. The most significant alteration was the 1919 installation of organ lofts and grilles in the sidewall arches.

Above: The replicated proscenium cartouche hovers over the lower stage while being raised into position. This feature, along with others which had disappeared during a major renovation in 1960, was modeled by sculptor Andrew Andrechuck.

Above: The regilded grand staircase leading to the Winter Garden, photographed in October 1989.

Right: View towards the Winter Garden's proscenium arch in 1975, looking much the same as it did in 1914.

Replicated opera boxes of the lower theatre, in the process of being regilded. Fascia ornament of the box on the left has received a preliminary coat of shellac. Corresponding ornament of the central box has advanced to an application of aluminum leaf and gold stain.

The regilding process. Plaster
of the opera boxes prior to
application of shellac and
aluminum leaf [Upper left]; a
patina glaze being brushed onto
gold-stained and silver surfaces
[Left]; and the glaze being wiped
off with cheesecloth rags to
produce a rich, burnished finish.
[Above]

Above: A vaudeville flat slightly damaged in storage being touched up and repaired

Above: The cleaning of fragile Winter Garden murals, executed in water-based scenic paint. Rolling across the surfaces small balls of bread dough removed decades of accumulated grime but left painted decorations intact.

Right: A view of the Winter Garden's original beech leaves, artificial blossoms, and garden lantern. These leaves were too brittle to survive the removal of their heavy coats of soot.

The reaping of beech branches was best accomplished early in the morning, at the tree's highest water retention level, and during late June and early July, before the onset of any recession into winter dormancy. Trimmed and loaded into vans, the branches were sprayed with water to forestall wilting. On arrival at the studio, their long stem ends were trimmed, crushed with mallets to increase absorbency, then dunked into solutions of glycerin and water. There they remained for five to seven days, until glycerin had replaced the water content of the branch, and the branches and leaves had turned a butterscotch colour. They were then spray painted in original colours in appropriate proportions.

These preserved branches have been woven into and suspended from new wire grids, and intermingled with cotton blossoms dyed in sprightly yellow, pink and blue hues, reproduced to match the originals. Adding to this multicolored vision are close to 200 suspended garden lanterns, in yellow, red, green and orange stained glass.

The painstaking and complicated restoration process with its acres of leaves, gilding and marbleizing as well as the planning and construction of new additions occupied a period of more than four years and cost $29,000,000 .

The cost of construction and the constraints Loew's theatre- building project faced in 1913 were altogether different. The original building cost about $500,000. Ground was broken in April, and the lower theatre opened on 15 December 1913. Marcus Loew, the owner of the circuit, came by special train from New York with some special guests for opening night, including theatrical tycoons Lee Shubert and A.L. Erlanger. Master songwriter Irving Berlin and the classic comedy team of Weber and Fields were guests in Loew's box and augmented the opening programme with performances on the lower stage before an audience dotted with posh people . Toronto politicians and millionaires turned out in force with their families. The "class" of the opening night audience — according to a newspaper report "one of the most fashionable ever witnessed here" [1]— challenged the relatively low status and admission price of the type of mass entertainment for which the theatre was built.

Lieutenant Governor of Ontario Sir John Gibson and his daughters occupied pride of place: the left centre box, which was draped with a large Union Jack. Among other Government big shots in attendance were Ontario Prime Minister Sir James Whitney (with his wife and daughter), Attorney General of Ontario the Honourable J.J. Foy, and the Mayor of Toronto, Horatio C. Hocken and members of the City Council.

Unfettered by conflict of interest guidelines, some government officials in attendance had leading roles in various financial institutions with vested interests in Marcus Loew's Toronto enterprise. Lieutenant Governor Gibson represented not only the Crown, but likely his Directorship of the Canadian Imperial Bank of Commerce. Attorney General Foy served as a Director of the Dominion Bank, the Toronto General Trusts Corporation and the Canadian Surety Co. Foy shared his stage box with Sir Lyman Melvin Jones, who was at once a Senator, President and General Manager of the Massey Harris Company, and a Director of the Canadian Imperial Bank of Commerce. In another box was Sir Edmund B. Osler of Osler and Hammond, stock brokers. He was a Vice-President of Dominion Bank, and a Director of Toronto General Trusts, Consumers Gas, Confederation Life and several other large corporations. In his party was Wilmot D. Matthews, a grain dealer and financial powerhouse who was the President of the Canada Foundry Company, a Director of Toronto General Trusts, and a Vice-President of Dominion Bank, Canada Permanent Mortgage Corporation, and Canadian General Electric.

Left: Original beech branches being removed in 1984. The restoration crew wore respirators for protection from the clouds of choking dust.

Below: Beech branches and leaves being preserved in troughs of glycerin and water. About 50 wooden troughs, 2 meters long and lined with plastic were used.

Left: Reaping beech branches. The trees felled were those already destined to be culled in a forest management programme.

Above: Spray paint cubicles devised for green and purple painting of preserved beech branches.

Above: The new backstage addition serves as a leaf painting studio in October 1989. Hanging branches have been spray painted green. Two shades of plum paint are being used to colour a smaller proportion of leaves, to match original Winter Garden samples.

Left: Hanging the painted beech leaves on a new wire grid.

Opening night dignitaries, 15 December 1913: Lieutenant-governor Sir John Gibson, Premier of Ontario Sir James Whitney, and Mayor of Toronto Horatio C. Hocken.

Other box and loge seats in the theatre were generously sprinkled with other members Toronto's commercial and financial elite and their families and friends, and with partners and chief executives of firms which had done or were expecting to do business with the theatre. Among the city's luminaries in attendance were John Ross Robertson, proprietor and publisher of the Evening *Telegram*, Joseph Atkinson, Managing Director of the Toronto *Star*, David R. Wilkie, President and General Manager of the Imperial Bank and another Director of Toronto General Trusts Corporation, Colonel George Sterling Ryerson, physician, author, retired member of Parliament and a founder of the Red Cross, and Royal Alexandra Theatre architect John Lyle.

The upper theatre opened two months later, on February 16, 1914. There was less fuss and few celebrities, though the Winter Garden was supposed to be the class of the operation. It charged up to 50 cents for a box seat, while tickets to the lower theatre's identical show ranged between 10 and 25 cents. By installing in the Winter Garden a policy of reserved seating, one evening show, and higher admissions, Loew was seeking to attract patrons of "big time" vaudeville.

Opening night audiences were introduced to a new, hybrid type of theatre building in Toronto, and a different, hybrid kind of entertainment. Loew's combined the numerous acts, the orchestras, fancy buildings and creature comforts of vaudeville with the cheap admissions, movies and continuous shows of the nickelodeon, or early makeshift cinema. The whole project was calculated to make Marcus Loew's competitors in Toronto, New York, and across the continent sit up and take notice.

Left: Before Loew's: the block of Yonge Street between Queen and Shuter selected for the entrance to the new theatres.

Below: View of Toronto skyline, about 1910. The roofs of two Toronto theatres on Adelaide Street, the Majestic (left) and the Grand Opera House, can be seen in the foreground.

Toronto in 1913

Between 1900 and 1913 Toronto had more than doubled its population — to about 500,000, occupying an area of some 30 square miles. This increase had been caused by Toronto's annexation of outlying municipalities and a flow of immigrants to the city who came from Ontario farms and overseas. As a result, many large banking, insurance, retail and manufacturing establishments in Toronto grew and flourished. A boom was very conspicuous in Toronto's construction industry, and in the expansion of its streetcar system, road paving, sewers and water mains. A 20th-century cityscape was heralded by two new 20-storey skyscrapers at King and Yonge Streets. A downtown business area devastated by the great fire of 1904 had been rebuilt, and an unprecedented number of new buildings — 10,217 — were recorded in City permit books in 1912.

The city's new affluence was reflected in recent cultural and recreational developments. Among these were the founding of the Toronto Symphony Orchestra, the building of the Mutual Street Arena and a new Central YMCA. Plans for the establishment of the Art Gallery of Ontario, the Royal Ontario Museum, and a zoo in Riverdale Park were well underway. Notwithstanding these proliferating recreational opportunities, Sunday diversions were strictly limited, and even tobogganing in High Park was prohibited on the Sabbath.

A 1913 publication summarized: "The city is well supplied with places of amusement, having 33 public parks, three beaches, free Zoological Gardens, an island devoted to summer amusements, a number of athletic fields, yachting, rowing and canoe clubs, 6 large theatres, and Massey Hall, seating 5,000 [sic]... It has the best annual exhibition in the world..."[2] Toronto also boasted "some very fine musical organizations," including such choirs as Mendelssohn's, Schubert's, and the National Chorus.

Toronto's sophistication in 1913 could also be seen in its 6 daily newspapers, 60 weeklies, and over 100 semi-weeklies and monthlies. There were three morning papers: the *Globe*, the *Mail and Empire*, and the *World*, with a combined circulation of over 150,000. Each evening, the *News*, the *Star* and the *Telegram* competed for a total of close to 190,000 readers.

Toronto publishers of an assortment of literary, society, religious, professional and trade weeklies and monthlies catered to a remarkably literate population. 1911 Census takers assessed that over 95% of the city's population could read and write. Toronto's women were slightly more literate than its men: 96.38% of females could read and write, compared to 95.94% males.

In spite of this picture of a leisurely and educated citizenry, Toronto's pockets of poverty should not be overlooked, nor the consideration that many of its citizens had little money, nor opportunity to indulge in literary pursuits and other entertainments.

According to *The Canada Year Book* for 1913, a typical family of five in the city lived on an income of $800 a year (or about $15.40 per week). The cost of living was rising steadily, as rents in Toronto had risen an astonishing 35.9% since 1910. This family spent, on an average, $11.70 weekly for food and rent, and $2.02 for "fuel, lighting, etc.", leaving little surplus for purchasing theatre tickets.[3]

CHAPTER ONE

SETTING THE STAGE: THE THEATRE BUSINESS IN TORONTO AND NEW YORK, 1913-14

In 1913 Canada's growing population and wealth were attracting the attention of American theatre entrepreneurs. A January article in *The New York Dramatic Mirror* raved about the new possibilities across the border:

> In point of fact, Canada has taken such a stride forward in her theatrical life during the past five years...its people, through necessity — and without much balking — have merged their amusement interests with those of the United States until today New York is as much the source of supply for Toronto and Montreal as for Pittsburgh and Buffalo. ...this is the day of a *theatrically new Canada*. Optimism is rampant. Towns and cities have almost gone delirious upon suddenly found wealth from land speculation. Thousands of eager spenders have been created, as it were, overnight ... Hence musical comedies and vaudeville have taken a vigorous vogue, likely to continue indefinitely.[1]

An upstart New York theatre tycoon, Marcus Loew, may have been encouraged by such a report to announce the building of his double-decker theatres in Toronto.

In 1913 the city's population was served by seven other live theatres, each booking a variety of stage entertainment and seating over 1,000. For the most part, they were "road" houses, with touring shows. Most of the buildings were not fireproof or up to the mandated standard for public safety. Only one of these was a large and modern vaudeville theatre, and six of the seven did not directly compete with the theatres Loew planned to build. Of these, two were classed as "legitimate" theatres, two offered comedies and melodramas, while two others hosted burlesque.

Loew's also contemplated entering an entertainment market in Toronto which included a burgeoning number of increasingly pretentious movie houses. Toronto then possessed about 60 movie theatres, and could count an additional 25 or so under construction.

Though fairly substantial movie theatres were being designed by architects, in 1913 Toronto's movie theatres continued to be widely regarded as "lower" class venues, as were its two large burlesque theatres, the Gayety and the Star.

Left: The Comique movie theatre, 279 Yonge Street, which operated from 1908 to 1914. The film advertised here was released in September 1910.

Right: Another of Toronto's five-cent movie theatres: the 1914 Big Nickel, 373 Yonge Street. It seated about 600, was architect-designed with a display of movie posters in mind, and had "a mechanical organ... [with] all the stops needed to imitate the natural sounds." (It is still standing, and operates as the Rio, showing triple and quadruple bills of second-run 'action' pictures.)

TORONTO MOVIE HOUSES IN 1913

The experimental nature and newness of the movie business had been reflected in makeshift, raw, and wildly eclectic early movie houses. It was not easily foreseen that multi-million dollar buildings were to be especially designed for a product which had just recently been treated only as a "dumb act" on a vaudeville bill, and exhibited in arcades, fairgrounds, and converted stores.

Among movie theatres in Toronto in 1913 was the Beaver, designed by Neil G. Beggs of the City Architect's office for owner William Joy. In a December advertisement, the Beaver claimed to be "Toronto's leading motion picture and vaudeville theatre," with the best and latest films and the "most up-to-date vaudeville acts procurable."[2] This theatre was described in *Construction* as "somewhat more pretentious than the average moving picture building." It seated 800 in orchestra, balcony, and balcony boxes, and was equipped with four dressing rooms.

The novelty of the movies, as well as the independence and the variety of early exhibitors were reflected in the names given to early movie houses. Among those advertising in the *Toronto World* in December 1913 were the Colonial, Ryan's Theatorium, the King George and the Prince George, the Aster, the Eclipse, the Iola, the Onoka Theatre, the Maple Leaf, the La Reta, the Midway, the Cum-Bac, and the Idle Hour. Such diverse and idiosyncratic names contrast with the multitude of "Capitols" and "Orpheums" which resulted later from the erosion of the independents exhibition business and the concentration of theatre ownership.

Right: Up another notch in the scale of increasingly pretentious movie houses, the 1913 Beaver Theatre, 1784 Dundas West, Toronto.

TORONTO'S LEGITIMATE THEATRES: THE ROYAL ALEXANDRA AND THE PRINCESS

At the top of the scale, in terms of class and admission prices, were Toronto's two legitimate theatres, the Princess and the Royal Alexandra, whose seats in the evening cost between 50 cents and $2.00. These theatres hosted the touring productions of two mammoth theatre-owning and producing concerns based in New York: the Princess received the shows produced by theatrical magnates Marc Klaw and A.L. Erlanger, while the Royal Alexandra embraced the touring productions of brothers J.J. and Lee Shubert. Local managers of these theatres were, respectively, O.B. Sheppard and Lawrence Solmon, both of whom became heavily involved in the business of Loew's theatres in Toronto. Sheppard became Vice-President of Loew's Canadian company after his retirement from the Princess in 1915, and Solman was enmeshed from the beginning as an investor and director.

The most respectable of these two theatres was the Royal Alexandra, designed by Toronto architect John M. Lyle in 1907 and built by local interests, though later it served as the Canadian headquarters of Shubert operations. The Royal Alexandra is said to have been the first fireproof theatre in Canada, and the first with a system of air conditioning. It seated 1525, and had a balcony and gallery said to be the first in Canada built on the cantilever principle. The 1600-seat Princess theatre was of less modern construction. Built as the Academy of Music in 1889, it was renovated and redecorated in 1901 and 1907. Still, it left much to be desired as a modern theatre, as the building was not fireproof and lacked reasonable fire escapes.

MELODRAMAS AND COMEDIES: THE GRAND OPERA HOUSE AND THE MAJESTIC

Further down the scale were the Grand Opera House and the Majestic theatres. These neighbored each other on Adelaide Street West and formed links in two associated Ontario chains which offered run-of-the-mill melodramas, comedies and musicals in touring shows to mostly middle- and working-class audiences. The Grand seated about 1750, and was originally built in 1874, though it was rebuilt after a fire in 1879. It had been Toronto's leading theatre but had not managed to maintained its earlier class. It was described in a 1913 report for the City of Toronto as "an old non-fireproof building of inferior construction" with no sprinkler system and dreadfully inadequate exits[3].

Notwithstanding , at the time the Grand was the headquarters of a chain of some 40 Canadian theatres owned by Toronto's Ambrose Small. Some of the Grand's entertainment was supplied by other local entrepreneurs, brothers Peter and John Griffin, while some of Small's shows were booked into the Griffin's

Historic interior view of the Royal Alexandra Theatre. For many years a Shubert house and mostly used for touring road shows, the Royal Alexandra is now owned and operated by Torontonians Edwin and David Mirvish. It is one of the oldest theatres in the city and continues as a very significant venue for live performances.

"pop" vaudeville chain of about 20 theatres. One of the Griffins' houses was the 1700-seat Majestic, which had been rebuilt in 1903 from the ashes of the 1886 Toronto Opera House. In safety and comfort, the theatre fell well below modern standards in 1913.

SHEA'S VAUDEVILLE

Marcus Loew's vaudeville theatres were not designed to compete for the patrons of these Toronto theatres, but for those who frequented Shea's Victoria theatre, a middle-class venue which charged up to 75¢ admission. It was a unit in a small chain operated by Ontario-born Buffalo tycoon, Mike Shea and his brother, Jerry[4]. Shea's was affiliated with United Booking Office (known as U.B.O.), an arm of Keith-Albee, a vast New York-based chain masterminded by Edward Albee. In 1913, this chain and its booking office virtually monopolized "big-time" (or high class) vaudeville theatres and vaudeville acts.

Shea's Victoria was the only capacious and luxurious vaudeville theatre in Toronto in 1913; it was purpose-built and designed by architects Leon H. Lempert and Son of Rochester, New York. It had been opened in August 1910, seated just over two thousand, and was located at Richmond and Victoria Streets. Interior decorations were by New York's Rambusch Studio, and included a sounding board mural called "The triumph of youth." According to opening publicity, the auditorium was decorated in crimson, with gold trimmings and oak wainscotting. Windsor Castle was depicted on its act curtain. The theatre had a movie projector, but it was almost an afterthought, located on the edge of the top gallery. Patrons "...sometimes meddled with the machine until a railing was built around it."[5]

Following Loew's announcement of his invasion of Shea's and U.B.O.'s vaudeville territory, Shea rushed to compete by building a massive new theatre which offered the same programme — continuous vaudeville and movies — at the same low admission prices as Loew's downstairs theatre. It opened in April of 1914, within two months of the Winter Garden's debut.

Construction on Shea's Hippodrome at 440 Bay Street had begun during the summer of 1913, as Loew's complex was rising. Shea again employed Rochester architects Leon H. Lempert and Sons. Unlike Loew's example, Lempert and Shea did not favour a narrow façade and a long lobby corridor from the main street. Instead, the Hippodrome imposed its presence on Bay Street. Its enamelled brick and terra cotta facade was massive and strikingly visible from a distance, fortified with an illuminated glass and copper dome topping each corner.

Like the new Loew's theatres, the Hippodrome had no gallery or second balcony, but it was larger than Loew's. It seated 2,622 (the largest capacity in Toronto). Its auditorium was flashily ornate, encrusted with plaster relief work in ivory and gold, and with direct and indirect electric lights "...introduced into the decorations at all available points." [6]

Though the Hippodrome had less restroom and promenade space than Shea's Victoria, it had more than Loew's, and included a powder room on the main floor as well as in the mezzanine lobby. Other triumphs were the Hippodrome's pipe organ or "invisible symphony orchestra" imported from Leipzig, Germany, and its 12-piece orchestra, accompanying the "cream of vaudeville and photoplays." These were offered in continuous shows between 12.30 to 11 p.m., at the same scale of admission as Loew's downstairs theatre. By taking on Loew's on his own turf, Shea was attempting to teach Loew a lesson, and to frighten him away from the "big-time" policy he had launched in the Winter Garden, as its reserved seats and one show per day were a direct challenge to Shea and to Albee's United Booking Office.

Below: Two interior views of the Beaver Theatre, showing its six tiers of balcony boxes, central aisle, and original theatre organ. Later, this theatre was the proud owner of a second-hand Wurlitzer.

Left: The Princess Theatre on King Street West, about 1910. This theatre burned to the ground in 1915, although it was immediately rebuilt as the New Princess. This reincarnation was demolished in 1930.

Left: The Grand Opera House, where its owner Toronto theatre magnate Ambrose Small made one of his last appearances before his mystifying disappearance in 1919. The theatre's furnace was vainly sifted for his remains. The building was pulled down in 1928.

Left: The Majestic Theatre on Adelaide Street (with the Grand Opera House in the distance). Though a second-rate venue in 1913, the Majestic was rebuilt by Thomas Lamb in 1916, renamed the Regent, and became the flagship of Famous Players Canadian Corporation. The theatre was demolished in 1938.

Grand Opera House and Majestic Theatre, Adelaide Street, Toronto, Canada

Below: Façade of Shea's Hippodrome on Bay Street. It was opened in 1914 and closed in 1957. Its site now accommodates the new City Hall.

Above: Façade of Shea's Victoria, Victoria Street, the first large purpose-built vaudeville theatre in Toronto, built in 1910 and demolished in 1956.

Above: Portrait of Mike Shea, owner of a chain of 23 theatres in the Buffalo region and three important vaudeville theatres in Toronto: Shea's Yonge Street, Shea's Victoria, and Shea's Hippodrome. Mike was born in St. Catharines, Ontario, but moved to Buffalo as an infant.

Above: Auditorium of Shea's Hippodrome.

THE CIRCUIT BUSINESS: CAPITALISM ON STAGE

The period 1912 to 1914 was a turning point for the Loew circuit and the history of mass entertainment. This was reflected in the hybrid structure Loew built in Toronto, as the building was symbolic of Loew's collision with big-time vaudeville and the uncertainties and upheavals of the age. Just on the horizon was a new entertainment product — the feature-length film — which would contribute to the eventual downfall of the older vaudeville circuit, and to the rise of new amusement monopolies.

When Loew's Toronto complex was planned and constructed, the commercial theatre business on this continent was in a state of considerable flux. In 1912, three other big-time vaudeville circuits had capitulated to Edward Albee's United Booking Office. Complicating the picture was the "wonderful boom" simultaneously enjoyed by small-time vaudeville[7]. Thus, old theatre wars were dying and new ones were being born, and new alliances were being formed and discarded. Competition between chain owners was characterized by intermittent theatre building or buying sprees, which were punctuated by mergers and complicated agreements to reduce competition.

In league with some traditional enemies of U.B.O., the small-time Loew circuit would continue a recent and aggressive expansion which challenged the big-time vaudeville monopoly. The escalating war was spilling into Canada. In January 1913, *Variety* announced that new Loew houses would open in Philadelphia, Boston, Baltimore, and Toronto. Loew's expansion into the territory hitherto claimed by U.B.O. and Shea's vaudeville theatres was calculated to unnerve. The new complex in Toronto would be a direct and conspicuous challenge to circuit owners across the continent, as it portended to be the flagship of a chain of Loew's theatres in Canada. That the double decker theatres were patterned on the American Theatre and Roof, Loew's headquarters in New York, conveyed for all to see Loew's expansionist ambitions.

A February article in V*ariety* added more details, including investment data and news of two construction sites for new Loew theatres in Toronto. (A 3,000 seat Loew theatre predicted for College Street would not be built.)

> Toronto is to have two new vaudeville houses according to plans just announced. Both will be booked by the Loew-Sullivan-Considine offices, New York.
>
> One, seating 3,300, will be built on Victoria street...with a lobby and entrance on Younge [sic] street. This house (with a roof garden) will have a larger area than any house in Toronto....
>
> The site cost $600,000 while the theatre will cost $300,000. In the company behind the theatre are Marcus Loew, with $100,000 worth of stock; Geo. W. Cox, Cincinnati, $50,000, and Joseph Rhinock, $50,000. Local capital is also invested. The other house will be on the south side of College street, 200 feet west of Spadina avenue. Its capacity will be something like 3,000 and will cost about $150,000.
>
> The new Shea Hippodrome looks also like a reality as the Shea people intend to go ahead the minute a certain piece of property comes into their possession.[8]

Several earlier conflicts were entangled with Loew's 1913 expansion and his contest with big-time. Among these were an enduring struggle between New York booking agent William Morris and U.B.O., the uneasy truce between the Shubert brothers and the older Klaw and Erlanger theatrical syndicate, and an earlier attempt by these legitimate operators to break into big-time vaudeville.

Morris, the Shuberts, and Klaw and Erlanger, tough and experienced theatrical magnates, might have thought that Loew could be used to serve their purposes and that they had the upper hand. Instead, Loew used them to enormous advantage, and the size of his business empire was eventually to eclipse them all.

MARCUS LOEW AND FRIENDS

Nicolas Schenck, Marcus Loew's right-hand man and General Manager of his theatres in 1913, who became President of the circuit on Loew's death in 1927.

Only a few years before 1913, Loew might have been seen as a relatively unsophisticated small businessman who had failed three times in the fur business. His management of an apartment building for actor David Warfield introduced him to "show business" and penny arcade ownership. Loew added the novelty of moving picture exhibition to a second floor room of one of his Cincinnati arcades in about 1904. This beginning may even have contributed to a certain sentimental attachment on Loew's part to the idea of two operations in the same building.

In 1909, Loew bought his first "real" theatre, a burlesque house in Brooklyn. He had made or was making friends and connections which would manifest at the 1913 opening of his theatres in Toronto: Lew Fields (half of the comedy team of Weber and Fields and a theatre owner himself), songwriter Irving Berlin, and theatre mogul Lee Shubert. Loew had also linked his fortunes in 1908 with Nicholas and Joseph Schenck, brothers who helped him to forge the multi-million dollar corporation. Like many others in the exhibition field in its earliest days, the Schencks came to it from amusement park interests. Loew happened upon and invested in one of their ventures, Paradise Park in lower Manhattan, and he inveigled the Schencks into investing in a couple of theatres. (They maintained a soft spot for amusement parks, purchasing Palisades Park in New Jersey in 1911).

Joseph ran Loew's Booking Office while Nicholas was "General Manager of all the theatres." Nicholas, who succeeded Loew as President, claimed he ran the whole show even in 1914. As he put it, "I represent Mr. Loew in every respect; Mr. Loew is not very active; I do all the work for Mr. Loew." [9] This statement contradicts all Loew's publicity in this period and the conventional view of the extraordinary and overriding influence of Marcus Loew's genius and business instincts.

Schenck testified in Toronto in February 1914 on the extent of Loew's theatre operations: "I am operating 83 theatres, and half of them we built ourselves."[10] The circuit had just extended its theatre and booking operations from coast to coast absorbing in 1912 the mid- and west-coast Sullivan-Considine circuit. Though this merger was the least successful of Loew's ventures, it is worth noting that Loew thereby had gained a foothold in Canada, as Sullivan-Considine booked vaudeville attractions into Vancouver, Victoria, and Montreal. Expansion to Toronto must have seemed logical.

Marcus Loew in 1912 "who began life as a New York newsboy, became a proprietor of penny arcades, and now owns or controls nearly a hundred moving-picture theatres."

MARCUS LOEW'S THEATRES LIMITED, TORONTO

Marcus Loew's Theatres, Limited, was incorporated in Toronto by letters patent dated 11 February 1913, and its capital stock was divided into 10,000 preferred shares and 7,500 common shares with a par value $100 each, or $1,750,000. In this period, Loew's was proud of the small local investors and the common man who purchased its stock, though Loew's took gradual control of the Toronto company. It was incorporated "to construct theatres and other buildings," to "manage, maintain and carry on the said theatres and other buildings," and to provide for the production and presentation of "operas, stage plays, operettas, burlesques, vaudevilles, ballets, pantomimes, spectacular pieces,...musical compositions, photographic films and other dramatic pictorial and musical performances and entertainments...." [11]

NETWORKING AND COMPETITION IN THE THEATRE BUSINESS

A Dun and Bradstreet report in Toronto in August 1913 provided the following financial history of Marcus Loew:

> He gradually got into the moving picture business and was very successful organizing various companies of which he was an officer and heavy stock-holder.... [On] Feb. 9th, 1910 he organized Loew's Consolidated Enterprises and later Loew's Theatrical Enterprises, a $5,000,000 corporation. At the start he had the backing of a local politician and realty operator, but also interested numerous small investors and has generally earned them substantial dividends, but competition in the field in which he is engaged in has been steadily increasing and is expected to become particularly pronounced in the near future. He is to some extent associated with the Shuberts. Has invariably declined all specific details as to his various ventures particularly as to the identity of those whom he has interested in the theatrical field. The propositions have been successfully financed and carried out in the past. [12]

Loew was more than "to some extent" associated with J.J. and Lee Shubert's theatrical empire. It was one of his most important affiliations in the 1912-3 period: his company's expansion from 1910 was attributed to their clandestine financial backing and was a significant factor in the building of the Toronto complex.

This Shubert financing for the Toronto project can be discerned in the *Variety* announcement of February 1913, which credited an $100,000 investment to two Shubert front men, an amount equal to Loew's investment. The silent partners named were former Kentucky Congressman Joseph Rhinock and George Barnsdale Cox, a retired Cincinnati ward politician and theatre owner. Cox and Rhinock confirmed their involvement by attending the opening of the lower theatre in Toronto in December 1913, as did Lee Shubert and A.L. (Abraham Lincoln) Erlanger. That Loew had the power and influence to bring together way up in chilly Toronto the frequently warring legitimate theatre magnates must have alarmed yet impressed Edward Albee and U.B.O. The Syndicate and the Shuberts had called a truce to renewed hostilities only in the previous month, and in April 1914 the two were to announce that they would not compete with each

Above: Brothers J. J. and Lee Shubert of New York, formidable theatre owners and producers, and clandestine backers of the 1913 expansion of the Loew circuit.

Board of Directors of Marcus Loew's Theatres Limited, Incorporated February 1913.

Letters Patent listed the Board of Directors of Marcus Loew's Theatres Limited:
Marcus Loew, New York City, U.S.A. Gentleman
Lawrence Solman, Toronto, Gentleman
Robert B. Bongard, Toronto, Broker
R.S. McLaughlin, Oshawa, Manufacturer
T.P. Birchall, Montreal, Financier

Solman was the manager of the Shubert's Canadian operations and manager of the Royal Alexandra Theatre. Apart from his work for and with the Shuberts, Solmon was an important figure on the Toronto scene. He was heavily engaged in providing amusement to its citizens. He owned or managed baseball, lacrosse, and hockey interests, the Mutual Street Arena, Hanlan's Point Stadium, and Sunnyside Amusement Park and Toronto Island ferries. (Later Solman was a vice president of Loew's Canadian chain .)

Thomas Perrin Birchall of Montreal was a banker and broker, the President of the Canada Industrial Bond Corporation, director of Bras d'Or Coal Co., and later a director of Loew's Montreal Theatres Ltd. Robert Ross Bongard was President of Bongard, Ryerson and Co., brokers and underwriters.

The inclusion of automobile manufacturer Robert McLaughlin as a major investor is interesting, and can perhaps be understood by noting that the President of General Motors in the United States was one of four directors of Loew's Incorporated. McLaughlin himself was not entirely remote from the affairs of the complex, as is testified by a letter he wrote in 1920 to its manager Jules Bernstein:

"Delighted to learn by yours of the 29th that the car which I arranged for you was so satisfactory, and that it contributed to the enjoyment of your good wife and yourself on your recent holiday.

"I was very glad to reciprocate, in a slight way, for your many courtesies to me."[13]

Right: Lawrence Solman of Toronto, Manager of the Royal Alexandra and Canadian manager of Shubert interests, a prime mover in the development of the Loew circuit in Toronto.

other in Montreal or Toronto. Some level of cozy and profitable arrangement probably existed between the Syndicate and Loew's Toronto theatres — Klaw and Erlanger films were being shown there in 1914 — though the level of involvement did not rival that of the Shuberts.

Money was not the Shuberts' only significant contribution. Their Canadian manager, Lawrence Solmon, can be credited with masterminding Loew's invasion of Toronto. The specific idea for the large theatre and its location seems to have been Solman's (contrary to a later publicity claim that Loew himself had picked out the site half an hour after his first arrival in Toronto)[14]. Solman had engaged local architect Stanley Makepeace, who had been working "for local people" designing a theatre on that site "for about a year" when "the local people and the Loew's combined...."[15]

But there were limits to the Shuberts' support for Loew's in Toronto. The Shuberts and Solman saw Loew's and the Royal Alexandra's shows as parallel and not competing operations. However, in 1914, when Percy Haswell's stock company, occasionally at the Royal Alexandra, was rumoured to be interested in "Loew's roof" for the summer, J.J. Shubert wrote to Solman, "In reference to Haswell going to Loew's roof, you have more to say about that than anybody else, but I would not permit her to do so as it is only making opposition for us." [16]

CIRCUIT WARS

The reasons for the Shuberts' secret backing of Loew's expansion were complicated and rooted in earlier theatre wars. They used Loew as a front for their vaudeville stratagems because they were prohibited from doing business in vaudeville by the terms of an earlier agreement with U.B.O. This agreement had followed a period of fragile truce when the Shuberts and Klaw and Erlanger had ganged up on Albee's United Booking Office, in league with Albee's sworn enemy William Morris. Together they tried to challenge its monopoly by organizing their own big-time vaudeville circuit, while in retaliation, U. B. O. threatened to invade their legitimate field. To end the contest in 1907 and in order to "freeze out" William Morris, U.B.O. paid a handsome sum to the Shuberts and the Syndicate to call off their plans.

William Morris, left in the lurch, tried to continue his struggle by aligning himself with Loew, but by 1911 Loew had absorbed the theatres Morris controlled. U.B.O. was gratified by the withdrawal of Morris, an enduring thorn in its side, and may have been persuaded that Loew's continued expansion was not harmful to its business. U.B.O. had not considered Loew's early theatres to be particularly alluring to big-time's genteel, urbane, and mobile patrons. These early theatres were classified as "neighborhood." They catered to the working class, and were dedicated to small-time "combination" vaudeville in continuous shows or what was known as "family time."

By 1912, Loew was enticed to compete with U.B.O. with its harsh blacklist policies towards acts which rejected lifelong indenture or which did not play by Albee's rules. Because big-time performers were seeking refuge in small time, Loew threw down a gauntlet. He added expensive headliners to some of his cheaper shows and raised his prices. This policy was notably installed in the circuit's headquarters — a double-decker theatre acquired from Morris — which he had intended as the showcase of his would-be theatre circuit: the American Theatre and Roof on 42nd Street in New York. Loew's also used this double-decker complex to go head-to-head with U. B. O. While the lower theatre catered to Loew's traditional small-time patrons, the upstairs theatre was placed in direct competition with big-time. In the American Roof, Loew offered a programme of twelve acts of vaudeville for a top price of 75 cents, in contrast to his usual range of 10 to 35 cents. In this use of the American Roof to test public reaction to new policies, Loew was following a roof garden tradition. Such experiments, subsidized by admissions to a lower theatre, were less risky than the prospect of going out on a limb with a new policy which absorbed all admissions. Loew extended the type of scheme used in the American Roof to his Winter Garden in Toronto in 1914, where higher admissions and one show an evening were meant to attract relatively well-heeled patrons who normally attended U.B.O. shows.

U.B.O. finally creaked into action. After failing in attempts to lure Loew into agreements to divide their respective territories or to merge booking offices, the decision was taken to go after Loew's small-time patrons. U.B.O. and Loew's crossed over into each other's turf in a number of cities. The building of Loew's Toronto complex spurred U.B.O. to mount determined and specific opposition to Loew's Broadway theatres. *Variety* rumoured, "Mike Shea of Buffalo is said to have been brought into the Broadway theatre deal, through argument brought to bear on him that Loew, in invading Toronto against Shea there, should have a lesson taught in return. " [20] In revenge, U.B.O. affiliates Mike and Jerry Shea immediately built Shea's Hippodrome in Toronto to compete for Loew's small-time audiences.

Right: Interior of the Shuberts' New York Winter Garden.

The New York and the Toronto Winter Garden

In spite of the web of intrigue which bound Loew and the Shuberts, the upper theatre in Toronto shared no connection with the Shuberts' New York theatre and its legendary Winter Garden shows. The 1911 Winter Garden Theatre still stands, and was designed by William Albert Swasey. It was so named expressly to compete with the popular roof garden follies shows. Though it does not much resemble a garden, a description provided in a 1911 issue of *Architecture and Building* suggests an affinity with the Toronto Winter Garden's decor:

"The entire auditorium is finished to give the effect of open-air trellis construction. The side walls behind the trellis work are decorated with landscape painting with concealed green light...The entire audience thus appears to be witnessing a theatrical performance on a roof high above the city sidewalks and in the open air, protected from the sky by a huge pergola with trellised roof."[17]

Even before the Shubert's Winter Garden opened, Marcus Loew reportedly had "passed by and smacked his lips." [18] Loew unsuccessfully tried to lease the theatre in April 1913. Naming his Toronto theatre the Winter Garden was a kind of consolation, perhaps. More importantly, Loew took this liberty because the Winter Garden name, used in advertising, was known to increase receipts, and because it eminently suited the Toronto Winter Garden's decor.

J.J. Shubert later did not approve and did not appreciate this appropriation. He complained about the misleading appellation when it came to his attention in 1919. Enclosing an ad from the *Toronto World*, J.J. opened to "My dear Marcus," "Don't you think it is unfair to use the name of 'Winter Garden' in the ads?" Loew provided a long and misleading reply to "My dear Jake," pretending that the Toronto Winter Garden predated the New York Winter Garden:

"This has been named before your Winter Garden was opened. As a matter of fact, the American Roof used to be called the Winter Garden and we changed it when you opened yours because it meant less to us and meant a great deal to you. Now, who do you think has got the nerve? The fellow who copied the name or the originator? I am surprised that this is the first time that you knew that we called our Roof Garden the Winter Garden in Toronto. It is matter of 7 or 8 years now and I certainly will have to get after my press man. If a man with the interest that you have never heard of it something must be wrong.

At any rate, you probably are right. When the Winter Garden shows are playing... [at the Royal Alexandra], I will instruct ...[Loew's] manager not to use...['Winter Garden'], if you will let me know in advance so as to avoid misunderstanding." [19]

POST SCRIPT

U.B.O.'s strategies did not work, and, uncharacteristically, it would be unable to swallow or ruin this vaudeville opponent. Loew's continued to expand and prosper, in league with the Shuberts, and to assimilate and invest in the new entertainment, feature-length movies. In 1919 the circuit purchased Metro pictures, and became Loew's Incorporated, reorganized at $100 million.

The business for Loew's in Toronto seems to have been profitable. According to *Motion Picture News* in 1919, "In the 5 years of operation, the preferred stock of Loew's Toronto Theatre has paid 35% in dividends (7% per annum) and the common stock 49%, or an average 10% per annum." [21] In this light, Lawrence Solman provided a bombshell in a June 1921 letter to the Shuberts: "Four of us here had to put up a large sum of money in order to keep Loew's Toronto Theatres from being sold by the sheriff. We put up $20,000 each; Mr. Loew was one of us and we had to do it in a hurry...You know you cannot sell in this market at present, the vaudeville business is in a terrible shape. Loew's for some time back have been showing a deficit every week." [22]

The difficulties in 1921 might be attributable to the post-war theatre building boom and the competition of other chains and notably in Toronto theatres built by Pantages and Famous Players Canadian Corporation. Loew's had also expanded in Canada to encompass seven theatres in six cities: the Uptown in Toronto, Loew's Court (previously the Français) and Loew's theatre in Montreal, and Loew theatres in Ottawa, Hamilton, Windsor and London, Ontario.

After 1921, Loew's would almost withdraw from the field in Canada. But, along with its theatre in London, Loew's would cling to its extraordinary double-decker theatre in Toronto, which, in the beginning, had so elaborately symbolized and entailed the history and the future of the circuit.

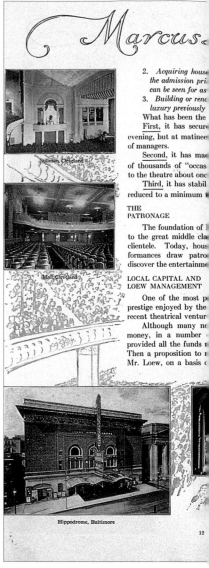

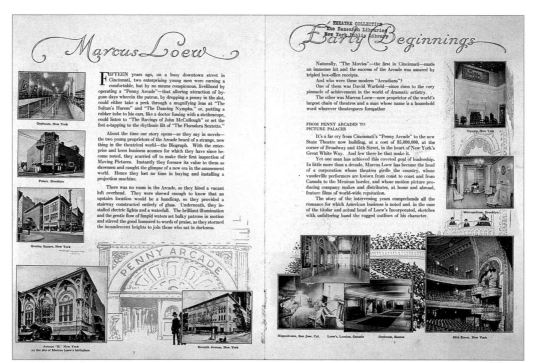

From "Marcus Loew: Entertainer of a Nation", a brochure which celebrated the 1919 multi-million dollar incorporation of Loew's Inc. and the purchase of Metro Pictures.

Patrons as Partners

fifty per cent of the profits. Wherever the venture seemed justified, in Mr. Loew's opinion, this proposition has been accepted. Today Loew controls several houses in which his only investment is brains, experience and the value of the name.

REAL PROFIT-SHARING

Loew's Incorporated is a recently organized stock company, formed to take over all of the Loew enterprises and their management.

All the shares are of common stock only. *There are no preferred shares to take precedence in the distribution of dividends.*

This means a genuine and generous sharing of profits among *all* stockholders, regardless of how much or little each investor holds.

ESTIMATED EARNINGS

Based on current earnings, a conservative estimate of Loew's net income, after taxes, for the year ending August 31, 1920, is $3,000,000.

This estimate is based on the present rate of earnings, as computed by the Federal Accounting Corporation, certified public accountants. Based on the same consideration and the use of new capital in the contemplated development program, it is estimated that for the year following the completion of properties now well under way, the net income of Loew's Incorporated will reach $6,000,000.

A CASH BUSINESS

Loew's Incorporated conducts a strictly cash business. Every theatre in the vast chain of Loew enterprises pays all

[left column, partially cut off:]

...ing capacity, and pulling ...ach of all. A Loew show ...s. ...on a scale of richness and ... history of theatricals.

...attendance, not only at ...the traditional bugaboo ...heatregoers of hundreds ... Formerly, folks went ... they go oftener. ...ss of entertainment and ...financial hazard.

...was the appeal he made ...this was exclusively his ...me theatres, Loew per-...priced attractions who ...y of its luxurious setting.

...of the brilliant business ...is the way many of his ...nanced. ...being built with Loew ...capital has cheerfully ...uild and equip a theatre. ...erate has been made to ...y per cent ownership or

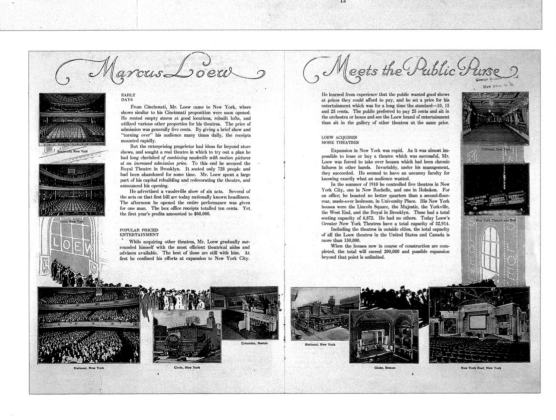

Loew's, Hamilton, Ont. Stillman, Cleveland Loew's, Hamilton, Ontario Winter Garden, Toronto, Canada

13

Marcus Loew Meets the Public Purse

EARLY DAYS

From Cincinnati, Mr. Loew came to New York, where shows similar to his Cincinnati proposition were soon opened. He rented empty stores at good locations, rebuilt lofts, and utilized various other properties for his theatres. The price of admission was generally five cents. By giving a brief show and "turning over" his audience many times daily, the receipts mounted rapidly.

But the enterprising proprietor had ideas far beyond store shows, and sought a real theatre in which to try out a plan he had long cherished of *combining vaudeville with motion pictures at an increased admission price.* To this end he secured the Royal Theatre in Brooklyn. It seated only 728 people and had been abandoned for some time. Mr. Loew spent a large part of his capital rebuilding and redecorating the theatre, and announced his opening.

He advertised a vaudeville show of six acts. Several of the acts on that first bill are today nationally known headliners. The afternoon he opened the entire performance was given for one man. The box office receipts totalled ten cents. Yet the first year's profits amounted to $60,000.

POPULAR PRICED ENTERTAINMENT

While acquiring other theatres, Mr. Loew gradually surrounded himself with the most efficient theatrical aides and advisers available. The best of these are still with him. At first he confined his efforts at expansion to New York City.

He learned from experience that the public wanted good shows at prices they could afford to pay, and he set a price for his entertainment which was for a long time the standard—10, 15 and 25 cents. The public preferred to pay 25 cents and sit in the orchestra or boxes and see the Loew brand of entertainment than sit in the gallery of other theatres at the same price.

LOEW ACQUIRES MORE THEATRES

Expansion in New York was rapid. As it was almost impossible to lease or buy a theatre which was successful, Mr. Loew was forced to take over houses which had been chronic failures in other hands. Invariably, under his management, they succeeded. He seemed to have an uncanny faculty for knowing exactly what an audience wanted.

In the summer of 1910 he controlled five theatres in New York City, one in New Rochelle, and one in Hoboken. For an office, he boasted no better quarters than a second-floor rear, made-over bedroom in University Place. His New York houses were the Lincoln Square, the Majestic, the Yorkville, the West End, and the Royal in Brooklyn. These had a total seating capacity of 6,872. He had no others. Today Loew's Greater New York Theatres have a total capacity of 52,914.

Including the theatres in outside cities, the total capacity of all the Loew theatres in the United States and Canada is more than 150,000.

When the houses now in course of construction are completed, the total will exceed 200,000 and possible expansion beyond that point is unlimited.

Roosevelt, New York Circle, New York National, New York Circle, New York Columbia, Boston National, New York Globe, Boston New York Roof, New York

Orpheum, New York New York Theatre and Roof

MARCUS LOEW
ENTERTAINER OF A NATION

BOX

Headquarters 1907
Third Avenue, N.Y.

Headquarters 1920
Loew Building·Broadway, N.Y.

CHAPTER TWO

"A COMPLETE THEATRE ON TOP OF ANOTHER."

In 1914 the *Toronto World* wrote in an enthusiastic article on the Loew's new theatres in Toronto: "Several theatres have been built with open air roof-gardens or dance halls on top, but the feat of building a complete theatre on top of another has only been attempted a few times." This statement, though essentially correct, requires some elaboration.[1]

Numerous open-air performing spaces or amusement centres were located on the roofs of theatres, but these were not substantial structures of brick and mortar, architect-designed from the beginning as permanent theatrical operations. And likewise many cities and towns were dotted with above ground or second storey auditoriums in non-theatrical buildings. But the piggyback accommodation in one building of two full proscenium theatres, each with stage house and balcony, was rare. Only a handful of counterparts existed in 1913, all in Manhattan.

Within the decade, four additional analogous or somewhat similar double theatres were in operation: the Riviera and Japanese Garden in Manhattan, Proctor's in Newark, the Orpheum and Sky theatres in Cincinnati, and the Century and Valencia in Baltimore. Still, the operation of the double-decker theatres in Toronto was unusual enough to elicit the following comment from F.H. Richardson, an expert correspondent for *Moving Picture World* on a multi-city tour in April, 1918: "Loew's theater presents an excellent picture and a very odd arrangement, in that there are two distinct, complete theaters, one above the other, having a combined seating capacity of 3,500." [2]

THE ROOF GARDEN THEATRE IN THE 1880S AND 90S

The concept of a *summer* roof garden theatre on the roof of a theatre below was developed by New York impresario Rudolph Aronson in 1881-83. He was inspired by the summer concert gardens of Europe, together with a burning desire to make twice as much money on a theatre lot. Steel construction and the elevator had made the commercial use of roof-top space feasible. The prospect of obtaining a measure of relief from summer heat and a spectacular view would help to induce attendance. As New York and other cities became more crowded early in the century, roof gardens were exploited by department stores, schools, hospital buildings and hotels as well as theatres.

Aronson's Casino theatre at 39th and Broadway in 1883 had an open-air roof, with tables and refreshments, along with shrubs, flowers and rustic seats. These adornments came to characterize most of the later roof theatres. The Casino was acknowledged in a 1913 book on New York theatres as "the first venture of this kind" and "...a little two-by-four affair, which was considered more in the light of a novelty than a serious enterprise, though it continued to run for twelve and thirteen years."[3]

The Casino's roof remained the only such theatre space in New York until the 1890s, a decade which experienced a "craze" for rooftop entertainment and the roof garden's progression into a complete and year-round theatre space. Though open-air summer roof theatres embellished with foliage and coloured lights were opened in 1892 on the rebuilt Madison Square Garden and atop the American Theatre and the Manhattan Theatre in 1893, the serious enterprise of roof gardens got underway in 1896 and 1899 with Oscar Hammerstein's operations at the Olympia and Victoria Theatres, both designed by New York architect J.B. McElfatrick. The Olympia, opened in 1896, encompassed a music hall, smaller theatre, concert hall, and refreshment areas. (Billiard rooms and a bowling alley were also planned). It had a covered roof theatre, though this roof was glass with water running over it, which supposedly contributed a cooling effect. The roof theatre was heated and, for a time, was named the Winter Garden. It was the first to attempt year-round operation. Not only did it defy winter, it was the first roof garden to deny that it was on the top of a building and in a city. Instead, it presented an artificial world, with no elevated city view, no city sound, and sometimes no summer breeze. Imitation rocks, grottoes, landscape murals, bridges, a miniature lake, and live swans and ducks formed part of its decoration, along with the more conventional roof garden foliage. When the roof theatre was renovated in 1901, its columns were decorated as tree trunks.

The roof theatre of the Victoria, opened in 1899, was expanded onto the roof of the adjoining Republic Theatre next door. Against New York building regulations, it was a makeshift and non-fireproof structure which was gradually and surreptitiously transformed into a covered variety theatre. The adjoining open air roof of the Republic was tarted up to resemble a "Dutch farm," with a windmill, a miller's cottage and stork's nest, a stable with two cows[!], a duck pond, a ruined castle, and a grist mill.

Hammerstein and McElfatrick had gone beyond the idea that a roof theatre was open to the elements and restricted to summer operation, and they firmly allied the experience of the roof theatre to the realm of imagination. Like the later "atmospheric" theatres, their roof gardens created another world: they were to "...lift [the patron] above the little conventionalities of every-day life."[4] Potted plants and coloured lights and the view on an open roof were no longer sufficiently enticing. Neither were the simple variety entertainments originally found in the roof garden, like "dumb" acts with few acoustical requirements. The trend was towards more elaborately constructed covered roof theatres, with larger, more versatile stages. Roof gardens played an important part in the history of popular theatre, as they became "venues for experimentation, a place to try out new performers and new kinds of performance...." and they served to funnel into the mainstream black musical theatre, small-time vaudeville and film, aspects of the little theatre movement, and the modern revue.[5] Roof gardens contributed to changing theatre-going habits. Patrons began to become accustomed to the idea of going to the theatre in the summer in the city, and vaudeville performers no longer necessarily expected summer layoffs.

THE NEW AMSTERDAM AND THE AMERICAN THEATRES

The movement towards more sophisticated and elaborate roof garden theatres and entertainment had culminated with the 1903 building of the New Amsterdam Theatre and Aerial Garden for the Klaw and Erlanger syndicate by the distinguished architectural firm of Henry Herts and Hugh Tallant. The building was steel skeleton construction housing two substantial proscenium theatres equipped with cantilevered balconies. The decorative conventions employed by other theatre architects were abandoned with the stunning art nouveau embellishment of the lower theatre.

Right: The Casino's open air roof theatre, bedecked with foilage and lights. It opened in July 1883.

Below: Oscar Hammerstein's 1895 "multilevel entertainment center" on Broadway between 44th and 45th, photographed in 1910. Originally named the Olympia, its auditorium, concert hall and roof garden theatre were all renamed several times. The building was destroyed in 1935.

Left: The Casino Theatre, 39th and Broadway, New York, the first with a roof garden theatre. The lower auditorium, seating about 1300, opened in September 1882. The buliding was demolished in 1930; its roof theatre had been abandoned decades before.

Right: The glass-covered roof garden theatre of (what had been) Hammerstein's Olympia, with fixed seating and decorations of flowering trees, palms and vines, seen in about 1901.

ROOF THEATRES IN TORONTO

The concept of a roof garden theatre for Toronto had existed since at least 1892. In September, the *New York Clipper* reported that H.R. Jacobs, the operator of the Toronto Opera House, had completed arrangements for the building of a new theatre on Yonge Street to be named the Imperial which would have a roof garden and be open winter and summer.[6] Since most Broadway roof garden theatres were still open-air, this concept was a rare and sophisticated one.

The *New York Clipper* also reported in August 1895 on the affairs of a Toronto Island roof garden. Though early in the month cold weather had almost paralyzed business at "this resort," by the end of August, "packed houses" were reported at each performance.[7] Open-air vaudeville shows during the early 1900s could also be experienced at Hanlan's Point, Munro Park and Scarboro Beach. Still, outdoor theatres were not the norm in Toronto for obvious reasons.

The closest thing in Toronto to Loew's "double-decker" and contemporary with it was the Garden theatre at 290-2 College Street, designed by J.H. Stanford. The Garden was opened in 1911 and offered an open-air show on the almost undecorated roof, where chairs and tables were arranged for refreshment and talking. The theatre below seated about 550. This theatre, however, and had little or no impact on the design and operation of Loew's Yonge Street and Winter Garden theatres. The important precursors were two double deckers in Manhattan, built during the first decade of the new century.

Above: View from the covered theatre of Hammerstein's Victoria towards the open air roof of the adjoining Republic Theatre, with its "miller's cottage" and "windmill". A species of its resident livestock is standing at the top of the stairs.

Right: Façade and open air roof garden of Toronto's 1909 Garden Theatre, 290-2 College Street. Note its flower-filled hanging baskets and window boxes, and its lattice decoration.

Upstairs, Herts and Tallant also served notice that this was a roof theatre like no other. No garden setting or refreshments were offered in the auditorium itself. Patrons were supposed to go to the Aerial Garden primarily to attend a show, not, as in the open air roof theatres, to see the view, chat, dance, or consume refreshments. The Aerial Garden presented "...the highest class of legitimate productions ever seen in a place of this kind," and, as the *New York Times* recorded, it was "...not a half-way amusement hall, such as are the various roof gardens in New York."[8] The concession to roof garden norms was the promenade behind the stage house, "...laid out among flowers and ferns, with tables scattered here and there for the purpose of serving the patrons with refreshments during intermissions in the programme."[9]

Façade and entrance of the New Amsterdam. The Aerial Garden's large pivoting windows can be seen above the roof of the store on the left.

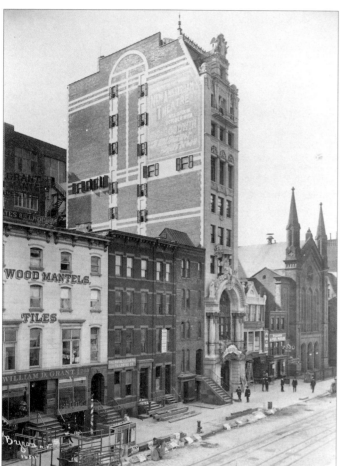

Though the roof theatre seated about 700, in contrast to the 1700 capacity of the lower auditorium, the same show could readily be staged in the two theatres. Later, "...production numbers were often first tried upstairs before becoming part of the [show] downstairs and likewise, popular numbers...would be moved upstairs to continue their run..."[10] Though it had an art nouveau flavour to its decoration, the Aerial Garden was not treated to the sensational sinuous swirls and naturalistic forms or the murals and intense colour of the lower auditorium. Instead it was decorated in tints of old rose, with pivoting windows on three auditorium walls which could transform it into "almost an open-air theatre."

Architect Thomas Lamb may have patronized these establishments before he designed in 1908 his first roof garden auditorium for the American Theatre, an existing 1893 theatre in the same block as the New Amsterdam. It was the first of his theatres written up in a major architectural journal. The American Theatre was originally designed by architect Charles C. Haight with an open-air roof garden decorated with coloured globes, potted ferns, ivy, and other plants. Lamb tore out its small roof-top stage and built above the lower auditorium a "fully equipped two-storey concrete and steel theatre" seating about 1400, with a stage almost as large as that downstairs. Lamb's design had been commissioned by William Morris, who had leased the building to serve as the hub of his future independent vaudeville circuit. Marcus Loew would take over the building in 1911, and would use it as his headquarters and, in turn, integral to his challenge to big-time vaudeville.

West 42nd Street entrance of New Amsterdam in 1986.

Perhaps, however, an important influence on the decor of the American Roof and, later, the Toronto Winter Garden and subsequent "atmospheric theatres" was Murray's Roman Gardens, a restaurant opened in 1907 in midtown Manhattan and designed by Henry Erkins. A contemporary description of its atrium dining room read: "The scheme of decoration...is to produce an outdoor effect, and to carry this out, the side walls are festooned with climbing vines, plants and trees, the ceiling is decorated to represent a blue sky in which electric stars twinkle, while by an ingenious arrangement of optical apparatus, the effect of clouds sweeping over the sky is produced...".

The *New York Times* provided a description of the "scheme of sylvan architecture" of Lamb's addition to the American at its opening in July 1909:

Above: Art nouveau elevator doors in the New Amsterdam lobby, 1986.

Above: Auditorium, New Amsterdam Theatre, 1986. While much of the theatre's splendid mural work survives, its boxes have been destroyed. Each had represented a different flower: violet, heliotrope, and buttercup were among them.

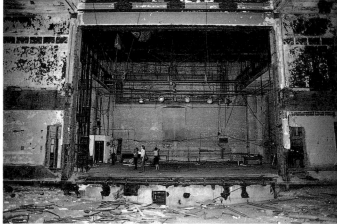

Right: Two views of the gutted auditorium of the Aerial Garden, 1986. The space has served, variously, as a radio theatre, television studio and rehearsal hall.

Trunks of imitation trees form the proscenium supports to the stage, and the roof, studded with tiny twinkling electric lights, is designed to carry out the impression of being under the stars....tree-entwined and foliage-hung walks lead to two open-air gardens where patrons may sit at rustic tables for refreshments ....The woodwork is disguised with real birch bark, and scores of palms and shrubs add to the attractiveness of the outdoor setting.[11]

Further description and photographs were provided in the *Architects' and Builders' Magazine* in 1909. The interior of the American roof was decorated to resemble an 'Adirondack Lodge' and its balcony and box fronts were tricked out in lattice decorations. According to this account, "...the decoration applied directly on the surface of the concrete is of light color, with scenic effect on the walls." It continued:

The supporting columns at the sides are encased in plaster, a very good imitation of large trees, which seemingly rise from the floor through the balcony and branch out into the ceiling at the lower web of the trusses. At this level a screen of leafy foliage breaks the view of the ceiling above. All the upper part of the trusses, which are unprotected, and the under surface of the roof, are painted a deep blue. Suspended from this, about two feet down, are tiny, half-candle power electric bulbs, the flickering illumination of which gives the effect of the night sky. Thus, although the roof garden is entirely enclosed and the patrons are protected from a chance shower, the nearest approach to the outside air is given.[12]

In the Toronto Winter Garden, Lamb departed from the American roof's single box on either side, its decorative awnings, and its refreshment promenades, with their rustic chairs and tables. The Winter Garden was not a pale imitation or a carbon copy of its New York predecessor, and the decorative themes that Lamb had explored and experimented with in 1909 seem to have found a full and unique expression in Toronto in 1914. That Lamb's American Roof was the direct

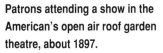
Patrons attending a show in the American's open air roof garden theatre, about 1897.

Below: Longitudinal section of Haight's American theatre, showing its original open air roof garden.

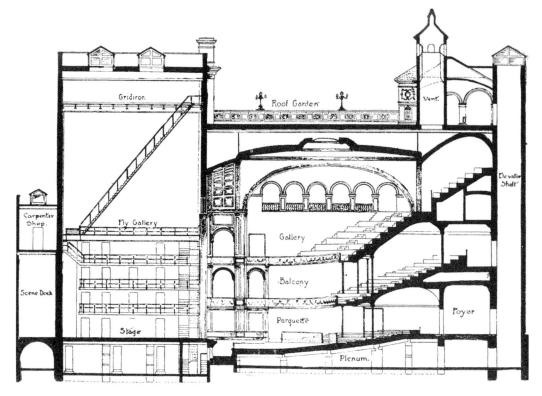

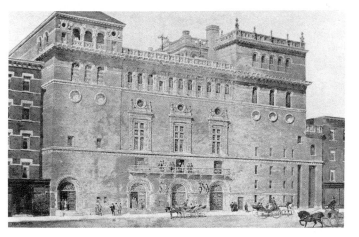

Left: West 41st Street facade of Charles C. Haight's 1893 American Theatre, New York, later the headquarters of the Loew circuit. The building was closed by fire in 1930 and the site was a parking lot by 1932.

Above: Lamb's 1909 American Roof added to Haight's American Theatre, the prototype for the Toronto Winter Garden.

ancestor of Toronto's Winter Garden was confirmed in pre-construction publicity in February 1913, when an article in the *Toronto World* promised: "There will be a roof garden on the house, with elevator connections, and constructed on the same lines as that in the new American Theatre in New York."[13]

Another double-decker designed by Thomas Lamb for William Fox, the Riviera and Japanese Garden, was a fraternal twin to Loew's Yonge Street and Winter Garden, and was built concurrently. Its erection was announced in *Variety* in January 1913:

> *Double-decker theatre.* The contract was let Monday by William Fox to build a double-decker theatre on his site at Broadway and 97th St., adjoining the present Fox Riverside house. The ground floor theatre will have a seating capacity of 2,400. Above it will be another, called the Japanese Gardens, glass enclosed, to play the year around, and seating 2,100. [14]

The Riviera and Japanese Garden opened in 1914. Like the Toronto complex, a more conventionally decorated movie and vaudeville lower auditorium was topped by a full scale, exotically decorated theatre. This time, flowers, trees and plants did not dominate the fanciful "other world" upstairs. The most important decorative elements were the curved Chinese roofs over sidewall boxes and proscenium arch, stained glass windows depicting an oriental countryside, a red and green ceiling, a "score of Japanese lanterns," and a mountainous proscenium mural, hypothesized as Mount Fuji.

Below: Longitudinal section of the Riviera and Japanese Garden Theatres, New York, Thomas Lamb, architect.

Below: View of the lower auditorium of Proctor's in Newark in 1986. The theatre is sometimes occupied by squatters and the tour guide is carrying martial arts weapons.

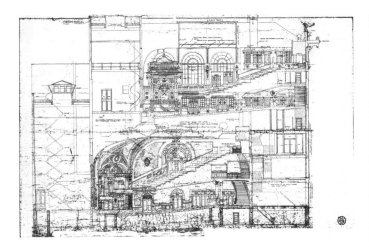

Left: Exterior of Riviera and Japanese Garden, Broadway and 97th Streets, and the adjacent Riverside Theatre, also designed by Lamb in 1911, to which he added an open-air roof garden theatre in 1912. All have been lost to demolition.

Right: Another Lamb double decker: the National Theatre and National Winter Garden Roof in New York's Lower East Side, opened in 1913 and owned by the Minsky Realty Co. The lower theatre seated 1901. The 963-seat roof theatre hatched Minsky burlesque. The building was razed in 1958.

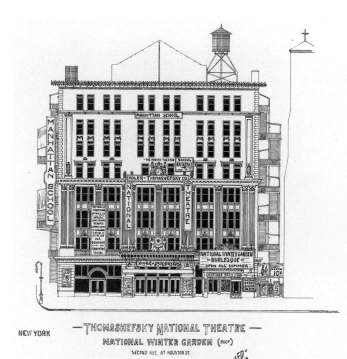

Left: Present condition of abandoned upper auditorium of Proctor's in Newark. In 1961 it was the Penthouse Cinema, offering the "best of international films."

Right: Façade of Proctor's in Newark, New Jersey, one of three surviving historic double-decker theatres.

Beyond Broadway

A large number of New York theatres had open-air roof gardens, including the Alhambra on 14th Street, whose roof theatre inaugurated movie shows in 1910 and the Metropolis Theatre at 142nd Street and 3rd Avenue.

Among a handful built with a complete, covered proscenium theatre on top of another were the National Theatre or National Winter Garden at Houston Street and Second Avenue, which used its roof theatre for burlesque shows. This double-decker was designed by Thomas Lamb. It was announced in 1911 by the *New York Times* as a "$250,000 theatre and roof garden for the lower east side". The roof garden was to seat 1500, and to have a large balcony and a stage.[15]

Cincinnati had the Orpheum and Sky Theatres, two stacked theatres in a multi-purpose building which included offices and a ballroom. These theatres were not opened simultaneously. The Orpheum was opened by a local entrepreneur in December 1909. It offered vaudeville and movies and a "cafe on the roof." According to one retrospective account, a "glass-enclosed theater on the roof later was added for the convenience of smokers."[16] In 1915, both auditoria were equipped with new Wurlitzer theatre organs, and two elevators were in constant operation, taking patrons both to the balconies of the lower theatre and to the roof garden.

Proctor's theatres in Newark, New Jersey, post-dated Loew's in Toronto. This complex, opened in 1914, seems to have been designed from the beginning as two substantial proscenium theatres by architect John W. Merrow. The lower theatre seated about 3,000, with two balconies of vertiginous height. The upper theatre was comfortably smaller. Its canvas-covered ceiling originally had Chinese motifs and a salmon and green colour scheme. This was painted over in the 40s with a scheme of rock-like clouds. (The complex is still standing, though it is vacant and in decrepit condition.)

The Century and Valencia theatres in Baltimore seem to have comprised the only North American double-decker built in the 1920s. There were two auditoria in the building when the Century opened in 1921, but one was more of a ballroom or cabaret than a theatre. Then, the Century below seated 3,450 for motion picture shows, and the upper house seated about 3,000, and had a dance floor and a telescoping stage.

The operation of two theatres in one building dated from Loew's take over in 1926, when the Valencia, "a wholly new theatre," was created in the former Century Ballroom by architect John Eberson[17]. The Valencia had a tented canopy over the proscenium, rough stucco side walls, and strolling guitar players, and ushers dressed as bullfighters adding to the ambience. It was an "atmospheric" theatre, whose ceiling simulated the sky. This was a specialty Eberson claimed as his own. In the Valencia, the "atmospheric" had returned to its roots — the 1890s roof garden theatre. Like the originals, the Valencia was built on top of existing theatre space, and revelled in the alfresco and the simulation of an outdoor environment indoors.

Right: Auditorium of Cincinnati's Orpheum Theatre above which the Sky Theatre was built. They were demolished in 1952.

Below: Upper theatre of the last double decker to be built, the atmospheric Valencia, opened in 1926, jestingly said to be "over a Century." They were levelled in 1962.

Above: Marquee of the Century and Valencia in Baltimore.

CHAPTER THREE

THOMAS W. LAMB: AN ARCHITECT'S PROGRESS

In 1913, the architect of Loew's Toronto complex, Thomas White Lamb, was an experienced designer of stacked theatres. He had drawn plans for two substantial double-deckers in Manhattan: the 1909 American Theatre Roof and the 1912 National Winter Garden. His Fifth Avenue firm was also concurrently engaged in designing the uptown Riviera and Japanese Garden theatres and in adding an open-air roof theatre to his 1911 Riverside Theatre next door.

But more importantly, in 1913 Lamb was on the threshold of defining a building type and would soon hit his stride as a movie palace architect. He was to become one of the most prolific and successful as well as the patriarch of his speciality. He was then 42 years old and largely self-taught in commercial theatre architecture.

EARLY LIFE, EDUCATION, AND CONTACTS

Lamb was born in 1871 in Dundee, Scotland, and crossed the Atlantic with his parents before he was a teenager. A family story relates that the Lambs first came to Canada, but settled in New York by 1883.[1] Nothing is known of this Canadian interlude.

In 1894 (at the age of 23) Thomas Lamb enrolled in the General Science Program at New York's Cooper Union for the Advancement of Science and Art. He, with all the other students at this private institution, had a full-tuition scholarship. Lamb graduated in 1898 with a Bachelor of Science degree, not a degree in architecture or engineering, and took only two courses related to his career: mechanical drawing and acoustics.

The first employment usually reported for Lamb was as a building inspector with the City of New York. He is said to have begun his architectural practice while still a building inspector and a student at Cooper Union. However, he opened an architectural office as early as 1892 — before he entered Cooper Union, as Lamb is recorded in the directory of the American Institute of Architects in 1892 doing "general work" and with an office at 487 5th Ave.

Lamb was employed by New York City's Bureau of Buildings for five years, first as an inspector and then as a plan examiner.[2] His experience in the Bureau of Buildings was to serve him well: there he "...encountered a wide variety of building types and construction problems." He also met future moguls of movie theatre empires like Marcus Loew and William Fox who were seeking permits as well as young architects open to designing their novel type of building. Lamb soon developed a theatre specialty, based on "his ready knowledge of the building code and quick solutions to the nagging problems of sight lines, acoustics and structure [and crowd safety] posed by theaters..."[3]

William Fox and Marcus Loew are both credited with setting him on the path of a theatre-designing career, though neither name occurs among early clients in Lamb's job book which records his submissions and projects. Lamb implied in a

Portrait of Thomas W. Lamb, about 1927.

1928 article that he received his first theatre-designing assignment from William Fox in 1909. But in an obituary notice his baptism in movie house architecture is ascribed to Marcus Loew: "In 1908 he was called on by Marcus Loew to draw up specifications for the motion picture houses of the company, which was then beginning to expand..."[4] The Loew chain was to become Lamb's best customer over a long association. Like some of the top Loew executives, Lamb was often paid in stock, with the result that he was the third largest Loew shareholder at one time.

LAMB'S JOB BOOK – THEATRES UP TO JOB NUMBER 368

Lamb started a "job book" in 1895 which provides a chronological record of his projects and an indispenable key to his drawings (now at Avery Archives of Columbia University). Entries in the job book are, however, scarce and haphazard until about 1905, when Lamb was beginning to receive a few theatre renovation assignments. Though the book was systematically enumerated, many job numbers were left blank, especially in the early period, and many were used for proposals not realized, for inspections, and even for filing drawings by other architects. The Toronto complex is listed as the "Victoria Theatre" and job number 368 in the job book, though only 108 numbers had been utilized up to this point. It is the 49th theatre listed, though perhaps the 22nd actually built from the ground up to Lamb designs. It was his first known foray as a theatre architect beyond the northeastern United States and the borders of New York, New Jersey, Pennsylvania, and Maryland.

Many of the path-breaking theatres which Lamb designed prior to his Toronto project have not survived. One of these was the City Theatre at 116 E. 14th Street, the first large theatre Lamb designed from scratch in 1909 for William Fox. It was elaborately reported in 1910 in the *Architects' and Builders' Magazine*. The architectural style of this 2,267-seat house was described as French Renaissance, a scheme familiar in some of Lamb's later theatres. The auditorium walls were wainscoted in scagliola marble, and topped with rose damask. Gilding encrusted the richly moulded plaster frame of the proscenium and the capitols of the interior columns. The sight lines of the theatre were held to be remarkably good, as there was not a post or supporting rod anywhere.[5]

Another important pioneer lost to posterity is Lamb's "Nicoland", a small theatre on Westchester Avenue near 156th Street in the Bronx. Its plans were filed with the City in February 1908, the structure reportedly to cost $14,000. (Its arched façade persisted until only recently though the theatre closed in 1914.) It is now attributed to have been the first "purpose-built" movie theatre constructed in New York City.[6]

One of the most important of his early theatres which has been only recently lost to demolition was the Strand Theatre at Broadway and 47th. What disappeared was one of the most influential theatres Lamb would ever design: the spectacular mid-town blossoming of the movie palace.

Right: One page of Thomas Lamb's job book, showing job 368, "Victoria Theatre, Toronto, Can." for Loew. The columns on the right indicated storage locations for drawings. Later entries in the job book provide more dates and annotations.

The New York Strand

Though the site of the Strand was leased in December 1912, ground was not broken until July 1913. Construction took only 9 months, and this million-dollar theatre devoted exclusively to motion pictures opened in April 1914. Senior theatre architect George M. Keister was engaged with Lamb to draw plans.

The revolution embodied in the Strand was recognized at the time, and has been discussed in secondary works on the history of the movie palace. It may be instructive, however, to note some of the differences between the Strand and the Toronto theatres Lamb built almost simultaneously.

In many ways, the Strand was much less of a hybrid. It was considerably larger, seating 3,300 on two floors. It accommodated more spacious lobbies, promenades, and rest rooms, along with furniture which completed the picture of luxury and comfort. The Strand was said to have three theatre organs, four moving picture projectors, a thirty-piece orchestra, three ticket booths, and 32 flaming arc lights on its massive facade. By contrast, the Toronto theatres were less generously equipped. They had no organs, and each was served by perhaps two projectors, a 7-10 piece orchestra, and two ticket booths. Only four flaming arcs accentuated the narrow Yonge Street façade.

Though the Strand was built "with accommodation for any change of policy," it was primarily designed for movies, with a shallow stage and new obsessions with movie sight lines. To a large extent, the building was close to developing into a prototype. As a respected architectural journal put it, "The evolution from the converted store building and other makeshifts, to the specially designed 'moving picture theatre,' finds in a sense a culmination in the Strand Theatre..."[7]

Left: The arcaded façade of Lamb's 1908 Nicoland in the Bronx, New York's and Lamb's first purpose-built movie house, photographed for city assessment purposes in 1939.

Left: Exterior of New York's and Lamb's first full-blown movie palace opened in 1914: the 3,300-seat Strand, Broadway and 47th St., New York.

Right: View of the New York Strand's 3,300-seat auditorium.
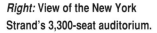

SURVIVING LAMB THEATRES BUILT BEFORE 1914

Eight Lamb theatres in New York City which predate Lamb's Toronto complex survive as of this writing, though some are in substantially altered condition or are threatened with demolition.

Two early Lamb theatres standing relatively intact in the theatre district — the Empire and the Cort — were designed for legitimate productions. The Empire opened in September 1912 as the Eltinge, a 900-seat legitimate theatre with two balconies and exemplary sight lines. (It was named for Julian Eltinge, one of the era's most popular female impersonators). Closed recently after years of serving up West 42nd Street's menu of violent and pornographic movies, the Empire awaits the realization of plans for 42nd Street's renaissance. (Present plans are for its terra cotta façade to be saved, and its interior converted for other purposes.) Lamb's Cort Theatre on West 48th Street, opened in December 1912, is in better condition It still operates as a legitimate theatre and is among the oldest surviving theatres in New York. The theatre's design and decoration was inspired by the architecture of the Louis XVI period: its façade modeled on the Petit Trianon and its interior based on "the style of Marie Antoinette."[8]

The rest of Lamb's survivors are further uptown. Only one is still used as a theatre. The façade and some interior elements remain of Lamb's 1913 Orpheum Theatre at 86th Street and 3rd Avenue. This theatre is still operated by Loew's, though as "twin" movie houses. The Boulevard Theatre, opened in 1912 with 2100 seats on Southern Boulevard in the Bronx operated as a movie house until recently, but now survives as a jeans store.

One of the most intriguing early Lamb survivors is the Audubon Theatre at 165th and Broadway, dating from 1912 and assigned job no. 322. It is remote from the theatre district, and calculations of real estate economies apparently did not affect this low-slung, sprawling building. Its exterior was dotted with windows and garlanded with colourful terra cotta, and the theatre's interior was tricked out with scagliola, gilded columns, red damask, stained glass, and swarmed with protuberant plaster decorations. One of its most unusual elements was its patriotic proscenium mural representing George Washington, his horse-backed entourage and the Jumel Mansion. The theatre, now owned by the City of New York, is abandoned and fire damaged. Any day, it may be demolished.

The earliest surviving Lamb theatre is his Washington Theatre at 149th Street and Amsterdam Ave, designed in August 1910 (Job 291) and opened in 1911. At the time, it was apparently managed by William Fox Amusement Co., and seems to have been a suburban variety theatre seating about 1,200, offering 15 to 25-cent shows. Little has been written of its early history. The theatre is substantially intact, and now serves as the New Covenant Temple of the United Holy Church of America. Another early Lamb theatre in the same category is the Bedford on Bedford Avenue in Brooklyn (job 354), whose interior has been painted white to function as a church.

The most important of the early Lamb theatres in New York and the third now used as a Church is the Regent, which, since Ben Hall's *The Best Remaining Seats*, is generally heralded as the primeval movie palace. It now serves the congregation and minister of the First Corinthian Baptist Church. This uptown theatre seating 1800 and listed as job number 344 in August 1912 was opened in February 1913, before plans were drawn for Loew's Toronto complex. Its "Spanish-Moorish" decorative scheme was rendered in gold, blue and red, with satin wall panels and heavy carpets of dark blue, and its proscenium mural reproduced "The Surrender of Granada" by Francisco Pradillo.[9] At its opening it had an organ and an 8-piece orchestra.

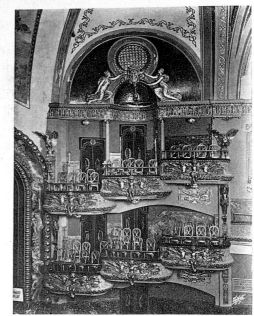

Left: View towards the proscenium arch of the two-balcony Cort Theatre, West 48th Street, New York, opened in 1912. The Cort still operates as a legitimate theatre, one of the oldest in the Broadway district.

Above: "Washington" mural and boxes of New York's Audubon Theatre.

Above: Exterior of Audubon Theatre, 165th Street and Broadway, New York, opened in 1912. To the left of the theatre entrance is a second-floor ballroom, now more renowned than the theatre because it was the site of the 1965 murder of black activist Malcolm X.

Right: Dome and balcony of New York's Audubon Theatre.

Arguably, the most unusual and interesting survivor among early Lamb theatres is his double-decker complex in Toronto. It was built during Lamb's most diverse and experimental period as a commercial theatre architect, when he established, rather than followed trends. His office was not yet manifesting a production line of similar theatres, and each project seems to have been a new adventure and opportunity, one which merited unique attention.

The Toronto complex is also significant as the earliest (and one of the few remaining intact) Lamb theatres in Canada. Together, Lamb and Loew embarked on the first of many ensuing theatre projects outside of the United States. But at the beginning, it was enveloped in controversy and scandal, perhaps contradicting the notion of the *New York Dramatic Mirror* that Toronto was just like Pittsburgh or Buffalo.

Right: Interior of the New York Regent and its sounding board mural depicting the surrender of Granada.

Right: Façade of the 1913 Regent Theatre, 116th Street and 7th Avenue, New York, listed as job 344 in Lamb's job book.

CHAPTER FOUR

LOEW'S INVADES TORONTO

NEW YORKERS COME TO TOWN

Though many of the subcontractors employed to build, equip, and decorate the theatre were local, Loew and Lamb resorted to a general contractor and foreman from New York City. The contracting firm was Fleischmann Brothers, of 507 Fifth Avenue, New York, run by brothers Leon V. and Gustav J. Fleischmann. Fleischmann Brothers had built between 40 and 60 theatres in American cities, including some for Loew's and a number for the Shubert chain. Fleischmann would have been familiar with Lamb's practice and standards, and the new breed of theatre building being erected for movies and vaudeville. Lamb and Loew's inexperience in Canada may have mitigated against the employment of a Toronto firm. (The general contracts for subsequent theatres they built in Canada were awarded to local Canadian firms.)

Later, in 1916, the Toronto Chapter of the Ontario Association of Architects complained bitterly of the "greater share of the work" being awarded to familiar foreign contractors by American architects freely practicing in the city. It stated that a concomitant "great injustice" to "our business and manufacturing industries was done because the American architect tended to specify his native building materials in preference to similar Canadian building materials...."[1]

This charge was borne out in the building of Loew's Toronto theatres, as other familiar New York contacts provided face brick, ornamental terra cotta, interior plastering, and decorating. Carter, Black and Ayres, brick dealers located at 1182 Broadway, was credited with supplying facing brick for the Victoria and Yonge Street elevations. Ornamental terra cotta was supplied by The New York Architectural Terra Cotta Company on Long Island. Cathcart and Kissell of West 34th Street was responsible for plastering. (Significantly, Joseph M. Cathcart of Cathcart and Kissell, Leon and Gustav Fleischmann, and architect Thomas Lamb were all domiciled in 1913 in the same apartment building at 601 West 156th Street.) Loew's and Lamb also employed the Rambusch Decorating Company of New York City. Founded by the Danish-born Frode Rambusch in 1898, the company had decorated several theatres, including Shea's Victoria Theatre in Toronto and, even more significantly the American Theatre in Manhattan.

Advertisement of Carter, Black and Ayres, supplier of the yellow face brick used on the Yonge and Victoria Street façades of the Toronto complex.

Advertisement for Fleischmann Bros. Co., the general contractors for Loew's Toronto complex. This firm advertised in 1911 that it had built New York's Folies Bergere (later the Helen Hayes Theatre) "in the record time" of 3 months and 27 days.

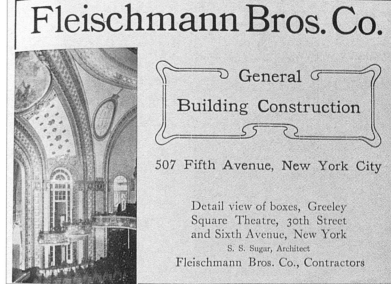

Loew's remarkable theatre building in Toronto was constructed in what now seems like record time. Only eight months elapsed between the issuing of the building permit and the opening of the lower theatre. Nevertheless, Loew's may have been disappointed at the length of this interval, since in February 1913 an opening date in August, six months later, was predicted. The building permit was issued on 5 April. It assessed the cost of the building at $250,000, though architect Lamb later admitted that the figure approached half a million dollars. Work on the site began about a month before the permit was obtained.

The process of obtaining the permit turned out to be a complicated one, coloured by hectic conditions prevailing in the City Architect's Department. At a period of frenetic construction in the city, the Department was engaged in a comprehensive rewriting of all of Toronto's building bylaws. The health of the City Architect had consequently broken down, and he was on leave for long periods during Loew's negotiation for the permit. On 1 April 1913, bylaw 6401 governing theatres and public buildings was passed by Toronto City Council. Thomas Lamb would have been already familiar with many of its provisions, as it mirrored, sometimes word for word, sections of New York City bylaws on theatres. The bylaw affected the design and equipment of Loew's Theatre and Winter Garden, though several of its sections were circumvented by Loew's and Lamb.

CORRUPTION IN TORONTO THE GOOD?

Concessions from the Mayor and Council and a trip to New York for city officials were required, because the building was unorthodox, with features which did not conform to updated Toronto bylaws. Most controversial were the length of the Yonge Street lobby corridor and the adjoining store, and the height above street level of the upper theatre.

The building of Loew's deepened a suspicion already present because of a pattern of irregularities and suspected corruption in the workings of the City Architect's Department. A cavalcade of complaints brought about a judicial investigation in 1914. The City's treatment of the unorthodox new theatres was just one of many important issues under review. The investigation found no evidence, however, that any City Official had been bribed by Loew's or had otherwise profited from the building of the theatre.

The conduct of Stanley Makepeace, Lamb's local architect on the Toronto complex, helped to trigger the investigation, though no wrong-doing on his part with respect to the Loew's project was established. But, during the enquiry, Makepeace was revealed to be unscrupulous, with low ethical standards. He admitted that in early 1913 he had pirated and plagiarized another architect's plans for an apartment building, aided and abetted by an unnamed person in the City Architect's Department. The 33-year-old Makepeace, who had moved to Toronto from the United States in 1911, was castigated by the investigation. He left town shortly thereafter.

Portrait of Frode Rambusch, founder of the Rambusch Decorating Company, another New York subcontractor employed in the Toronto complex.

1906 advertisement for the Rambusch Decorating Company. It developed a close working connection with Thomas Lamb and the Loew circuit. In all, the firm was responsible for the decoration of about 50 Loew theatres.

NEW YORK MODELS

In the course of the judicial investigation, presiding Judge Denton queried Acting City Architect G.F.W. Price whether Loew's Theatre was a building "the like of which has never before been constructed in Toronto." "Yes", replied Price, "I don't know of any City where they have the double-deck, a double-deck theatre like that, with the exception of New York, it is absolutely new to me."[2].

Price reported that both Toronto Fire Chief Thompson and City Architect Robert McCallum had opposed the idea in the beginning: "they did not know anything about this roof garden business, they had never seen it before." To win their approval, a trip to New York was arranged to investigate and to report on public safety in roof garden theatres there. Price, McCallum's Deputy, was substituted at the last minute because of the latter's illness. Another feature under investigation on the tour by the Toronto officials was the type of fire tower proposed for the fire escapes of the new Loew's theatres.

In New York, Nicholas Schenck, General Manager of Loew's, took Price and Thompson around and showed them "the different theatres," but at the City's expense. The offer of reimbursement for the $90 cost of the three-day visit was rejected. Most of Schenck's time was well spent. Price developed boundless enthusiasm for the fire towers, asserting that they were "the very best thing I have ever seen in that line."[3] More importantly, approval was won for the double-decker theatres. Board of Control sanctioned the building, notwithstanding that the Toronto bylaw permitted an upper level auditorium only if it seated under 500 and had no stage scenery.

From Loew's point of view, the trip was only a qualified success, as the two Torontonians refused to go along with other New York standards proposed for the Toronto theatre. Schenck had seized the opportunity to offer as a model the fire proofing system of cinders, cement, and sand used in the floors of New York theatres, in contrast to the concrete required in Toronto. Price and Thompson stoutly resisted, and Schenck complained later that Toronto's requirements for concrete cost three times what a comparable theatre in New York would have cost. Likewise the City's excessively stringent steel regulations had augmented construction costs by seventy five or one hundred thousand dollars.

During construction the City Architect's Department was stubborn on other issues. It reacted negatively to the seemingly unbridled desire of Loew's to stuff patrons into their new theatres. Because Price declined to use his discretionary power to allow Loew's to space seats 30" apart from back to back, instead of the bylaw's 32" spacing, in September of 1913 Loew's successfully filed for an amendment to the bylaw.

In other instances, the plans devised by Loew's and Lamb were revised at the Acting City Architect's insistence. Price demanded the removal of some of the seats in the lower theatre, a change which General Contractor Fleischmann considered was not required by code and resulted in a loss of revenue. He thought that Price was "really exercising wide discretion," and also resented the City's rigid or wrong-headed adherence to another bylaw provision. Price had insisted that the widths of certain balcony stairs be expanded from seven to eight feet. Fleischmann had complied "very reluctantly."

CONTROVERSY ERUPTS: THE LOBBY FROM YONGE STREET

Toronto City Council had not specifically approved the long lobby corridor from Yonge Street, which, with its adjoining store, seemed to violate the new Toronto bylaw of 1 April. This issue was more contentious than the height of the upper theatre, and did more to fuel rumours of unsavory dealings by City officials.

It was not the lobby itself, but the store attached to the long lobby which contravened a section of the bylaw. This stated that the front part of a theatre building might be used for stores if the stores were not more than 30' in depth from the street. Instead, the lobby corridor was 169 feet long, and the store measured 95 feet in length, more than triple the limit specified for stores in a theatre building.

Loew's Yonge Street was the first in Toronto to have a lengthy lobby colonnade leading to cheaper back land. This arrangement, already common in New York and elsewhere, required the minimum investment in prime real estate. Patrons were led by a narrow corridor to the large and less expensive block of land on which the auditoria were planted, half a block away on Victoria Street. Half the width of this expensive corridor would earn money by being rented out as a store, which, in turn, would benefit from the crowds attracted to the theatre.

The issue of the lobby from Yonge Street had festered since the early months of the theatre's construction. A group of Yonge Street merchants petitioned the City Council in May 1913 to "take all necessary steps to prevent the possibility of danger to our citizens, which might ensue, if the new proposed theatre on Victoria Street, proposing to run a continuous performance, is allowed to have an entrance or exit by means of a long arcade running from Yonge Street to such theatre on Victoria Street."[4] The question was referred to City Architect McCallum and to the Fire Chief, who provided a garbled and evasive reply on 14 May:

> ...the theatre referred to has the legal entrances and exits
> required under the By-law independent of the 20'0"
> passageway which leads out to Yonge Street, and we do not
> think it would be advisable to close up this additional means of
> ingress and egress, as the space provided has a tendency to
> afford a greater protection to the public in case of fire or panic.[5]

The *Toronto World* real estate columnist had taken up the cudgels on Loew's behalf, and had argued rather speciously on 11 May 1913:

> About the weirdest thing heard in realty circles for some time
> is the complaint from Yonge Street property owners that the
> new Loew theatre should not be permitted to use a narrow
> passage to bring its crowds in from Yonge and let them out
> again. All theatre audiences sift out through narrow passages,
> and so the one argument of the complaint, that congestion risks
> would be increased, is lost. But the unaccountable part is the
> desire to keep people off Yonge Street. Next thing Yonge Street
> merchants will be protesting against street cars and any sort of
> traffic. The objections were engineered by moving picture
> theatre owners, and that leaves the complaint valueless, except
> for comment.

Instead of seeking the Mayor and Council's approval for the store and lobby scheme, Loew's had resorted to subterfuge. To this purpose, in April the theatre's plans were drawn up as "Victoria Street Theatre," with no Yonge Street address.

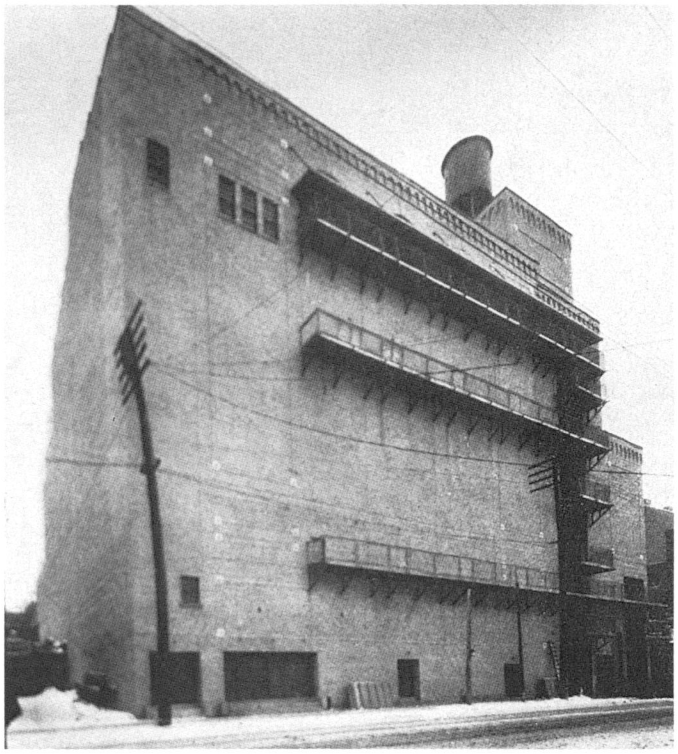

Right: **View of Victoria Street façade in 1913, photographed before the complex was completed. Note the exterior fire escapes and the 'fire tower' which enclosed their linking stairs.**

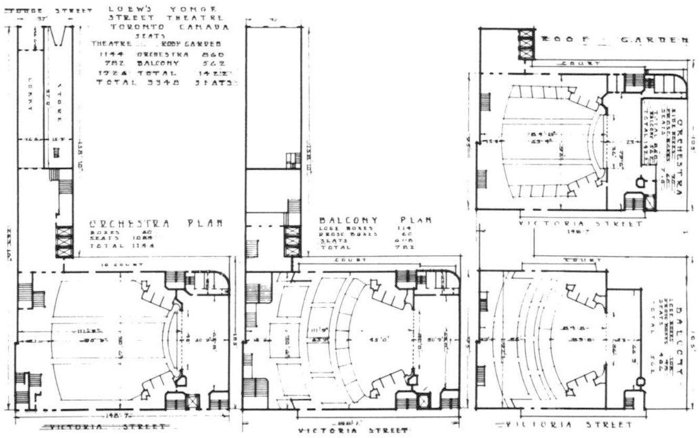

Left: **Lamb and Makepeace's floor plan of Loew's Yonge Street Theatre and Winter Garden, showing long lobby corridor and store.**

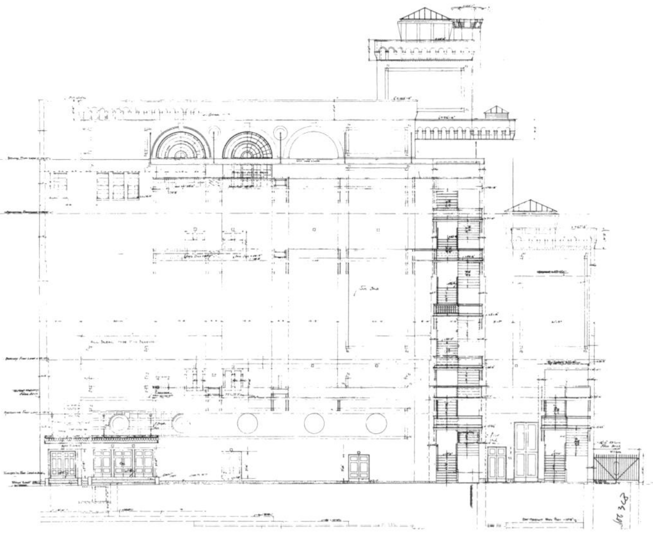

Right: **Lamb drawing of the Victoria Street elevation. Note the marquee shown over doors on the left. The Victoria Street box office was located behind the wall between these sets of doors. To serve both theatres, one of its windows faced the enclosed fire stairs to the Winter Garden while the other opened directly into the rear of the lower auditorium. This box office was removed in a 1928 renovation.**

Local Architect: Stanley Makepeace

Born in Watertown, N.Y. in 1880, Stanley Makepeace grew up in Syracuse, where his father, Mervale, had an architectural practice. Stanley withdrew before his graduation from Syracuse University, and received his B.S. in architecture from the University of Pennsylvania in 1905. According to a 1915 account, his career had begun as chief draftsman for a Chicago firm specializing in hotels, theatres and high-class apartment buildings. He had then reportedly designed "the new houses of the Marcus Loew syndicate throughout Canada" - a distortion of the truth.[6].

In Toronto, Makepeace initially worked as a draftsman in the office of Burke, Horwood & White. In 1912, he formed a partnership to practice architecture with Arthur W. McConnell, a lecturer at the University of Toronto. The business was manifested in a few permits for small commercial buildings, most of which were cancelled. Among these was one issued in May 1912, for a three storey brick "theatorium" and apartments at Bloor and St. Clarens. His partnership with McConnell had dissolved by the time Makepeace began work with Lamb on the drawings for Loew's complex, and his firm was then Makepeace and Makepeace. In this arrangement, Stanley's father was his partner.

Makepeace admitted to the judicial investigation that early in 1913 he had illicitly borrowed and copied drawings by the architectural firm of Edwards and Saunders of the College Heights Apartments. G. F. W. Price, the Acting Chief Architect, was implicated, as he had introduced Makepeace to his client in this affair. Makepeace brought even more attention to it by suing for his commission on the plagiarized apartment building built on the corner of King West and Dowling Avenue.

Makepeace was already involved in drawing plans for a theatre on the site. He had worked for local people on the project in 1912, before Loew's and Lamb's involvement. During the investigation, Lamb was non-committally distant on the subject of Makepeace. They were not acquainted before the project: Lamb "believed" and "supposed" that Lawrence Solmon had suggested taking advantage of Makepeace's former work, but denied that the City Architect's office had any role in getting the job for Makepeace. (Lamb acknowledged that working plans had been drawn up by "Mr. Makepeace and myself." Lamb had visited the site "about once a month keeping in touch and Mr. Makepeace made reports every other day." [7] It is unlikely they ever worked together again.)

Although thoroughly discredited by the investigation for his plagiarized plans, Makepeace still managed to obtain commissions for at least six dwellings in Toronto between March and August 1914. He left the city and the country by the end of the year. He surfaced in Detroit in 1915 where he tried to forge a brilliant career as a theatre architect. In that year he designed the 973-seat photoplay house, the Knickerbocker Theatre, located across the street from an amusement park. Here, he did not copy his own and Lamb's designs for Loew's Toronto complex. Notwithstanding his splashy Detroit debut, Makepeace faded from the scene and his whereabouts after 1920 are a mystery. He dropped from sight in the annals of the profession and in city directories thereafter.

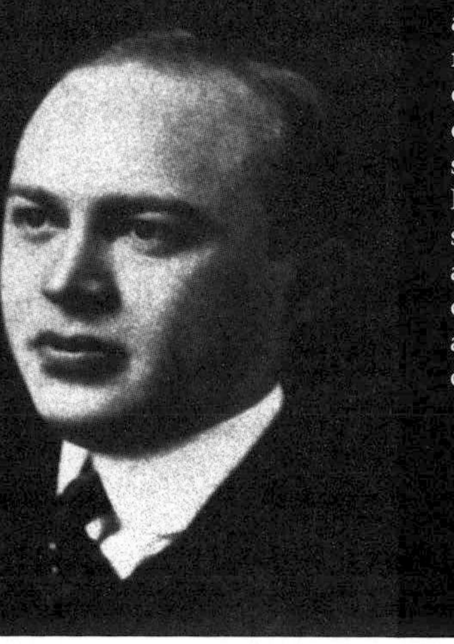

Right: **Portrait of Stanley Makepeace, local architect of Loew's Toronto theatres.**

A marquee and ticket booth on Victoria Street contributed to this impression. The ruse was effective, as Acting City Architect Price testified in 1914, "I know my idea of the thing was that the building was to front on Victoria Street."[8]

That this Victoria Street entrance and ticket booth were a sham was observed by the City's Solicitor during the 1914 investigation. He noted that patrons would have to "step right from the street into the body of the [lower] theatre," and added, "I don't suppose there would be one person in a hundred that would come from Victoria Street..?"[9]

Lamb would argue later that the bylaw regarding the length of stores in front of theatres did not apply because 189-91 Yonge Street was not only not the front of the theatre building, but it was not even part of the theatre: it was "...a separate building entirely."[10]

General Contractor Leon Fleischmann was just as outrageous in his testimony before the 1914 judicial enquiry:

> The front of that building we do not consider at all as Yonge St., we consider Victoria St. the front of that building and I feel we would have a perfect right according to the bylaw simply to shut that building off altogether and we would be still within the jurisdiction of the bylaws.
>
> Q. You mean shut the entrance from Yonge St. off altogether?
> A. Yes; we simply put that in, that is additional exit.
> Q. Or additional entrance?
> A. Yes, it works both ways.

Terra cotta mask on the Yonge Street facade.

BUILDING FOR ILLUSION

The builders of the complex wanted to have things both ways. They wanted a building on the main street, without main street expenses, and a building that looked more expensive than it was. Costly face brick was used sparingly, only in portions of the façade visible from the street. A low grade of common brick, supplied by Don Valley Brick Works in Toronto, sufficed for the remainder of the elevations and the brickwork in the theatre. This type of cost-cutting was typical in commercial theatres. The minimum screen of face brick, applied for the benefit of creating an illusion and for an audience, perhaps exhibited a kinship with a stage or a movie set.

Certain building materials played an important part in the construction of 20th-century fireproof theatres built for mass audiences and the movies. Concrete, hollow terra cotta, and terrazzo were relatively cheap as well as durable and waterproof. In particular, ornamental terra cotta had been enthusiastically embraced for the decoration of movie theatre buildings. Terra cotta decoration suited commercial theatre builders because of its flexibility and cheapness. It had endless possibilities for being modelled into elaborate and fanciful shapes. Gaily coloured and mass produced, it was suitable for dressing up exterior walls with few or no windows, and was light, resistant to dirt and the elements, fireproof and easy to handle and clean.

Steel was another prerequisite. Each theatre in the complex had a separate structural system, though the steel in the rear columns of the downstairs theatre performed double-duty in bearing the load of Winter Garden columns above. These theatres differed from run-of-the-mill vaudeville and legitimate theatres of the day in their gigantic steel trusses and single cantilevered balconies. The structural steel system in the complex was considered worthy of detailed attention in an article, "Loew's Yonge Street Theatre, Toronto," published in *Construction* in April 1915, and its author marvelled at the "striking...absence of obstructing columns" in both houses, a relatively new and welcome deficit in theatre architecture.[11]

According to Charlotte Kopac Herzog, "although steel frame girder and cantilever construction had been used for a long time, extremely long trusses were peculiar to the movie palaces." Long trusses were required because there was "...no girder long enough to span the one hundred or hundred fifty feet between the side walls of most palace auditoriums..." Within five years, a movie palace (the Capitol in New York) designed by Thomas Lamb would hold the record for "the greatest steel truss ever used in a building up to that time: one hundred seventy feet long."[12]

Interior ornamental plaster and "scagliola," or plaster imitating costly marble, were also important and emblematic components in theatre decoration. Ornamental plaster was a pliable and inexpensive method of decoration. With elaborate relief details and richly covered with burnished gilt, its surfaces reflected artificial light and contributed to the entertainment, grandeur and glamour of the interior, at relatively low cost. Relief decorations also impacted favourably on the acoustics of the auditorium. Prefabricated scagliola panels and columns contributed further to an extravagant impression at reasonable cost, and befitted buildings dedicated to make-believe.

While the lower theatre and lobbies were lavished with plaster which imitated marble, the Winter Garden ceiling was covered with beech branches and leaves which many assumed were artificial. These had been preserved, crated, and transported to the theatre, probably in the dead of a Toronto winter, after the lower theatre had opened. Many of the branches were woven through the grid from below, but others were tossed onto the accumulation. To this was added one artificial plum, one pear and one orange, made of cloth and papier mache, along with a few Christmas decorations and garlands. These were probably thrown on in the customary haste to open the theatre.

THE RUSH TO OPEN

Though the building of this complicated and unprecedented complex could have enkindled numerous newspaper articles, very little was written about it while it was under construction. Perhaps the furor caused by the long lobby from Yonge Street caused Loew's to be reticent about press releases in this period, or perhaps the chain was otherwise preoccupied. One of the only press items published was the *World*'s photograph of Loew's new theatre "nearing completion" , published on 10 September, but obviously taken several months before.

A *Star Weekly* article of 22 November was one of the earliest to provide details the new theatre, "rapidly approaching completion," though it was "taking longer to finish than was expected." The opening was predicted for the Monday before Christmas.

A flurry of press releases followed the announcement of the 15 December opening of the downstairs theatre. A 13 December newspaper article referred to the complex having been built "at astonishing speed in only seven months." The second warmest November on record — with an average temperature of 42°F must have assisted the drying of plaster and paint. Likely the theatre was rushed to open before Christmas, a profitable season, and building trades had worked night shifts to meet this goal. A *World* article on Saturday referred to every workman finishing his duties to meet the Monday opening deadline by "12 o'clock tonight".

The last-minute blitz was evidenced in the date of a 22 December newspaper which was found stuffed under the capping of the plaster balustrade of the grand staircase on the mezzanine level. On opening night a week earlier, this portion of the staircase and any other incomplete elements were probably veiled with colourful bunting or draped with patriotic flags. Other confirmation of this rush to open was supplied by the vivid oral reminiscences of the late Walter Stockdale who was directed by the local painters' union to Loew's site superintendent shortly after the theatre opened. On successive Sundays, when the theatre was dark, he worked on regilding sections of the dome of the lower auditorium. This was necessary where the lacquered metal leaf had been applied to "green" plaster which had not been allowed sufficient time to cure.

This kind of haste in building theatres was quite normal. Frequently, painters and chair installers were being surreptitiously ushered out just as opening night guests were being greeted by impressive camouflage of unfinished plaster work. No time could be lost in launching a commercial theatre towards its destiny and most exalted purpose: to return money to its owners.

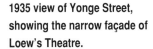

1935 view of Yonge Street, showing the narrow façade of Loew's Theatre.

CHAPTER FIVE

"UNIQUE FEATURES OF TORONTO THEATRES"
ENTRANCES AND FOYER SPACE:
FORM FOLLOWS FUNCTION

The design, decoration and equipment of the new Loew's theatres had rationale and purpose, and responded directly to uncompromising money-making ideas or money-saving economies. The materials and layout of the building observed (somewhat more flexibly) municipal bylaw requirements. Design features also reflected many conventions of the day, along with convulsive changes then taking place within the mass entertainment industry. Many elements of the design augured a new building type — the movie palace.

FACADE AND ELECTRIC SIGNS

The decorative treatment of the Yonge Street façade was fairly standard for small-time vaudeville theatres of the period. Other than by the dramatic masks on the keystones, one would not know that the facade was that of a theatre. This conservative approach, seeking to appeal to tradition and respectability, differed from some of the highly original and eclectic façades of the earlier nickelodeons and later movie palaces. The façade of the Victoria Street elevation received relatively extensive decorative treatment, probably only because of the elaborate pretence contrived by Loew's and Lamb that it was a facade, and of commercial significance

But this type of façade on Yonge Street, fronting only the lobby corridor and store, not the whole theatre building, was a new phenomenon for large Toronto theatres. A façade which was the "shortest distance between two stores" would become a movie palace prototype because it maximized profits. Any loss of conspicuousness for the theatre because of the narrow façade was more than compensated by the addition of huge upright signs and light-studded marquees, both of which became signatures of the movie palace.

The theatre's original marquee, a relatively modest one, was built over only the theatre vestibule and not the adjoining store. It was delineated by white electric bulbs, while four brilliant carbon arc lights defined its corners. Massive, colourful, swirling marquees which were unique to the movie theatre would await the 1920s.

The only available photograph of the original marquee. The photograph was taken of armistice celebrations on Yonge Street on 11 November 1918. (Lamb's drawings of the original façade and marquee are among those missing from the present collection.)

The Yonge Street façade, as seen in 1942. The second floor above the lobby was not accessible to the public. Initially, it was rented to the tenants of the store which adjoined the lobby corridor. Later, Loew's used it as storage and workshop space.

The original upright, a Loew standard, was a much more ostentatious affair than the original marquee. The sign could be seen from blocks away, advertising the price of the show, as well as the name and product of the theatre. This billboard type of upright, full of information, would yield later to vertical signs conveying only the name of the theatre.

EXTERIOR VESTIBULE, LOBBY COLONNADE AND BOX OFFICE

The exterior vestibule on Yonge Street and its free-standing box office were nickelodeon features which would carry over into the later movie palace. With its durable and easy maintenance terrazzo floor and marble faced walls, the exterior vestibule served several functions. It contained advertising material, and sheltered people buying tickets, waiting for friends, or perusing publicity, and it indicated the decorative splendours awaiting in the theatre, once a ticket was purchased. Its most important function was the accommodation of the outside box office, a domain in which theatre owners were mightily interested.

Owners of pioneer movie theatres had built ticket booths on the sidewalk to attract attention, and to lure patrons to their fly-by-night businesses and shows not otherwise advertised. The exterior booth catered to more impulsive ticket buying, considered to be a trait of movie show patrons, in contrast to the less impetuous habits in evidence at legitimate theatres with their reserved seating and interior ticket windows.

The outside booth would later be embraced by movie palace architects. The 1927 volume *American Theatres of Today* was explicit:

The exterior vestibule and outside box office in 1913. Note the opalescent glass transoms and glass panelled entrance doors which lead to the lobby corridor.

> Psychology enters into the placing of the ticket booth at the center of the entrance near the street. It must never be necessary to pass through doors or by any other obstructions to purchase a ticket. The larger theatres have additional ticket booths inside the lobby, but invariably a ticket booth is located at the street entrance also....The whole appeal of the exterior design is to sell the passerby a ticket. The entrance lures him, but the booth must actually sell him. Its design must be such as to hold the interest which the entrance has aroused.[1]

The outside ticket booth installed at Loew's in Toronto in 1913 fulfilled this function. The tent-like appearance of its colourful glass dome hearkens back to the carnival or circus origins of early movie shows. Like the nickelodeon booth, it was colourful enough to grab the attention of passers-by, and accessible enough to seize their money, before they changed their minds.

The gay opalescent art glass transoms over the entrance doors reflecting the artificial light behind helped to attract customers and introduced the interior colour scheme. They also gradually lowered daytime light levels in the lobby corridor. Glass panels in the entrance doors titillated would-be patrons with views of the interior. In 1913 no airlock (or second set of doors) was provided to buffer cold and drafts, though the airlock was not a new concept. This omission was later seen as a mistake, and airlock doors would be added during the first major renovation in 1919.

The original lobby corridor, with terrazzo and tile flooring. Lamb's detailed drawings show wall mirrors in each arch, instead of the brocade wall fabric and gas fixtures seen here. The radiator covers and the bases of the columns and walls are faced with marble. The fluted columns are imitation marble or scagliola.

The lobby corridor in 1942. The arched wall mirrors were added in a 1935 renovation. The terrazzo floor has been covered with linoleum and rubber mats and the original chandeliers replaced.

The purpose of the long lobby colonnade was not so much to provide amenities as to lead to the cheaper real estate where the auditoria stood, and to the grand staircase and elevators. Still, the lobby managed to perform several functions. It could accommodate long lineups and inside box offices and was profitably used to exhibit advertising posters to those waiting.

It was always hoped that an outside booth alone could not manage the throngs seeking admission. Inside box offices offered a warm, dry, welcoming alternative to the possibilities of a damp, cold, or otherwise threatening line up outside. Later movie palaces with huge capacities would maintain the convention of one or two inside box offices in addition to an outside ticket booth.

The box office in Loew's lobby corridor likely served another purpose. Following traditional theatre practices, it was the source of reserved seats. The complications involved in selling reserved seats to both theatres in 1914 must have contributed to an additional Winter Garden box office being established under the grand staircase, in a space originally planned by Lamb as an office.

The decorative scheme of the lobby colonnade prefaced that to be found in the downstairs theatre and grand staircase. Scagliola columns, arched, panelled and coffered forms, gilt, terrazzo, and brass were extensively used. The decoration included numerous references to the entertainment purposes of the building, and helped to create a receptive mood in the audience to be admitted. Ornamental allusions in plaster included flutes, clarinets, and tambourines. Inscribed on panels in the frieze above the fluted Corinthian columns on one side were the names of writers and composers: "some illustrious person whose work contributed towards the betterment of the stage." On the other side were the "various phases of theatrical life." These were uncovered during the 1984 restoration of the lobby corridor and read as follows from the entrance:

South wall	North wall
Burlesque	Goethe
Comedy	Mozart
Opera	Shakespeare
Tableau	Lizt [sic]
Tragedy	Schiller
Dance	Wagner
Drama	Schubert
Vaudeville	Ibsen
Music	Beethoven

Certainly, the list conveys the impression that this is a theatre of class and elevated refinement, one which the most well-bred should have been proud to patronize despite the misspelling of "Liszt". It also reveals a preference for Germanic culture on the part of those directing the decorating effort.

In 1913 and in subsequent renovations, opalescent glass lobby chandeliers beckoned patrons to the grand staircase and elevator hall. These and other fixtures did more than illuminate the theatre. They accustomed patrons to low light levels in the auditoria, and introduced the decorative glories there. The lobby was supposed to echo some of the glitter and brightness of the exterior, and to be attractively visible to potential patrons passing on the street.

Theatre architects also had to consider how the building might be used and abused. The terrazzo floors in the lobbies and grand staircase were cheap and easy to clean, and could easily withstand the detritus of tobacco users — of both the smoking and chewing variety. Brass railings used to guide lineups in the lobby needed to be sturdy enough to support leaning adults and acrobatic children, while being removable to sockets in other locations.

FOYER SPACE AND PASSENGER ELEVATORS

Though the theatres' staircase and elevator halls were neither notably spacious nor luxurious, they were unusual and dramatic in that they proffered a seven-storey climb to the Winter Garden, or, for the unwilling, open-cage passenger elevators which bore patrons seven storeys upwards. Lamb's drawings show three passenger elevators, a number corroborated by contemporary reports in *Construction* and the *Toronto Star*. In fact, only two passenger elevators were installed in 1913, in the two shafts near the staircase hall. The third was installed in April 1918.

The staircase hall, showing original configuration of the grand staircase and Winter Garden box office. The elevator hall lies directly ahead.

Above: The grand staircase to the Winter Garden. The enclosed stairway visible at the rear was a fire exit to the Winter Garden, mandated by City bylaws.

Above: Entrances to the double entrance lobbies photographed in 1934. In 1919 the original store was supplanted by an adjoining long lobby corridor which matched the original. Note that the opalescent glass transoms and entrance doors have been duplicated. The original outside box office has been replaced and its location moved to the left.

A MATCHING LOBBY 1919-1935

A post-war boom probably inspired later alterations which removed the controversial long store adjoining the long lobby corridor. The store at 191 Yonge Street was replaced by an additional entrance and lobby which matched the original at 189 Yonge Street (although a smaller store was rebuilt in the space in 1935).

The decoration of the duplicate 1919 lobby carried over the idea of frieze panels with inscriptions relating to "various phases of theatrical life," but with a difference. Instead of the 1913 model of names of writers and composers and different types of theatrical entertainment, Shakespeare plays and operas were named in four surviving inscriptions: Othello, Henry IV, Pagliacci, and Carmen.

Lamb had planned arched mirrors in the original colonnade, a scheme which was finally realized in 1935 renovations. The series of mirrors conveyed a more spacious and open vista, instead of the rather claustrophobic tunnel seen in the original photograph. Then, colonnade arches were treated to "imported red tapestries of floral pattern," the same fabric used in wall panels in the lower auditorium. In 1919, three of these arches were opened to the new matching lobby.

The addition of the new lobby in 1919 had other implications. The grand staircase was redirected to face the new lobby. Four steps were removed, a landing added, and the newel turned. The original cove and plaster panels in the staircase hall were redesigned and realigned to meet the adjustment and addition.

Right: A vestige of the matching lobby, left behind after a new, shallower store was installed in 1935. The grand staircase leading to the Winter Garden lies beyond the doors. Above the telephone directory stand can be seen a box office built in 1919 to match one in the original lobby corridor.

OTIS-FENSOM ELEVATORS

Symbolize the Spirit of the Age

OTIS-FENSOM ELEVATOR COMPANY, LIMITED
Head Office, TORONTO   Works, HAMILTON, ONT.

1913 advertisement for Otis-Fensom, suppliers of the elevators in the complex.

The elevators were of the open cage type, each capable of carrying about 20 people including an operator. The cages had additional gates between the elevators, facilitating a ride to the rescue by another elevator if one was stuck. The elevators stopped only on the orchestra level of each theatre, and were not self-service. The *Toronto Star Weekly* of 13 December 1913 referred to the elevator accommodation as "another novel feature, as far as Canada is concerned..." Elevators, as such, were no novelty in Toronto in 1913. But the passenger elevators in the complex were a first for Toronto's theatres, and they now are among the oldest extant in the city.

According to Edward Renton's 1918 volume on the vaudeville theatre, lobby and foyer space had to be arranged so as not provide "a loafing place for the populace." He recommended that "toilets, check-rooms, smoking rooms, etc., should not be planned with entrances off the lobby, but all such facilities placed within the theatre, so that those using them must have passed the door man..."[2]

Similar thinking probably had influenced the layout of Loew's, whose lobby and foyer were not expansively welcoming to idlers, and whose public washrooms were located a considerable hike past the doorman. No furniture on which to loaf was provided in the lobby corridor and foyers in 1913-14. Such furniture was inappropriate in their restricted spaces and because of continuous shows. Ontario regulations also specifically limited furnishings in "halls, passageways, stairways and approaches," and required these areas to be "kept free and unobstructed by any camp stool, chair, sofa, hinged seat or other obstruction."[3] The virtual absence of lobby furniture contrasted sharply with opulent lobbies and foyers in later movie palaces.

There was no check room in the minimum lobby space at Loew's. An attended check room was established at orchestra level under the stairs to the balcony of the lower theatre, while patrons of the more expensive Winter Garden had to be content with a row of coat hooks (behind a curtain) on the rear wall of the orchestra, in space that could not be used for anything else.

Theatre architect Clarence Blackall had observed in 1908, "A foyer on the ground floor is in a sense a spectacular necessity. The average American audience does not go out, to any extent, between the acts, but it has come to be considered the proper scheme to elaborate the decoration and the arrangement of the main foyer, and to give it a festive character, quite aside from that demanded by practical requirements."[4]

However, a minimum amount of crush space provided was regulated by some municipal bylaws. For each hundred in seating capacity on a particular floor, Toronto bylaw 6401 required 150 feet of floor space on that level in the "aggregate capacity of the foyers, lobbies, corridors, passages and rooms for the use of the audience, not including aisle space between seats."[5] (New York City, on the other hand, required no lobby at all. Boston was at the other extreme, demanding that each division of the theatre be preceded by a lobby or foyer big enough to accommodate standing the audience in that section.)

According to Blackall, contemporary theatre architects in America usually omitted "...everything in the way of approaches and lobbies which the law does not absolutely insist on." Still, he ascribed limited or non-existent lobbies and the "profound difference in the plans of our theaters as compared with what obtains abroad" to the theatre-going habits of the American public. While a European opera house would "empty itself almost entirely between the acts, the audience flocking to the promenades and foyers," in American theatres "ladies rarely leave their seats during the performance, and only a slight proportion of the men make use of the foyers."[6]

The evolution of concession space at Loew's.

Left: A relatively inactive candy counter in the early 40s. Neither drinks nor heated and frozen products are sold, and all candy is discreetly wrapped. Note the new configuration of the grand staircase.

Right: Loew's vigorous concession stand in the early 50s, now engaged in cooking popcorn, freezing ice cream bars, dispensing soft drinks, and generating attendant sticky messes. Note two large flanking trash cans, absent from the earlier photograph.

Left: Loew's concession stand in the early 60s: a new popcorn maker, a bigger and more visible freezer with more kinds of ice cream, and two soft drink dispensers. There are fewer candy bars for sale, recognizing the far greater profit margin in soft drinks and popcorn.

THEATRE CONCESSIONS AND REFRESHMENTS

Early in this century, ordinary theatres in North America did not usually accommodate refreshment stands in foyer space. If refreshments were offered at all, they were likely to be brought down the aisle by attendants. *The Illustrated London News* carried an article in 1891 complaining of pestiferous "ice-sellers and chocolate-vendors and stale-cake providers" who edged into theatre stalls and wantonly interrupted couples seated in boxes. These vendors, with their "poisonous drinks, musty buns, and stale chocolates" trod on toes and made havoc of hairdos. Further, the author protested, "They don't care if they dig you in the eye with an ice-tray, or powder you with the refuse of sponge cakes, or bury you under chocolate boxes." [7] Enterprising hawkers of sweets and soda also appeared in the aisles of nickelodeons.

No such aisle vendors and no foyer snack bar existed in Loew's complex during its vaudeville period. Further, there were no intermissions during which refreshments might be profitably offered. Instead of a foyer refreshment bar, each seat in both auditoria was equipped with a cylindrical chocolate dispenser. Each device contained one tube of Tobler's milk chocolate discs.

A coin inserted in the slot would cause the spring-mounted cover to flip open. The dispensers were supposed to be refilled nightly. If a seat had been just vacated by a chocolate-loving patron, one needed to search adjoining dispensers for a treat.

This type of use for the "wasted space" on the backs of theatre chairs was being advertised in *The Moving Picture World* in April 1914 . Not only would the "Midget Automatic Penny Vendor" turn the back of the theatre chair into a "gold mine," but its "beautiful nickel-plated appearance" would enhance the decor of the house.[8]

No drink other than water was routinely available in the theatres. There were two water fountains in the theatres, one in the rear of each auditorium. According to the far-fetched theory of a "Clow Bubble Drinking Fountain" advertisement in *The Moving Picture World* in July 1913, the lobby or foyer were more lucrative locations. It promised that while the patron's thirst was being quenched, "the desire for entertainment is being awakened," with the result that he or she will "go straight to the ticket window".[9]

The sale of refreshments in a theatre produced litter and mess, more work for the staff, and damage to seats and other furnishings. For these reasons, long-time Manager Jules Bernstein, who was notoriously fastidious about cleanliness, opposed and resisted having a lobby candy and drink counter in the complex until the 1930s. He did relent at least once: pink lemonade and peanuts were available during "Loew's Mighty Vaudeville Circus" in December 1924, an event atypical enough to warrant being advertised.

Bernstein's prejudice would have won the approval of Edward Renton, who commented in 1918 that candy and other concessions had been discontinued in many "first-class houses," though a few still had a candy case in the lobby or foyer. He admonished: "A peanut or popcorn stand, or similar enterprise, does not belong in the lobby of a well conducted theatre, and if candy is to be sold at all, it should be dispensed from a case in lobby or foyer, instead of by vendors passing up and down aisles."[10]

Popcorn had not yet won its niche in large variety theatres by 1913, though it had certainly arrived a few years later. Th*e Moving Picture World* of May 1919 contained an advertisement for a Butter Kist Pop Corn and Peanut Machine . It predicted earnings of $600 to $3120 yearly from a "little waste space," 26 x 32 inches. The machine, "an ornament any place," was said to pay four ways: its motion made people stop and look, its "coaxing fragrance" made them buy, its "toasty flavor" brought trade for blocks, and it was a "drawing card" to the theatre.[11] Still, the sale of concessions was a long way from its present status, when their earnings rank only just below or even exceed admission revenues.

LOUNGES AND RESTROOMS

According to a 1927 article by Harold Rambusch, the American public was gradually acquiring these European habits of visiting lounges and rest rooms.[12] The movie palace would signal an end to the practice of providing minimum foyer and restroom space in commercial theatres. Instead, the pendulum later swung wildly in the other direction, towards the most extravagant and abundant foyer space and other facilities, even including libraries, playrooms, music rooms, dog kennels, and, in the case of the penultimate Roxy Theatre in New York, a small emergency hospital "equipped for surgery." [13]

A *Star Weekly* article of 22 November 1913 on the new Loew's theatre had promised, "the lobbies and general accommodation will be on a scale hitherto unknown here. The lobbies will be immense..." Nonetheless, by comparison with the later palaces, they did not exceed the minimum functional requirement.

Likewise, the restrooms provided in the complex did not approach the movie palace's lavish standards. Later movie palace restrooms and smoking rooms were usually designed and furnished to maintain the spell that transformed shopclerks into royalty. Movie palace restrooms tried to resemble the intimate rooms of the most pretentious private houses, and to avoid looking like public facilities. A few, like the African room in Lamb's Ohio Theatre, were as entertaining as a movie. As Lamb put it in 1929, "retiring rooms, smoking rooms and lounges, very little considered five or six years ago, ...today figure as a most important part of the plan and decoration of the theater itself."[14]

Marcus Loew supposedly had "a fetish" for "beautiful ladies' rooms," and "the first thing he did when bought old theaters or built new ones...was to order the ladies' rooms sumptuously decorated. It was said at one time that many ladies paid the ten cents' admission fee to his theaters simply to use his ladies' rooms."[15] This "fetish" had not surfaced by 1913, judging from the unadorned and austere facilities of his Yonge Street and Winter Garden theatres.

These were not even up to a standard described by theatre architect Clarence Blackall in 1908. "Where space permits," he wrote, ladies' rooms were "invariably in close proximity to the foyer." They made a "very ornamental feature of the theater, and elaborately decorated as an advertisement."

A ladies toilet room was established on the mezzanine floor of each theatre. No dressing tables nor provision for lounging were included; each room had only three toilets and one washbasin. Their stark white tile walls and wood toilet partitions differed little from those of the adjacent men's room.

One might suppose that the openings to the men's and women's restrooms, about ten feet apart, were decently located at either end of the toilet room area. They were not, as far as at least one guardian of public morals in Toronto was concerned. In May 1914, W.W. Pearce, the new City Architect and Superintendent of Buildings, was required to inspect the locations of the toilets, apparently in response to complaints. He wrote to Mayor Hocken:

> Referring to the toilets, I find that the entrances are about twelve feet apart and open onto a common corridor. I inspected these toilets and found them light and clean, but gave instructions that one of the screens in the men's toilet was to be made larger. The question of men's and women's doors being too close together is largely a matter of opinion, and I believe is outside my province to pass upon. [16]

One of the austere toilet rooms in the Winter Garden's mezzanine. Originally, the lower theatre's toilet rooms looked like this.

The needs of male patrons of the lower theatre were more abundantly provided for. They were afforded a toilet room on the mezzanine level and an additional toilet room in the basement, supplemented by a basement smoking room. Perhaps Loew's was anticipating a preponderance of male patrons. This deficiency in ladies' room space would be addressed in later renovations.

A "charming new dressing room known as the cosmetic room" was added in the course of later renovations in 1928. The *Star* reported that this room would enable "milady to repair her toilette and apply her 'make-up' at perfectly equipped little individual dressing tables." "Mauve moire" covered its walls and festooned its ceiling, and "mauve lacquer" dressing tables and chairs completed the "modernistic" note. Because this colour scheme was in vogue at the Governor General's residence in Ottawa, it was suggested that this addition should be named "The Lady Willingdon Salon" after the wife of the Governor General, Lady Willingdon.[17] In 1928 women also captured a section of the mezzanine corridor, which was devoted to an additional ladies' lounge, "handsomely" arranged with "period furniture." After this date (and until the the 1989 reopening), the privilege of crossing the mezzanine corridor of the lower theatre would remain exclusive to women.

The ladies' lounge on the mezzanine floor of the lower theatre, a 1928 addition, photographed in 1961.

CHAPTER SIX

GILT, SCAGLIOLA, BEECH LEAVES AND GARDEN MURALS: DECORATING THE LOWER AUDITORIUM AND WINTER GARDEN

THE LOWER THEATRE (NOW THE ELGIN)

In one respect, the lower theatre was a contradiction. Though it was more expensively decorated than the Winter Garden, and had a bigger stage and seating capacity and the "class" of an attended coat room, the upper theatre was the prestige house of the two, with a higher scale of admission. Still, the lower auditorium received more approval in architectural journals, and a bigger Loew's splash at its opening. Decoratively, it was more typical of Lamb's work in this period than was the Winter Garden. It was the first theatre in Toronto to offer for as little as 10 cents such extravagant decor. It was lavishly decorated with gilding, brass, marble, and scagliola, and rejoiced in a chandeliered dome and elaborately ornamented proscenium, boxes, and balcony front.

Lamb's drawings delineate the decorative treatment to be applied, though many details were not realized exactly as shown. He later reflected on the relationship between the architect and the decorator: "The decorative scheme is the most essential part of the house after the architectural background has been set, and the quality of this decoration, though inspired by the architect, is largely left for the decorator to complete." [1]

The theatre's adornments were predicted in a *World* article of 6 March 1913 as "...of the modern French Renaissance style, with marble and scagliola wainscoting and columns. The walls throughout will be covered with silk tapestry. The fronts of all boxes, the proscenium arch, and all ornamentation, will be treated in gold."

The decoration of the lower auditorium can be classified as a "beaux arts" interpretation of Renaissance architecture, involving Roman orders and ornament like arched forms, rosettes and scrolls. This decoration was a vaudeville standard, and *Contract Record* considered the decoration of the lower theatre quite ordinary: "The interior of the building is executed in a manner after the style of most theatres. The ceilings and cornice are finished in a handsome design of ornamental plaster." [2] Many of the major movie palaces built later were far more outlandishly and exotically decorated. For them, novelty in decoration was often a point of principle.

Many references to merriment and the entertainment purpose of the building were manifest in the lower theatre's plaster ornament. Representations of dramatic masks, festooned grapes, ribbons, and a

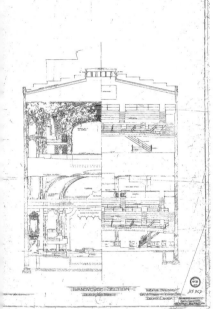

Lamb's transverse section drawing, dated 14 April 1913, showing decorative treatments not realized for proscenium and sidewall arches.

Detail of the original entablature and wall decoration above the boxes in the lower auditorium. Note the wall fan to the right of the column.

variety of musical instruments contributed to the festive ambience, and probably increased subliminally the receptivity and enjoyment of patrons.

In the lower auditorium, as in the lobbies, there was a profusion of gilding. This was not a meaningless frippery. The burnished metal surfaces reflected the auditorium's artificial light. Further, the use of gold served to make patrons feel glamourous and special, and was to help entice them to come again. The gold in the colour scheme caused the *Toronto Daily News* to be struck by the "warmth of color and coziness of the place," in spite of the fact that the theatre was "immense." Lamb explained in a 1928 article his continuing use of a great deal of gold. To him, it conveyed "the acme of wealth, warmth and coziness," and he agreed with a 19th-century Viennese decorator that there was no such thing as too much gold, as it was "pleasing and harmonious with any other conceivable color." Theatre decorator Harold Rambusch (son of Frode) agreed. Warm golden colours tended to make people glad and cheerful. Metal gold spelled richness, and made the most of subdued lighting. [3]

TEXTILES

Gilded plaster ornament was supplemented by "gold" or "fawn" draperies. The *Toronto Daily News* on 16 December 1913 acknowledged "...hangings of fawn velours, fastened back with tassels to match, and making a splendid background for the very elaborate gold balustrades." According to *Construction*'s description, "The heavy curtain is of embroidered valance made of gold silk velour and finished with a corresponding fringe."

Warmth and richness were also conveyed by the red silk brocaded damask fabric used to cover wall panels in the lower theatre. Toronto newspapers variously referred to this wall fabric as "rose-colored brocaded silk," "deep crimson brocaded silk walls," "red silk" "red floral tapestries," and "rich silk damask."

Red fabric panels were complemented by the choice of crimson Wilton carpet in the lower auditorium. The carpet's diamond pattern was effected in two shades of red. According to *Construction*, this carpet was "rich rose Wilton blending with the other decorations," while the *Daily News* referred to the theatre's "crimson carpets." The choice was prudent: Wilton carpets, with their close piles and tight weaves, are durable and resilient, and, in dark colours, do not readily show stains and dirt. Loew's purchased these original carpets, wall coverings and draperies from the T. Eaton Co. in Toronto. The contract allegedly "ran to $35,000."

Original photograph of the opera boxes of the lower theatre. The valances above the orchestra level boxes appear to be temporarily rigged up, perhaps in honour of opening night celebrities. Note the bent wood chairs in the opera boxes and the chocolate dispenser on the back of each orchestra seat.

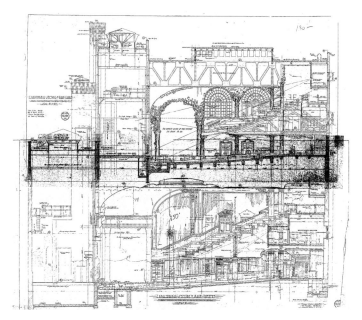

Lamb's longitudinal drawing of Loew's Toronto theatres.

THE PROSCENIUM ARCH AND SOUNDING BOARD MURAL

The proscenium arch shape of the lower theatre was a favourite of Lamb's: it is almost a signature. A unique feature for Lamb was its proscenium cartouche which sported the Coat of Arms of the province. The shape and decoration of the cartouche also conveniently echoed a lyre shape, and was flanked by two winged figures, posed as if ready to strum.

Above: Vew towards the proscenium arch of the lower theatre, about 1942. The area which once contained the mural of Simcoe greeting Indians is blank. In 1928 sidewall arches which accommodated Wurlitzer organ lofts replaced the original sidewall entablatures.

Above: View of the rear of the lower auditorium in 1914, including two sets of stairs leading up to the mezzanine corridor and balcony. The opening seen almost straight ahead leads down to the basement men's room. Columns, wainscoting and balustrades are scagliola. Decorations on columns and panel mouldings are richly gilded. The damask wall fabric and diamond patterned Wilton carpets are discernible.

Left: The Gilded dome of The lower auditorium in 1914. An assortment of musical instruments were included in its plaster motifs. The amber-coloured opalescent glass chandelier was removed by about 1935.

Above: The magnificently regilded dome of the lower auditorium, photographed in October 1989. (The slots in unornamented areas of the dome accommodate modern lighting instruments. Masking will camouflage them in future.)

Right: Close ups of motifs in the dome of the lower theatre.

An even more notable appeal to national and local sentiment appeared in the original proscenium mural, an icon of Toronto history lamentably lost. It was a unique creation which depicted Governor Simcoe meeting a group of Indians on the site of the city in 1793. Undoubtedly a standard or "generic" subject for a proscenium mural, with allegorical or classical figures, would have been a simpler option. The circuit must have imagined that financial benefit would accrue from their concession to local patriotism and history in Loew's first expansion outside of the United States. (The experiment was not repeated, however, in his later Canadian theatres.)

From the beginning, a proscenium mural exhibiting a heroic incident in Canadian history was planned. In March 1913, the *Toronto World* announced the Battle of Queenston Heights as the subject for this mural. By December, the theme was changed to one more peaceful and less inimical to Americans, the Simcoe meeting. The inspiration for the change may have been the realization that Queenston Heights was an American defeat in the war of 1812, or the decision may have been simply to favour a Toronto event— one less turbulent and gory as a mural subject.

The *Toronto Star Weekly* and other newspapers in December 1913 quoted in chorus from Loew's press release in describing "...a beautiful mural painting by the celebrated artist Rambusch, representing Governor Simcoe making terms with the Indians on the site of what is now the city of Toronto. The old block-house, which is still standing, near the Garrison Commons, is shown; and the color scheme is exceptionally rich."

If the muralist looked up accounts of important events in the history of Toronto, he would have learned that Governor Simcoe and a corps of Queen's Rangers first encountered two Indian families of the Mississauga tribe on the western bank and near the mouth of the Don River in the summer of 1793. The technicality that the Fort York blockhouse was not built until 1794 was overlooked. The "celebrated artist" Rambusch, the muralist to whom the press release referred, was Frode Rambusch of The Rambusch Decorating Company, New York City.

Only one Toronto reporter, writing for the *Evening Telegram*, departed from the otherwise slavish repetition of Loew's press release and critiqued the mural. Though he mistook its Indians for soldiers of the Queen's Rangers and misinterpreted the event as Simcoe's landing, the reviewer provided the most detailed description of this lost image. He was scathing on the muralist's depiction of local history and geography:

> A large painting has been executed above the lower stage, which is supposed to depict Governor Simcoe during his first landing on the site of our city. Artistically it is very creditable; but historically it is a miserable failure; for the Scarboro' Bluffs have been transformed into mountains and temporarily removed from their present position to the foot of Dufferin Street, which is meant to represent the mouth of the Don. The men of the old Queen's Rangers have apparently worn all their uniforms threadbare, for they have robed themselves with cow hide in order to appear before the Toronto audience. Governor Simcoe and some gentleman unknown have borrowed the King's uniform for the occasion, and the Island has been removed so as not to hide the view of the lake.

These newspaper descriptions provide the only detailed documentary evidence of the original mural, thus far. No original drawings or sketches of the mural have surfaced, and the batch of early photographs include vistas of virtually every elevation of the lower auditorium except one — the vanished sounding board mural.

WINTER GARDEN AUDITORIUM

The Winter Garden theatre was the first of its kind in Canada. It was the first full-scale auditorium with balcony and stage house built on top of another theatre. Added to its novelty was its spectacular beech leaf decor, garden murals, lighted moon, and tree trunk columns.

The supporting columns were decorated and painted to resemble tree trunks, though not with the smooth bark appropriate for the leafy beech canopy above. The beams of the ceiling were painted to resemble wood. Though presumably not visible to the public, the underside of the balcony and ceiling, above the dense network of leaves and flowers, was painted "sky blue." The garden decor was complemented by green curtains and "grass green" carpeting.

Though the leafy decor of the Winter Garden was obviously derived from the earlier scheme devised by Lamb for the decoration of the American Theatre Roof, it was applied on a much larger scale, and has no known counterpart.

WINTER GARDEN LEAVES AND FLOWERS

The botany of the Winter Garden was identified as "heavy screens in apple blossoms, roses and leaves" and "gay wisteria." The *Telegram* reported on "pastoral scenes that adorn the tower walls." The *Toronto World* and the *Star Weekly* reported on "bubbling fountains," and predicted that the decorative scheme would make readers think they had been transported to some "fairy bower."[4]

Except for *Construction*, no contemporary source noted the extraordinary fact that the Winter Garden's leaves were real. The ceiling and the soffit of the balcony and projection booth were hung with wire grids which supported about 5,000 real beech branches. More leaves were woven into the trellises of the balcony boxes. These were intermingled with artificial blossoms of coarse cotton, dyed blue, pink, and yellow which simulated wisteria. During ensuing years some of the original leaves easy of access were probably removed by souvenir hunters, and were replaced by the few anomalous specimens of oak and ivy branches found only under the balcony soffit near the rear exits and under the projection booth. One holly branch was found near the exit doors to the elevator hall.In addition, in the same accessible areas were some samples of artificial leaves, made of cotton, simulating maple, ivy, beech, holly, and oak.

Other theatres in this period were making use of floral and leafy decorations, though apparently not to the extent seen in the Winter Garden. *Motion Picture News* in August 1914 ran a few articles recommending and describing this decorating fad.

> A pleasing decorative plan, particularly appropriate during the present season, consists of outdoor effects obtained by the use of artificial plants, vines, splashing fountains and the subdued, mellow light of miniature incandescent globes hidden among leaves, with a few bold sweeps of sky tint on the ceiling, to complete the pastoral illusion. The effect is novel and the cost by no means prohibitive. [5]

An article in a later issue was entitled "Flowers as a basis of prosperity," and described the floral scheme enlisted for the redecoration of a Detroit theatre, involving garlands hanging from chandeliers, window boxes, wall baskets, and 20 palm trees framing the screen. The conclusion was drawn that "There is not

Above: Plaster tree trunks merging into painted branches and backlit moon in the Winter Garden.

Left: Another view of the Winter Garden's opera boxes.

a nature which is not appealed to by *flowers* and plant life in general."[6] This appeal, it was devoutly hoped, could be translated into increased box office receipts, the factor which most captured the interest of all theatre owners.

GARDEN MURALS

In the auditorium, garden murals brilliantly merged with leaves, tree trunk columns, and light fixtures. The Winter Garden's murals were realized in water-soluble scenic paint, and probably completed in 8 to 10 working days. Four or five scenic artists may have been employed, as distinct styles and talent are evident. One muralist signed Chinese characters. One of the most talented of the muralists was responsible for the murals in the stairs to the boxes on the west side and the rear of the auditorium. Murals in the mezzanine corridor are, for the most part, rendered with attention to detail and the spaces they occupy. Other murals less prominently located were more slap dash and less skillfully applied. They might have been painted in the last-minute rush before opening.

Climbing roses, morning glories and ivy were extensively represented in the auditorium. Ferns, daisies, clematis, mums and sunflowers occur, along with two irises, gladiolus, primroses, nasturtium, wisteria, black-eyed susans and wild flowers less readily identified. Small bushes, including sumac and juniper, pampas grass and other grasses appear in the mezzanine corridor. Except for an owl in the auditorium, the mezzanine housed the mural's woodland life: a snake, chipmunk, and birds.

Below: Mural decorations in the Winter Garden's mezzanine corridor.

Though the Winter Garden was one of the last of the roof garden theatres, it can also be considered a movie palace precursor. Its extravagant simulation of an exotic outdoor environment was the objective of the atmospheric movie

Above: A sampling of Winter Garden florals.

palaces built in 1920s by John Eberson and Thomas Lamb. Eberson explained the appeal of outdoor decor:

> ...In an out-of-door atmosphere, in addition to the 'warm' and 'friendly' foreign picturesqueness, the spectator enjoys the natural beauty of skies and flowers he has been brought up to love. He does not feel himself in entirely strange surroundings; he relaxes; he is interested; we appeal to his imagination and there you have a most modest assumption— a perfect and ideal theatre auditorium. [9]

Eberson later took full and exclusive credit for originating the "outdoor garden auditorium" in 1923. Surely the concept owed something to the simulated gardens of earlier roof theatres and those Lamb had created for the Toronto Winter Garden and the American Roof, though, unlike later atmospherics, these roof theatres were not decorated with extensive imitation sky ceilings, electric stars and scudding clouds.

The most accurate and detailed contemporary account of the decoration of the Winter Garden appeared in *Construction*:

> The scheme of decoration for the roof garden is novel in itself and depicts the idea of an outdoor theatre in striking reality. In order to produce the effect of tree trunks and foliage, the columns are covered with cement plaster modelled in the formation of rough bark and painted in all its true colors. The entire ceiling under the balcony as well as the main ceiling is covered by a wire lattice supporting the foliage, which consists of five thousand real beech branches dipped in a chemical preparation that renders them absolutely fireproof. The whole effect is greatly enhanced by the myriad of small wrought iron lanterns of vari-colored glass scattered throughout the foliage of the ceiling....The sounding board...has been painted with a landscape scene blending in with the foliage around the proscenium boxes.[10]

Based on the *Construction* article, the English journal *The Builder* formed strong opinions on the Winter Garden. In the first place, it seemed a "misnomer" to call it a "roof garden." Its decor "hardly commends itself to us," though the trellis treatment won some praise. "...the use of trellis in French design to suggest an outside effect is wholly admirable when employed, as it is by them, with restraint..." The writer abandoned any predilection for understatement in considering the use of actual foliage. It was denounced as "absolutely wrong and unfitting in a building, and belongs to the class of make believes which from time to time has disfigured the general sanity of architectural design, and is expressive of the instinct which led people in the middle of last century to call their houses `abbeys' or `retreats' and to ornament them with parapets and sham machicolations, or such eccentricities as l'Art Nouveau." [11]

But the decor of the theatre caused certain newspaper writers in Toronto to engage in unrestrained hyperbole. The *Toronto Daily News* reported on 17 February,

> The whole place is one mass of foliage. The ceiling is smothered with every kind of plant imaginable, while the walls are studded with flowers. And out of this mass of foliage twinkle the lights of multitudinous fairy lamps of almost every known colour.

The same rustic scheme of decoration reigns in orchestra and balcony, and at every turn of the head one is met by flowers, flowers, flowers. Even the pillars have been covered over with bark to resemble trees, while close to the stage the branches are made to taper until they meet the painted twigs on the walls, the effect produced being a highly realistic one. And above this flowery arbour floats a peaceful moon which suffuses its rays over the whole fairylike picture.[12]

HOUSE LIGHTING

House lighting provided other practical components of the decoration and atmosphere. In the lower theatre, *Construction* photographs reveal a jamboree of differing electric fixtures: chandeliers and lanterns which diffused light through opaque glass, clusters of exposed bulbs, and bulbs enclosed with knobs of diffusing crystals, along with unusual light fixtures attached to the rear columns of the auditoria.

This house lighting was a mix of the old and the new. The "old" included emergency gas lighting and direct electric lighting along with ornate, dust gathering fixtures. Even the central chandelier in the dome of the lower theatre was considered passé by some architects by 1913, as it interfered with balcony sight lines and was apt to centralize the lighting of the auditorium. The "new" was the "semi-indirect" which diffused illumination through translucent or opaque mediums in fixtures.

The most imaginative and effective example of diffused lighting in the complex could be found in the backlit moon in the Winter Garden. Its auditorium lighting was a festive affair with its myriad of opalescent glass lanterns in blues, greens, yellows and whites. These "multitudinous fairy lamps of almost every known colour" were probably derived from a catalogue, though they are now remembered to have been custom made. Similar opalescent glass lanterns can be seen in a 1915 General Electric catalogue, retailing for $11.25.

Most of the auditorium lights in both theatres could be turned up or down by backstage dimmers. House illumination in the Winter Garden was also in three colours — red, blue and white — though these colours could not be exhibited and mixed independently. House lighting in colour was of recent vintage. Effects lighting in the auditorium and shifting colour harmonies to suit the movie scene came to fruition in the movie palace, especially in those of the "atmospheric" type. These effects and changes were supposed to "...carry the audience on a veritable magic carpet to the `land of make believe.'"[13] And this was, after all, the purpose of going to the movies and to the movie palace.

A butterfly, a squirrel, birds and Chinese chracters found on Winter Garden walls.

DECORATION AND ACOUSTICS

Theatre decorations had a great deal of bearing on acoustics; sound-reflective plaster on balcony fronts and boxes, absorptive wall fabrics, drapes, seat upholstery, and carpets had an impact, as did coves and domed ceilings, sounding boards, and rounded corners. Materials of construction were also implicated, steel, reinforced concrete, heavy varnishes and hard white plaster being notorious reflectors of sound.

Undesirable sound wave reflection was broken up by arches, coffered niches, ornamental grilles, heavy stucco, relief decoration, fabric panels, and velvet draperies (as well as by the audience itself). When "modern theatres" swept away the respectability of the movie palace, architects scrambled to find acoustic compensations for these unfashionable features. These included such unprepossessing materials as "...fibre and sawdust boards, acoustical plaster, rock wool, punched materials,... Heerwagen tile [and] tiles that vibrate..."[7]

Still, even architects wedded to "honest" and "logical" modern style found it difficult to find suitable alternatives to such traditional decorations as damask wall covering, with its "light absorption surface and open weave," or draperies over doors and large openings. As one devotee of the modern acknowledged ruefully while such fripperies as decorative draperies blocked light in stairs and lobbies"...their sound-absorbing qualities were appreciated and they used to fit into the architecture. They have been discarded or reduced...but nothing has as yet been found to replace them with all their functions."[8]

Right: Directions for the Ladies' room on Winter Garden walls.

Below: Painted lattices, roses, branches, and leaves of the Winter Garden's sidewall arches.

Right: A gas and an electric fixture co-existing in the grand stair to the Winter Garden.

THE FIRST (AND ONLY?) REDECORATION, 1916

Apart from the 1915 enlargement of the Winter Garden's orchestra pit, only one other alteration of the Winter Garden was reported. Perhaps mostly for publicity reasons, it was "redecorated" in September 1916. As the *Globe* reported:

"Special preparations have been made for the fall opening of the Winter Garden in connection with Loew's Yonge Street Theatre, which will take place at 7.30 o'clock Monday evening next.... The Winter Garden, which affords 'all the comforts of home,' has been redecorated and is in readiness for the initial performance".

This redecoration may have been intended to give the Winter Garden a "new look" at the lowest cost, or to effect repairs and to remedy omissions. It seems to have encompassed the repainting of the elevator lobby, some additional mural signs pointing to mezzanine and washrooms, and some branch replacement in areas within the reach of patrons. After this, the Winter Garden remained remarkably untouched — except for losing its seats and small incidents of vandalism — a time capsule of the vaudeville period.

FIRE RENOVATION, LOWER THEATRE, 1928

The first major renovation of the lower auditorium was inspired by a midnight fire on 4 May 1928 which began under the stage. Smoke, flames, and water damaged the moulded plaster decoration of the proscenium arch and, likely, irretrievably ruined the Simcoe mural above. During the fire renovation, the proscenium arch was repaired, and new sidewall arches were built over the boxes to accommodate new organ lofts.

The fire also brought about a change of colour scheme and new carpets and draperies. The new scheme was described as "turquoise blue, ivory and gold...throughout the house with a beautiful pastel effect in the ceiling decorations." Walls were "richly covered in blue damask." Carpets blended "harmoniously," and "rich, soft blue draperies" hung in the boxes.

CHAPTER SEVEN

LAYING OUT THE THEATRES: PUBLIC SPACES

FLOOR PLANS OF AUDITORIA

The floor plans of the theatres were vital components of their commercial success. The importance of the design of marquees, ticket offices and lobbies paled in comparison to the architect's task of the satisfactory and economic arrangement of seats. As a 1908 article in *Architectural Record* stated, a commercial theatre architect was required "to plan his auditorium so that every inch could be stuffed as full of people as the law allowed."[1]

A SINGLE BALCONY

The lower theatre was the first of the large Toronto stage theatres built without a gallery or a second balcony. Its auditorium was wider, and its balcony larger and closer to the stage than those found in other Toronto vaudeville theatres up to that time. This was to be the wave of the future. And like the lower theatre, the Winter Garden was designed with a single, sweeping balcony, and no gallery.

Construction referred to Loew's Yonge Street Theatre as "a one balcony house which modern practice and wide experience has proven the most economical and satisfactory type." This "modern practice" and "wide experience" had not until then been seen in Toronto, though, as Gerald Lenton noted, "...galleries were being eliminated from most theatres constructed at that time, including those built for legitimate drama...."[2] The small range of admission prices to low-priced vaudeville had made the appeal both of building and sitting in a far-off and high-up gallery disappear. It was also a terrible vantage from which to see a motion picture screen. Another theatre architect, William Albert Swasey, writing in 1913, ascribed diminished gallery patronage to "the moving picture craze."[3]

Edward Renton's 1918 tract on the vaudeville theatre was emphatic: "The builder is strongly advised not to construct a gallery, or second balcony. They increase the cost of the building out of all proportion to the revenue derived from the seats. Gallery seats are the cheapest in the house and the increased height of the building is the costliest construction."[4]

BALCONY LOGES AND OPERA BOXES

Patrons seated in the front row of the balcony of the lower theatre were only 37' from the stage at the closest point. The concept of organizing good balcony seats into balcony loges was relatively new, arriving with the truss system and the deep cantilevered balcony, thrust forward close to the stage. Balcony loge seats,

View of the Winter Garden's side boxes. Note the platforms for ventilating fans on the "tree trunk" and in the lower opera boxes.

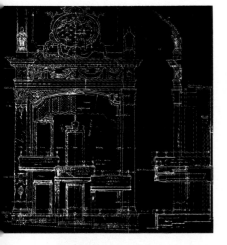

Drawing of the boxes of the lower theatre.

sold at the top of the admission scale, helped to make up any potential loss of revenue from the omission of the gallery.

By the time Loew's Yonge Street theatre was built, opera boxes no longer fulfilled their original function of providing the most commanding view of the stage and the most prestigious location for seats. Their siting had been compromised long before in legitimate theatres by the abandonment of the stage apron. Any benefit of their location was further eroded by the arrival of wider proscenium arches brought in the train of the large-scale cantilevered balcony.

Blackall had commented in 1908,

> The planning of proscenium boxes is a difficult task. Seldom are they of any practical value at all. Though they are nominally the highest-priced seats in the theater the boxes are more often given away by the management than sold, as they are really the poorest seats in the house....For a combination house, where the action takes place all over the stage, it is impossible to hope that the boxes will be much more than architectural ornaments, and as such they are best treated.[5]

That boxes appeared in this theatre and would continue to be built in the movie palace testifies to the conservatism of commercial theatre owners, and their reluctance to forgo the resemblance to older and presumably more respectable playhouses. Theatre builders also wished to take advantage of any possibility of additional seats, especially when patrons might be persuaded to pay premium prices for them.

The Winter Garden was to have been provided not only with the usual proscenium and balcony boxes, but with side boxes. The additional boxes in the Winter Garden testified to its role as the prestige house, and the one in which patrons were more likely to reserve their seats. The side boxes were thus arranged to make them more desirable to patrons, and provided more seats for which an extra tariff could be logically charged.

SEATING PLANS AND SEATS

By more comfortable standards of many legitimate theatres, Loew's was packed with seats, a common nickelodeon practice which helped to justify the low admission cost. In a 1913 seating revision Lamb drew for the lower theatre, some rows were squeezed between and behind rear columns, providing less than desirable vantages. The density of seats might have been a response to the unexpectedly high construction costs of the complex, or the seating revision may merely reflect the circuit's more generalized and permanent ambition to reduce the cost per seat in its theatres with maximum seating capacity.

Strangely enough, the highest priced seats in these houses and other theatres in the period were flimsy and uncomfortable looking straight-backed bentwood chairs, which can be seen in the high-priced boxes and balcony loges of both theatres in original photographs. These chairs were standard furnishing for proscenium and balcony boxes, and cost about $1.15 each. They were potentially an exit hazard when knocked over, as they were not fixed to the floor, but unattached box chairs were specifically permitted by Toronto bylaw.

The level of upholstered seat comfort provided by Loew's was also less than that offered in later movie palaces and less cost-conscious contemporary legitimate theatres. The seat of the one surviving original chair from Loew's lower theatre is 17" wide and deep. With arm rests, the seat was about 22" in width.

Though these seats, with padding and upholstery, were more generously endowed than the nickelodeon standard, they were not that far above it.

The backs of the seats were also closer together than any large Toronto theatre, though, according to Lamb, this did not mean less knee space. As he explained:

> Instead of making a deep seat we cut off our seat and make a shorter seat and make the handles of the chairs shorter, so that it gives as much or more room than under the old law, where they had a big comfortable seat. We sacrifice the comfort of the seat to the width of the aisle. [6]

Seating plan revision, lower theatre. This Lamb drawing reflects the 30" spacing between seat backs for which Loew's were obliged to apply for an amendment to the Toronto bylaw.

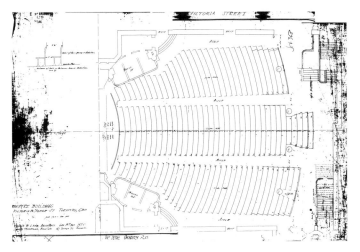

More importantly, the theatre owner gained about two more rows of seats. The shorter, less comfortable seats probably also served Loew's purposes in discouraging patrons from sitting through too many continuous shows. This slightly wider spacing between rows may have also helped the cause of those coming and going at any time.

Lamb's arrangement of two aisles dividing the orchestra seats conformed with current standards of many bylaw requirements in North America. One central aisle had been a tradition in many large legitimate theatres, and continued as a common plan in many 1913 movie theatres because the movie projector occupied that location and space. Various theatre experts now considered a central aisle disadvantageous for live theatre, as it eliminated some of the best seats in the house, and disconcerted performers looking down its empty passage and not at "a sea of faces."[7]

SIGHT LINES AND PROJECTION BOOTHS

Sight lines were affected by the obstructions of supporting columns, proscenium boxes, railings, chandeliers, cornice and other decorations, low-hung balconies, and patrons' heads. The architect's task was to lay out the theatre and its seating to minimize such obstructions, thus maximizing profits and satisfied patrons. An important element was the pitch of the auditorium and the balcony stepping.

In the days before the movie palace, the opportunity to see two-thirds of the stage was considered by some authorities to be adequate for the theatre patron, for the actor's voice could at least be heard, and he or she might move rewardingly into one's line of vision, whereas each patron in a picture theatre needed to see the entire screen and to read the titles.

Projection booth design and sightlines were new concerns for theatre architects, and would become increasingly important. In 1913 it was not self evident that the projection booth would soon be the source of the most important part of the entertainment programme. The projection booths in Loew's complex did not approach later movie palace examples, though they were considerably elevated above the minimum standard of the day and the makeshift and dangerous affairs known to the nickelodeon. The booths in the complex had no separate rewind rooms for highly combustible nitrate films, and did not even have toilets for their projectionists. Still, the two were among the first substantial, fireproof booths architect-designed from the beginning for large Toronto theatres.

ORCHESTRA PITS AND THEATRE ORGANS

The orchestra pits in the complex were from a more primitive age, and not a new era. As early as February 1915 the orchestra pit of the Winter Garden had to be enlarged when vaudeville was dropped and the theatre was converted into a "photo playhouse de luxe." (Its pit was to be expanded to "symphony proportions" to make up for the absence of live entertainers. The experiment lasted only five weeks.) Orchestra pits which could accommodate dozens of musicians and magnificent organ consoles would appear in the movie palace.

The original Winter Garden projection booth with a Simplex silent projector.

The original pits in the Toronto complex held no organ consoles. This was not an oversight on Lamb's part: few theatre organs were in existence in 1913, in comparison to their proliferation in the 1920s. Instead, Loew's patrons heard orchestral accompaniment for live acts and short silent movies, provided by 8 to 10 musicians. This number outranked theatres with cheap admissions and movies, many of which offered only a piano player. A lone piano player would soon be considered hopelessly inadequate, and huge, well-dressed orchestras would accompany feature-length silent movies in the grand palaces.

Five years after the opening, theatre organs were installed in both theatres. Loew's must have been responding to the competition from the snazzy organ at Shea's Hippodrome as well as to more recent contenders in new Toronto movie palaces like the 1916 Regent. The organ installations were also testimony to the increasing importance of the movie show in a variety bill. By 1918 theatre organs had become almost mandatory and they were cheaper and more practical than theatre orchestras for silent movie accompaniment. In many theatres, orchestras were displaced, though this was unlikely to have been Loew's intention. Still, the orchestra musicians must have had misgivings, as organ chambers installed in the stage basement of the lower theatre supplanted their musician's room. The organs installed in 1918-19 were 2-manual instruments, each with about 10 ranks of pipes, and were built in Woodstock, Ontario, by the Warren Organ Company, one of two companies in Canada manufacturing theatre organs. Loew's investment in Canadian enterprise might be seen as laudable, though Warren theatre organs would have compared unfavorably with organs produced by such American manufacturers as the Wurlitzer Company.

THE 1928 FIRE AND A NEW WURLITZER

The Warren organ in the lower theatre was burned up in a May 1928 fire which had started in its overheated blower. Loew's then opted for the prestige and panache of a Mighty Wurlitzer. The new "$30,000" Wurlitzer gloried in a gilded horseshoe console, three manuals and 13 ranks of pipes, 6 tonal percussions and 12 traps. Only eight other theatres in Canada could boast of Wurlitzer organs: two others in Toronto, four in Montreal, and two in Vancouver.

For the Wurlitzer, Loew's would avoid the under stage chambers of its predecessor, preferring to build organ lofts in new sidewall arches. This necessitated the removal of original entablatures and cartouches above the boxes. Lamb, who had been immediately called in after the fire, also designed an enlarged orchestra pit, rebuilt the front of the stage, and restored a musician's room to the basement. Such renovations probably would not have occurred two years later, when orchestra pits and musicians' rooms were becoming obsolete, and vaudeville and silent movies were more obviously on the wane.

PATRON COMFORT: HEATING AND VENTILATING A THEATRE

Even with heart-stopping music, splendid projection and exciting stage performers, theatres elaborately furnished and laid out profitably in every other detail would not attract steady repeat patronage if they were stuffy, smelly and hot when full, or drafty and cold when half-full. The heating and ventilating systems designed impacted on receipts, and became vital considerations for theatre architects.

Such concerns were relatively recent. The American Theatre, built in 1893, was said to be one of the first theatres heated and ventilated in New York City. Heating and ventilating systems would grow in importance in the movie palace era, when the uncommon comforts and air conditioning offered were often as important as their shows. By contrast, "nickel" movie shows had a notorious reputation for providing very little fresh, let alone cooled, air. An article in *Construction* in 1911 claimed that "the five-cent theatres on Yonge Street" were "...boxes with a hole in each end, unventilated pest houses: the odour, due to the lack of ventilation is sickening, and the contaminated air that patrons, mostly youthful, are obliged to take into their lungs, is almost as dangerous and disastrous as the obvious lack of fire protection."[9]

The ventilation system received special attention in the opening publicity for the lower theatre. It was important for the public to know that the fetid and stale atmosphere of the contemporary cheap movie house was absent, especially in a germ-conscious period of widespread concern that lack of fresh air was a serious impairment to public health. Many nickelodeons and other theatres for the movies invested in electric fans to respond to these apprehensions and to attract patronage. A G.E. six-blade oscillating fan "especially constructed for motion picture theatres" is advertised in a May 1914 issue of *Moving Picture World*. Such wall fans are clearly visible in 1914 photographs of Loew's Yonge Street and Winter Garden theatres. Whirring and distracting wall fans would be abandoned in the movie palace.

Though the ventilating and heating system in Loew's Toronto complex was cut well above those of the nickelodeon or nineteenth century theatre, its radiators and wall fans paled in comparison with the elaborate machinery of "creme de la creme" movie palaces. Loew's "upward" system of ventilation changed the air throughout the complex every 15 minutes, and circulated "iced" air during the summer months. Loew's patrons could expect to find theatrical entertainment all year round, as they were among the large Toronto theatres to remain consistently open all summer.

In the summer, the Winter Garden's open windows and roof clerestory provided ventilation and fresh air. *Construction* referred to the clerestory as "a large skylight in the main roof which may be opened in sections," and added, "...in conjunction with all the exit doors and side windows the garden becomes in reality an outdoor place of amusement as its name implies." Whether the numerous openings affected the acoustics of the Winter Garden was not reported in early accounts of its operation.

Above: Wurlitzer organ removal in 1958. It was transported to a barn in Picton, Ontario.

THE MIGHTY WURLITZER

Much newspaper hyperbole was attached to inauguration of the new organ in June of 1928 in the lower theatre: "Hear the Massive Wurlitzer Organ....EXTRA! A Superb Musical Program Will Be Rendered Daily on the MASSIVE WURLITZER, Canada's Most Magnificent Theatre Organ." The name Wurlitzer was known to have tremendous advertising value.

The investment paid off. Such was the interest in the reopening of the theatre and the new Wurlitzer that "Crowds thronged the lobby long before noon literally waiting to crash the doors, and when the second performance started, enough people to absolutely pack the house were already in line." [8].

The *Globe* reviewed the new organ's first public performance: "The new Wurlitzer organ pealed its harmonies to the public for the first time, and as its bass rumblings shook the house and rolled on up the scale into shrill ecstasies of the weird high organ notes, it was readily accepted as the tone-elegant instrument heralded by the management. 'The Indian Love Call' and other lilts were literally thrilling and, again, applause (from the body of the house) demonstrated real appreciation." [10]

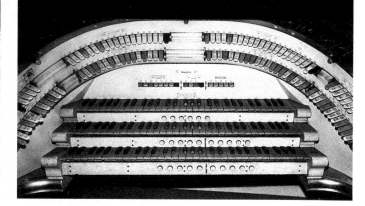

Above: Console of the 3-manual Wurlitzer installed in the lower theatre in 1928.

Right: Exterior of the original Winter Garden projection booth.

The Winter Garden's asbestos curtain. Backstage, a kitchen knife was tied to one of its ropes (or cut line). When this was severed, the curtain would fall immediately. Unlike some other cities, Toronto bylaws on theatres did not require the front of fire curtains to be reassuringly and prominently labelled 'asbestos.'

A 'fire drill' involving a queue of employees at Weber and Field's Theatre, New York City, about 1900.

THE FIRE: 4 MAY 1928

The *Globe* reported on 4 May that Loew's Yonge Street Theatre had been saved from destruction early that Friday morning. The blaze was said to have been started by "spontaneous combustion" in an area under the stage. Night watchman Isaac Thompson had detected the flames and hurriedly cut the rope to drop the asbestos curtain. He turned in the alarm, which was also sounded by the "automatic sprinkler gong on the wall of the theatre."

Fireman found a "ceiling high wall of flame leaping up in front of the stage from under the orchestra pit, where it had apparently spread from beneath the stage." In "bursting out into the orchestra pit," the flames had destroyed the theatre's "magnificent $12,000 pipe organ," along with "a number of valuable instruments left in the pit." The pit and the "front part of the lower floor" suffered the most in the fire. Sprinklers set off by the heat throughout the house caused heavy water damage, "particularly in the dressing rooms, back stage and among the properties and scenery." Damage was estimated at $30,000 to the "interior of the playhouse and its furnishings."

The *Star* published a photograph of hero of the hour Thompson, and added to the *Globe* report that the fire had been discovered at 1.15 a.m., and that damage had included "destruction of the pipe organ console and operating unit, injury to the stage and proscenium arch, and some scenic effects."

The Fire Department's report on the fire reads:

Fire report, May 4 1928   1.17a.m.
Part of building where fire started: under stage
Part mostly damaged: seats and decorations
Est. loss to building: $3,000
Loss to contents: $20,000
Amnt of insurance: $800,000
Insurance cos.: London, Lancashire and others
Time water was played: 55 mins.
Fire struck out: 2.55a.m.[13]

PATRON SAFETY: FIRE PROTECTION IN A THEATRE

The fire protection system was another important design concern of the theatre architect. While the system had little impact on the daily economics of a particular theatre, owners wished to keep at bay the frightful spectre of a fire in a crowded theatre. Twentieth-century municipal regulations also prescribed protection from fire for theatre patrons and employees. Such protection cost the commercial theatre owner money, while not adding a cent to his revenues. His recourse would be to add more seats, in order to recoup the investment newly required by most building codes.

In contrast to some large American cities, Toronto bylaws in 1913 did not make onerous demands on theatre owners relating to fire protection, other than regulations on fireproof materials for theatres seating over 1,000, self-closing devices for the projection booth, and an isolated boiler. Toronto did not regulate smoking in the theatre, did not demand a separate rewind room or storage room for volatile nitrate films, and did not require stage skylights or a "fire watch." Other of the city's regulations were concerned with automatic sprinklers and fire curtains, standpipes and fire-fighting equipment, a fire alarm system and fire exits.

The protection from fire afforded the public in Loew's complex was widely publicized:

> The new building is built of fireproof materials, and is
> provided with an elaborate apparatus for the extinguishment
> of fire and the protection of its occupants from accidents in case
> of panic. There is a sprinkler system and a powerful pump to
> provide a reserve supply of water for that system and the
> hydrants inside the theatre should the city pumping plant
> happen to fail in time of need. There are fire extinguishers, axes
> and the like in various parts of the house. Asbestos curtains can
> be lowered promptly in the event of fire on the stage. Skylights
> above the stage are so constructed that in the event of blaze
> they will open automatically or can be opened by the stroke of
> a knife, to carry off smoke. Numerous fire exits equipped with
> "panic" fastenings which open with ten pounds of pressure are
> provided. [11]

The boasting was justified, as Loew's considerably exceeded most large Toronto theatres of the time in fire protection. Toronto audiences regularly paid admission to firetraps, provided with little or no fire-fighting equipment and hopelessly inadequate exits. This was the conclusion of a Civic Survey Committee report at the end of 1913 which inspected six of the eight large theatres in Toronto. In at least four of these, not only was there "an absolute disregard for the by-law," but the absence of "the most commonplace fire preventive measures."[12]

Soon, uncomfortable and unventilated tinderboxes would no longer suffice as theatre buildings. Lamb's stacked theatres in Toronto helped to raise standards and expectations. He introduced a new kind of theatre to the people of Toronto and helped to usher in an era when the theatre-going public would expect to see and hear everything going on, even for the lowest admission price, and to do this in a safe, comfortable, and salubrious environment.

CHAPTER EIGHT

BACKSTAGE: WORKING SPACE

While the success of a theatre depended on the architect's design of public, money-making spaces, it also hinged on plans for the area which brought the building to life: the stage and stage house. A good theatre architect needed to understand thoroughly the work to be performed in backstage areas, along with the technical requirements of the shows to be presented. In a vaudeville theatre, these entailed the efficient storage and movement (if not the production) of a large quantity of stage scenery, and the appropriate distribution of basic elements of stage lighting as well as the dressing room accommodation of up to two or three dozen performers.

View towards the proscenium arch of the Winter Garden Theatre, 1914, with an exhilarating and exotic Oriental drop on the stage.

Lamb's drawings detailed the two rigging lofts in the complex — the areas above the stages (out of sight of audiences) where scenery, drops, and lights were suspended or "flown." Implicated in each was the gridiron — an open framework of beams located a critical and expedient distance below the roof and above the stage which supported blocks, pulleys, and ropes. Attached to suspended scenic units counterweighted with sandbags, these ropes (or "lines") were fastened to and operated from pin rails. Lamb's designs encompassed all these, as well as the fly galleries or large platforms mounted above and at either end of the stage on which pin rails were usually located. In each theatre, he also planned the connecting bridges and ladders between opposing fly galleries and the network of ladders which linked them to the stage and gridiron.

Drawings of the lower theatre and Winter Garden included such elements as footlights (at the front edge of the stage), border lights (suspended in parallel locations above the stage), stage pockets (receptacles set into the stage floor into which lighting instruments could be plugged), and the requisite space for the switchboard which controlled each lighting system.

Lamb's designs consequently had a pervasive impact on the working environment and productivity of the backstage crew, and on the morale and work of the vaudeville actors for whom he devised dressing room, trafficking, and playing spaces. Such spaces, on stage and in the wings, were considerably affected by one theatre being on top of the other. The stage houses were interwoven, each restricted by the theatre above and below. Wing space and depth were further complicated by the intrusions of features which spanned both stage houses: the stage elevator, the Victoria Street fire tower, and the chimney.

These were thus uncommon stages to begin with, but they were also built in a period of considerable flux in the design of proscenium theatres in North America. Several nineteenth-century conventions were being abandoned, and stage houses had begun to shrink. And, of course, many gigantic and magnificent movie palaces were built later with shallow stages, or, in extreme cases, with no stage at all.

STAGE DIMENSIONS AND LAYOUT

The size of stage openings was affected by the prevailing metamorphosis. In theatres built after the turn of the century, these tended to be lower and wider than their nineteenth century counterparts. The size of a proscenium opening also affected the dimensions of drops, curtains and flats. An opening which was higher and wider or lower and narrower than average could cause trouble for companies travelling with scenery of standard dimensions. The proscenium openings and stage depths in Loew's complex were relatively standard at the time, adhering to the "modern" school.

The depth of the lower stage, measuring "29.9'" from the fire curtain, was alleged to be carefully contrived for all possibilities, according to a report in the *Toronto Star Weekly* of 12 December 1913. The dimensions made it "...available for the average musical comedy and ideal for the modern drawing-room play, should at any future time the management desire to devote it to such purposes." The circuit was at least pretending to be skeptical about the future of motion pictures and vaudeville. Alternatively, this was a threatening bluff: Loew's may have been trying to frighten stock theatres away from its type of combination movie and vaudeville shows by offering to meet them on their own turf.

Another fairly modern and "American" feature of the complex was its level stage floors. At the turn of the century, an engineer's notebook with guidelines and statistics on numerous Canadian and American theatres had recorded that stage floors should be pitched "not more than 1/8" per foot." [1] Theatre architect Clarence Blackall made national distinctions. He noted in 1908 that the stages of European theatres were "...habitually sloped up towards the rear at the rate of one-half inch to the foot." At the time, he affirmed, most American stages were level, with a few raked exceptions. [2] The stages also differed from those in the traditional 19th-century theatre by not having numerous and elaborate stage traps and cuts for "disappearing" acts.

Right: A view of the lower stage in 1975, showing its switchboard and its stage-level cast iron pin rails and belaying pins. Manipulation of these ropes (or "lines") lowered or raised drops and borders normally suspended (or "flown") from the gridiron above the stage. The small platform above the switchboard is a "calcium balcony," used for spotlights. The fly gallery is not visible. The door seen in the middle of the wall opened to the dressing room corridor. Through this (and others in tiers above), performers' trunks and other paraphernalia could be hoisted by ropes suspended from the gridiron.

The fireproof fly galleries, pin rails and gridirons dictated by Toronto bylaw and installed in the complex also distinguished it from many 19th-century theatres and from English playhouses where everything backstage — including the gridiron, pin rails and pulleys. — was constructed of wood. [3] The location of a pin rail on each stage floor of the Toronto complex was another modern feature. It had been only recently discovered that this location meant that scenery could be operated "with fewer men and more promptly." [4]

A less "modern" element shown in Lamb's drawings was the "iron paint bridge," located twenty-five feet above the lower stage and linking its fly galleries. This large stationary bridge was presumably intended for a scenic painter, who would work on canvas drops suspended in a moveable frame at this level. The feature was not completed : a very substantial bridge was built (forty-four inches wide with a railing over three feet high) but with no accompanying paint frame. This anomaly reflected changing times and uncertainties. A traditional feature, the backstage paint bridge was almost defunct in commercial theatres of the day. Their use had been prohibited in some cities since the 1880s because of the fire hazard presented backstage by scene painting — caused by both the heating of paint size and the smoking habits of some painters.

The "paint bridge" was merely used as an oversized catwalk. Perhaps the idea of painting scenery in the complex was abandoned before construction was

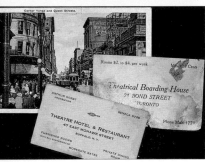

Backstage detritus found in the Elgin and Winter Garden complex.

completed, or the ample bridge was built just in case, with the prospect of a paint frame addition. There was no corresponding paint bridge planned for the Winter Garden. Instead, according to Lamb's drawings, an "iron foot bridge" was to link its fly galleries.

DRESSING ROOMS

Seven tiers comprising 23 dressing rooms were accessible to both theatres. The dressing rooms evidenced the modern age and bylaw concerns for the safety of patrons and performers. Unlike dressing rooms in many nineteenth century theatres, those in the complex were located at the side of the stage, instead of below it. They even had windows, were separated from each other and the stage area by fireproof doors and walls, and had toilets on each floor.

Though the City of Toronto and theatre experts might propose dressing room standards, many theatres did not live up to them. Basement dressing rooms with woefully inadequate ventilation and exits were commonplace. The small-time performer encountered theatres without toilet facilities or running water, theatres with one dank basement room divided by a sheet for male and female performers, and theatres with no dressing rooms at all.

Sophie Tucker described some of the dressing room facilities she encountered on her tours, most of these well below the standards of her accommodation in 1915 at Loew's Yonge Street Theatre: "Drafty old firetraps, no toilets, filthy dirty cracked walls that let in the wind and the rain, old broken floors....One hard jump and down into the cellar you went. Never enough heat." [5] She was used to covering rat holes with cardboard, and renting a heater to make her dressing rooms more liveable.

In the Loew's complex, there was no obvious star dressing room. Such an omission may have quelled some of the chronic dressing room contests engaged in by competing headline acts or may also reflect the fluid and more democratic nature of small-time vaudeville, where a performer might get top billing by appearing in his or her home town. Usually, however, stage-level dressing rooms served stars or the act with the most frequent quick-changes.

Each dressing room had a wash basin, a table, lighted mirrors, and coat hooks, along with a gas fixture and mantle. Gas was used for heating grease paint, and probably also served as emergency or supplementary lighting for the performers. Sometimes, the gas burner was employed by performers for cooking or for heating a kettle or baby bottle.

BACKSTAGE FURNISHINGS

In 1908 Clarence Blackall counselled that backstage furnishings should be rudimentary. He thought that finish and fixtures behind the curtain line should be "...of the most simple, durable, unbreakable character. If a thing can be defaced or ruined it is well nigh hopeless to expect it not to be."[6] Edward Renton's 1918 book on the vaudeville theatre presented a more humane perspective on the needs of vaudeville performers. He suggested that dressing rooms be equipped with "good-sized rugs," "substantial dining or bentwood chairs," a full-length mirror, and outlets for an iron, electric fan, and curling iron.

Stickers and cards touting boarding houses and restaurants for vaudevillians were omnipresent in dressing rooms and backstage areas across the continent, as were the doodles and graffiti of those awaiting their turns, union notices, and other messages.

Gas mantle, buzzer, and graffiti in one of the Winter Garden's dressing rooms, photographed in 1971.

Actors applying makeup in a crowded dressing room of an unidentified New York theatre. Note the combination gas and electric fixture, and admonition against defacement of walls (which appears to be working).

Remaining dressing room chattels were brought by the itinerant act. Sophie Tucker described the belongings which accompanied her as a black-face singer on the small-time circuit.

> I had a stage wardrobe....two dresses, one of red velvet, the other black, a pair of high-heeled black patent-leather pumps, a black wig, black lisle hose, and two pairs of black cotton gloves. Also a tube of brown paste, a can of brown powder, black pencil for eyebrows, and a red lipstick. In the same grip were packed my street clothes: two suits, one black and one brown, three white shirtwaist, two sets of underwear (cotton and linen mixture, no silk), six handkerchiefs (from the Five-and-Ten), two cotton wrappers (a quarter apiece — one for the dressing room, the other for the boardinghouse), two pairs of black cotton bloomers, and six ribbed sweat shirts (ten cents each). The only things I splurged on were three fancy frames for Mama's, Papa's and Son's pictures....The rest of my luggage consisted of a hatbox with a black and brown hat in it and a music case to carry my orchestrations. [7]

As a headliner later, she carried various textile furnishings in her theatre trunk to make her dressing room more homey: cretonne hangings, wall sheets, chair and table covers, and a cheap homemade rug for the cold cement floor. Other accoutrements accompanying many performers were several towels, perhaps a clothes line for stringing laundry across the dressing room, and whatever small items might be used for juggling, making magic, or otherwise showing off.

STOCK SCENERY IN VAUDEVILLE

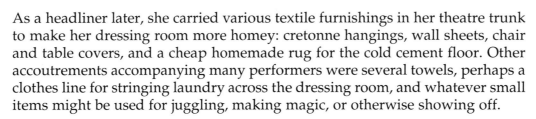

An efficiently run vaudeville theatre needed to be equipped with a battery of stage curtains and painted scenery. These were functional as well as decorative, providing appropriate backgrounds for the acts, cropping the stage opening, and shielding from the audience waiting performers and working stagehands. Drops, flats, and free-standing set pieces were the major components of stage settings. A front teaser and successive border drops masked gaps above. Flanking tormentor flats and the succeeding wing flats defined, respectively, the width of the stage opening and the stage entrances.

On a touring circuit, a theatre would be expected to possess a range of standard scenery. Included among these norms were drops which depicted a garden, a rocky pass, woods, a conservatory, a "palace," the exterior of a rustic cottage, and a streetscape. A theatre showing movies also required a drop on which a "picture sheet" (or movie screen) was painted. Another stock item was an "olio" or all-purpose drop, used by a great variety of acts. The decoration of this latter drop varied from theatre to theatre, but tended to exhibit a scenic vista behind a foreground portal. The olio, the picture sheet, and a streetscape and advertising drop (if any) were "drops in one" which hung just behind the first entrance to the stage, five or six feet behind the footlights. These drops tended to be used by soloists or song-and-dance duos who did not need much performing space.

Scenic drops to be hung further upstage — behind the second, third, or fourth entrance — were often accompanied by the matching wings. These were a succession of flats intended to be set at the sides of the stage parallel to the curtain line. Other connecting flats formed interior settings, some with practical doors and windows. These tended to be occupy the full stage. A vaudeville theatre required at least three different kinds of interior settings: plain, dark and fancy,

Right: A dark fancy interior which could convey a living room, library, office, or court room. Dark interiors were often employed for dramatic or serious vaudeville playlets. An unusual fancy border with swags of vines and purple beans is suspended above. The fancy backing drop seen through the openings appears in the 1924 Herzl Zion photograph.

Above: Drops and wings decorated with urns and flowers on the Winter Garden stage in 1924. These performers appeared in an amateur show staged by Herzl Zion Club.

Right: A pair of flats (framed canvas scenery) with peacock motif, used as wings with the olio and any other appropriate drops. "Palace" was written on the backs of these flats.

Right: A light interior decorated with butterflies, probably used for comedies and other light numbers. The garden drop is visible through its windows. This interior would have been accompanied by light furnishings.

Above: Urns and flowers seen in three pairs of conservatory wings, hinged together into "book flats" for extra stability and simpler installation. The taller pair of flats was destined for the larger lower stage while the remainder matched the lower proscenium opening of the Winter Garden. In each case, they would have been backed by appropriate conservatory drops, now missing from the collection.

Above: A remnant of the Winter Garden's "olio" or "all-purpose" drop. This exquisite example of the scene painter's art was unaccountably hacked to pieces during the vaudeville period.

Above: A traditional garden drop, used with any number of vaudeville acts.

Above: The remnant seen on the right was sufficient to permit a rendering of the scene on the complete olio drop — a vista of an exotic castle behind a foreground portal embellished with urns, flowers, and peacocks.

and light and fancy. The plain or kitchen interior could also be used as a prison. These interiors tended to serve the sketches and playlets on the vaudeville bill. The dark interiors tended to complement more serious dramas, while light interiors served comic or other light-hearted presentations.

A LARGE AND UNUSUAL COLLECTION

Representative examples of all of these scenic elements and norms managed to survive in the complex. Its surviving vaudeville scenery comprises a rare and valuable cache, as such items over the years have been little valued and routinely discarded. The collection contains fine examples of "generic" or standard vaudeville scenery as well as unique and unusual specimens of scenic art over a fifteen-year period.

The lower theatre and Winter Garden were equipped with much duplicate scenery in order to accommodate the same show in both theatres. Since the height of their respective stage openings differed, flats for the lower stage were eighteen feet high, while those intended for the Winter Garden measured sixteen feet. Flats were all five feet nine inches wide, a stock width determined by the measurement of an opening of a box car door in a train.

Some of these surviving flats have been overpainted with completely different designs. This recycling indicates vaudeville's appetite for novelty as well as the dedicated pursuit of money-saving economies by commercial theatre owners.

A few of the flats in the collection had small perforations in the canvas at eye level. These peep holes denote the curiosity of waiting vaudeville performers about the size and receptivity of the audience they would imminently have to impress.

SCENIC STUDIOS

In 1913, standard scenery was produced in New York for the Toronto complex and for all other new Marcus Loew theatres. The backs of original flats were identified: "Marcus Loew Studios, Albert Howard, Scenic Artist, New York." Albert S. Howard had joined Loew's in 1912. He "went up and down the circuit dressing up theatres and stages as new houses were acquired or built." [9] In the 'twenties — and possibly earlier — the studio was located at Loew's American Theatre.

The workings of Marcus Loew's Studio under Howard's direction were described in an in-house magazine in 1930 when it had just relocated to the Metropolis theatre in the Bronx, an 1897 roof garden theatre:

> A staff of seventy-five men and women under the supervision
> of Albert S. Howard are required to turn out the scenery,
> drapes and valances used in the Loew theatres.
> The department is located in the old Metropolis Theatre, New
> York, and each week turns out the scenic equipment of a com-
> plete unit show. Draperies, valances and act curtains for the-
> atres are also constructed in this department.
> Carpenter shop is located on what was the auditorium floor
> of the theatre, the floor being now built up to stage level. Di-
> rectly above the stage proper are three huge paint bridges with
> paint frames approximately 70 x 40 feet. Border lights about 60
> feet long illuminate bridges. Rigging department is quartered
> in dressing room sections of the theatre. [10]

The 1897 Metropolis theatre and open-air roof garden in the Bronx at 142nd Street and 3rd Avenue, converted in 1929 into Loew's Scenic Studios and Warehouse. Prior to this, Loew's Studio was in his American Theatre in Manhattan.

Loew's Scenic Studio, still in operation at the Metropolis in 1946 with Albert S. Howard in charge. At this time, the studio supplied upholstery fabric, wall damask, draperies, curtains, carpets and display frames for Loew's theatres around the world. More infrequently, stage sets and accessories were produced for live shows. At the lower right of the photograph, Howard is directing the preparation of a stage set and is leaning over a pile of vaudeville drops.

The scenic studio was generally a late-nineteenth and early twentieth-century development which entailed increasing centralization and trade specialization. In North America, before the development of chain theatres, travelling shows, and the railroad, most scenic artists had to travel from theatre to theatre to find work. In this period the artist was not likely to have made his living exclusively by painting scenery, and moved between easel painting, decorating, fresco, sign painting and scenic art.

Chain theatres brought increasing specialization and loss of independence for scenic artists, who were slowly absorbed into studios. While this may have favoured the unionization of scene painters, the formation of studios probably suited the chains even more. Instead of dealing with numerous itinerant artists for homogeneous scenery requisites for travelling shows, these could be met by one concern that organized a production line of scene specialists. The studio could also readily deliver the product continent-wide by means of railroad lines.

As Lance Brockman explained,

> Scenic artists were hired by these studios to paint interiors, palaces, or foliage according to their perceived talents. As the studio system became a reality, the age of the romantic travelling artist was doomed, and he became a part of a merchandizing and "factory" environment that placed emphasis on perfection of process and profit. [11]

THE PRODUCTION OF STAGE SCENERY

Drops and flats were painted on linen canvas which had been glued onto frames or tacked onto battens, then sealed and stiffened by applications of warm glue size. Frames, battens and profile pieces were pine. A fireproofing salt solution was mixed with the size and brushed or sprayed on to the back of the drop or flat, though this "fireproofed" the textile only. Wooden elements remained just as flammable.

After dry distemper colours were mixed with a binder of glue or size and simple monochrome areas were filled in, the scenic artist then began to work, often freehand, with brushes and sponge. When warranted, he would employ stencils and pounce patterns.

His colours and compositions were affected by and, in turn, influenced the development of stage lighting. Nineteenth-century scenery, with its "muted colors, romanticized compositions, and soft blended passages," [8] was illuminated by gaslight, and not very brilliantly or comprehensively. The comparative harshness of 20th-century electric stage lighting ushered in a different style of scenic art. It employed brighter colours and other effects which capitalized on the new possibilities. Among these was the use of gilt or bronzing powders which took advantage of the variety of colour available in stage lighting. These 20th-century developments are embodied in the surviving vaudeville scenery.

Canvas drops being painted in the studio.

A scenic artist and his assistants construct models.

Organized into studios, scene painters were categorized as "specialty" or "utility", the former being responsible for more imaginative or intricate work. A specialty artist might be further classified according to his particular expertise, say, in flora and fauna, or in architectural features. Chinese artists were in demand, as they were considered to possess an appropriately exotic sense of colour and design.

Some scenic studios employed their own carpenters to fabricate set pieces or wings, moldings, and curtain and drapery tracks. A scenic studio might also encompass drapers and salesmen, with paintboys at the bottom of the ladder. Its scenic artists might continue to travel from theatre to theatre, but only with their presold work. Perhaps one or two paintboys accompanied a stage carpenter and an artist to a client's theatre with large orders of scenery. On arrival, the carpenter would install and rig the scenery while the artist would touch up the drops. The artist was probably also required to paint an asbestos curtain on site, as painted asbestos fabric was difficult to ship and install.

Obviously, a team of scene painters who were floral specialists touched up scenery shipped from the studio and painted the asbestos curtain, along with the murals in the Winter Garden. The task probably took 3 to 4 weeks. These painters could have been local scenic artists, though it is more likely that Albert Howard sent in a crew from New York, consisting of 3 or 4 artists along with a paint boy for each.

SUPPORTING THE ACTS

A vestige of an archaic system which survived on the Winter Garden's stage were the two grooves which supported its tormentor wings. The groove system had been used in nineteenth-century theatres for suspending flattage and side scenery of uniform height on the same principle as a sliding door. It obliged scenes to be set at right angles to the side walls or parallel to the curtain line. Booth's Theatre in New York is said to have been the first (in 1868) to abandon this system. Though the groove system was out of fashion by the turn of the century, Blackall explained in 1909: "Such construction is still in use in some of the older vaudeville houses, and occasionally for the tormentors, but the grooves constitute a clumsy device at best and our scenery is now either built up and lashed together in box form, or braced to the floor with extension braces." [12]

A modern system, which used stage screws and braces instead of grooves supported flats in use on both stages. This new stage technology had affected profoundly scenic design and the appearance of stage presentations, because of the new flexibility allowed for flat placement. The system was described by Sachs and Woodrow in 1898:

> The "scenes," "profile pieces," etc., are fixed to the stage by means of a wooden brace with a screw inserted at one end in the wooden framework of the "flat," and at the other end in the stage floor. By this means the "scenes" are held upright, but the stage floor is being constantly pierced and worn with small holes, and looking as though it were worm-eaten.[13]

In addition to the small holes made by stage screws, there were numerous larger holes in the Winter Garden's stage, most of them grouped behind the second and third entrance and drilled at an angle. They probably accommodated the 5/8"-inch belaying pins used in the pin rails in the complex. These may have been inserted in the stage floor in order to brace and anchor the balancing, diving or bouncing apparatus of acrobatic acts.

"TAKING IN" THE SHOW

Such apparatus, along with cages of performing animals and scenery travelling with an act, would have entered the lower stage through a sixteen foot-high scenery door on Victoria Street. The transit of travelling scenery and a voluminous array of vaudeville properties to the Winter Garden's stage was more complicated. Small props and animals, along with performers, could travel in the stage elevator between the two stages. But the elevator's cab, with a clear height of 8' and measuring only 9' 3 1/2" by 4'4", was too small for large items like battens, flats, and diving tanks. Cables and wooden platforms left on the stage roof of the lower theatre testify that such items were hoisted or lowered outside the building, likely on the north side, where Victoria Street traffic did not complicate the process. This task would have been performed infrequently, as the duplicate stock scenery in the two theatres sufficed for most acts.

Vaudeville trunks belonging to performers did not take the elevator. These were raised and lowered by ropes suspended from the gridiron, and entered or left the dressing room corridor in each upper tier through an opening protected by a fireproof sliding door.

STAGE PROPERTIES

Acts travelling on the Marcus Loew circuit would always have been accompanied by the necessary unique props. The property man or stage carpenter employed in the complex would have been responsible for items not otherwise provided, some of which may have been contracted out. According to an August 1914 Winter Garden programme, stage furnishings were supplied by Reliable Furniture Co. of 36-8 Queen Street West, and Bell pianos were used "exclusively." This was a fairly standard kind of exchange, with local merchants being accorded theatre passes as well as advertising.

Miscellaneous props such as draperies, fake fireplaces and balustrades, furniture, statuary, and artificial plants contributed to interior stage settings. In his 1918 book on the vaudeville theatre, Edward Renton entreated theatre managers to avoid tired and shabby settings, as well as disharmonious ones.

> Observe carefully that there is harmony in the color scheme of the scenery, carpets and draperies; avoid the rather frequently encountered combination of a green carpet, red upholstered furniture, old-rose hangings and perhaps a blue rug or two....Never set an interior for instance, with a mahogany piano, white enamelled tabourets, oak table and mission settee. If part in mission, then all so....DO NOT set a sketch [with] action taking place in the winter with curtains and drapes of light and airy cretonne.[14]

Left: Tormentor wings, decorated with urns and flowers, and matching teaser on the Winter Garden stage in 1971. These are seen framing the "picture sheet" drop, or movie screen, which has its own draw curtains. These tormentor wings, always in place and fixed in grooves, defined the width of the stage opening and the location of the first entrance. (Teaser is the term used for the first top masking behind the proscenium. Subsequent ones are called borders.)

Renton probably divulged the common practice by advising vaudeville theatre managers to get rid of the "decrepit ... imitation marble clock on the dirty, dingy mantel," and the "time-worn, discouraged artificial palms," the "dejected lifeless old imitation-leather lounge", and the "dirty tablecloth."

One can only surmise the inventory of stage properties which was maintained at Loew's complex in Toronto. Two dark fireplaces and one tree stump were the only survivors. The dark fireplaces were supplements to dark interior settings (if maxims on harmony were observed), while the tree stump likely appeared in a rustic or woodland milieu, and was sturdy enough to be used as a seat or platform by performers.

TRAVELLING SCENERY

Only truly big stars in vaudeville transported their own curtains and sets. Such chattels were usually the responsibility of the act, along with the employment of any additional stage hands or any extra electrician required for an elaborate presentation. Few small-time acts on Loew's circuit would have bothered. Not only were labour and transportation costs a deterrent but the exact fit of such travelling settings could not be taken for granted as the dimensions of proscenium openings on the circuit were not uniform. Additional scenery, unusual lighting effects, and other equipment added work and complications to the Monday morning installation and rehearsal of the week's show, when less than an hour of rehearsal time was available for each act.

The son of Loew's manager Jules Bernstein remembered that most of the acts he saw weekly did not require any special scenery, and that the same scenery would be used for fifty different acts. He also recalled that numerous performers appeared in front of curtains rather than scenery. (Stand-up comedians and monologists were among those who did not seek the distractions of an elaborate setting.)

Still, specialty scenery was developed for various lead performers and production numbers, and various acts did travel with their own scenery on the Loew circuit. This is evidenced in the Winter Garden's printed programme of 31 August 1914 which acknowledges "Scenery by Valentine, Brooklyn" and "Ralph Hollingsworth, carpenter," in the context of Ed Ford and his Dance Review. In 1924, settings used for Loew's Amateur Minstrel Frolic were credited to Loew's Studio, American Theatre, New York. One drop used in another 1924 amateur show depicted the deck of a ship, complete with guns.

During the teens and early 20s, scenery used in the complex did not receive much comment in newspaper ads and reviews, with a few exceptions. *The Mail and Empire* noted on 25 March 1916 the elaborate setting of the diving and swimming act "Six Water Lilies." It presented the interior of a palace, with the huge tank masked in to look like a marble basin. [15] A nautical musical scenic production by the Pollard Musical Players was mentioned the week of 16 February 1920.

The Royal Pekin Troupe

After about 1924, settings were habitually noted in Loew's advertising. This sometimes entailed weekly or even bi-monthly references to "unique" or "original," "appropriate" or "pleasing," and "colorful" and "artistic scenery" along with "pretty" or "new" costumes and settings, and "special scenic effects."[16] Sometimes, specific settings were recorded. These may have travelled with the act, or may have been promoted because they had been recently acquired by the theatre, even if only by recycling.

In January 1924, a very pretty woodland scene was the background for an act called "Autumn Three" doing bird calls and animal imitations. A woodland setting was also singled out for "Their First Love," a duet appearing in May 1927, though such a setting must have been familiar to Loew's audiences since 1913. A shoe store setting was employed by the "Shoe Box Revue" on 8 September 1924, and Ensign Al Moore and his Jolly Tars Orchestra appeared with a setting which represented a picturesque boat scene in March 1927. A New York night club was the setting for "White Way Gaieties" in June, while an old barn setting backed Ezra Buzra's Rube Orchestra in September 1927.

Gautier's Toy Shop. This act appeared on the last vaudeville bill to be presented at Loew's on 2 October 1930.

Much of the scenery noted depicted foreign or exotic places. In November and December of 1924, "A Night in Spain" boasted of songs, dances, gowns and scenery "all in Spanish style," while a Venice setting complemented the song and dance revue of the Venetian Masqueraders. A "brilliant setting and becoming costumes" marked the presentation of Harry Elsworth and his Russian orchestra in August 1925. More of the same Russian scenery appeared with The Russian Master Singers in October 1925, and, again, to set off the fancy skating of Elsie Paulson in April 1928. Oriental costumes and settings were presented with the Royal Pekin Troupe in May 1926, and "10 different scenic settings" were cited for Toyland Midget Revue in January 1926, including Sunny Spain, Toyland, and the Land of King Tut.

The Venetian Masqueraders

CHANGING STYLES

The collection of scenery which survived in the complex encompasses changing scenic styles and entertainment over its 17-year history of vaudeville. It includes scenery typical of the early and late 'teens, which depicts representational and traditional settings, with soft shading and blended colours. These were often used by the traditional vaudeville sketch, singer, or comedian.

By contrast, settings which date from the mid-to late-20s settings have bright colours and hard lines. They are exotically decorated with large and abstracted features like butterflies and scarabs. The style reflects the cult of art deco in the 20s, as well as some of the permutations in a vaudeville programme which the movie palace had engendered. Its vivid and splashy revues, unit shows, and spectacles had little use for the traditional settings of forest and kitchen. The domestic sketch and its mundane settings had further waned in importance in the vaudeville programme because of the influx and popularity of the feature film and acts which featured modern music, fashion shows and dance crazes.

The style of scenic art in the 20s might also be seen as testimony to the increasing importance of extravagant lighting in theatrical presentations. Shaded, subtle and naturalistic scenery was best appreciated when illuminated simply by a wash of light from footlights and borders. Spotlights and "following" lighting, emanating from points in the auditorium, did not do justice to such scenery, and was more effective with plainer backgrounds.

STAGE DRAPERY

The most interesting survivor in the complex in the category of stage drapery was a satin act curtain, apparently made for the lower stage in the 20s, though its style and coloration is appropriate to the Winter Garden. It is a magnificently decorated specimen, with gold bullion fringe and studded with diamond dust. Its light-sensitive materials responded with infinite variation to subtle alterations in lighting, and it appropriately set the tone for the gaudy, glitzy variety entertainment which waited behind it.

Draperies and curtains did much to enhance the decoration and excitement of the theatre. (This purpose was extravagantly fulfilled in the later movie palace, whose curtains were laden with jewels, spangles, tassels, fringes, beads, rhinestones and appliques, in keeping with the unprecedented razzle dazzle of the rest of the house.) But even much plainer stage curtains and draperies contributed to the spell being cast on the audience. They provided the focus of attention in the theatre and created suspense and excitement. They concealed an upcoming act and its set and revealed it dramatically at the appropriate moment. Even the picture sheet drop came with draw curtains, perhaps to increase the sense of drama and theatrical experience.

The stages and scenery of the vaudeville house were recalled in the elaborate stage settings built in many movie palaces which had no stages. Often these settings merely framed the screen and served no dramatic purpose. The theatrical past of the movies is also acknowledged even in austere modern cinemas. They continue to drape their screens, though this seems equivalent to festooning a television set.

Below: The satin act curtain used on the lower stage, expertly painted on a shimmery fabric which is unforgiving of any mistakes or second thoughts by the scenic artist. Diamond dust, made from granulated glass or gelatin derivatives, highlights some of its decoration.

Below: Another light interior likely painted in the mid- to late 20s, with large, more abstract motifs. Performers appearing in front of this setting must have worked hard to hold the audience's attention.

Switchboard and dimmers of the lower theatre. The system operated on both ac and dc, and on 110 volts and 1800 watts.

LIGHTING THE VAUDEVILLE STAGE

The effective use of stage scenery depended upon the lighting system arranged for the theatre. In the days of oil and gas, stages were lit by footlights below and border lights above, and by bunch lights on standards in the wings. What changed, initially, with the coming of electric stage lighting, was its power and quality, not its locations.

Even so, the lighting in the Loew's complex and in and other vaudeville theatres of the period was dim by modern standards. Footlights and borders provided a uniform wash of low-intensity white or coloured light as well as numerous shadows. Spotlights and floodlights — carbon arcs, and incandescent olivettes and bunch lights — yielded side light, some of it brilliant. In the Loew's complex, all the stage lighting instruments were located in the stage area, though in this period stage lighting from the auditorium was not unknown. Red, white, and blue bulbs were used for stage lighting.

According to a 1918 article on theatre illumination, a vaudeville theatre revealed its class origins by its quantity and tones of its stage lighting:

> The stage equipment will vary depending on the character of the house. However, there are generally certain set principles covering the stage lighting which vary as a rule only in quantity. The cheap vaudeville house might have a footlight of simply white lights, and perhaps one or two borders of white lights only. The better class of vaudeville house will have a footlight of three colors with three or four borders, each of three colors, and in addition incandescent pockets either side of the stage, and from two to a half dozen arc or spot pockets. [17]

This lighting was controlled from switchboards and dimmers. The switchboards in Loew's theatres appeared to be marble, but were marbleized slate. Slate was used for the switchboard because it was easily cleaved at the right thickness, had the same strength, stability, and insulating quality as marble, and was cheaper.

The Winter Garden's switchboard supported a bank of 15 resistance dimmers. Incandescent stage lights were dimmed by decreasing (or resisting) the flow of current. This process generated considerable heat in the vicinity of the dimmer board.

FOOTLIGHTS AND BORDERS

Among the incandescent stage lights were 192 50-watt bulbs in each of the footlight and border troughs in the complex. Half of them were white, a quarter were blue, and a quarter were red. The interior of the trough was painted white, so as to provide a softer reflection, less hot spots and less eye strain for performers. Forty-eight red, 96 white, and 48 blue bulbs were also to appear in each border trough. (There were three borders on the Winter Garden's shallower stage, while four borders were accommodated on the stage of the lower theatre.)

White, red, and blue were the current norms for theatre lighting, though occasionally amber was added. In various combinations, the red, white and blue colours in footlights and border lights tended to improve flesh tones and flatter the performers. These colours could convey differing times of day, including sunrise, sunset, and evening, and could enhance the colours normally used in stage scenery. In 1913, these bulbs were dipped in lacquer. The frequent renewing of the stain was a recurring problem. The colour screen on the bulb —

especially the colour blue — deteriorated rapidly in the heat generated in the trough. Frequent redipping was required, which usually occurred without the removal of previous coatings. Vaudeville lighting was thus rendered dimmer. Loew's was built during the dying days of this system of dipped bulbs and undivided footlight compartments. High intensity mazda bulbs, introduced in about 1914, brought in their wake a compartment for each bulb. The bulb was no longer coloured: instead each compartment was screened by a frame containing coloured glass or gelatine media.

Lighting traditions of the 19th-century theatre were still in evidence in the gas footlights seen in the Winter Garden (and probably in the downstairs theatre). Like the rest of the gas lighting in the complex, these were probably intended only for emergency or back up. Gas footlights were not required in Toronto in 1913; in fact the bylaws demanded incandescent electric stage lights "where the current can be obtained." Theatres in large U.S. cities had been using electric stage light since 1885, though switchboards and gas tables coexisted backstage during the early years of the twentieth century. The gas footlights in the Winter Garden were probably never used. They were controlled by one valve near the dimmer board. They had no guard or screen, and would have been susceptible to breakage and to igniting nearby costumes. An additional hazard was that their "batwing" burners were easily removed or could be blown out of their sockets by gas pressure in the pipe.[18]

SPOT LIGHTING

A third type of lighting — carbon arc spotlights — coexisted in the complex. Powered by direct current and plugged into "floor pockets", these spotlights were struck and fed by hand, and dimmed manually by a stagehand. One stage hand might operate two only if they were stationed close together. These labour-intensive instruments, requiring constant attendance, provided the only intensely bright and specific stage light available. Carbon arc spotlights produced pure white light, but also contributed a fringing chromatic aberration, or a rainbow hue around the spot. The size of the spot light available would have ranged only from about 3' at the smallest, to perhaps 10 or 15 feet. Other than in the wings, spotlight locations in the complex were on the fly floor and on 12-foot high "calcium balconies" on either side of each proscenium. Such locations would have been used for lighting big or spectacular acts. Though some other theatres at the time arranged follow spots in the projection booth, Loew's Toronto complex maintained older traditions.

CONSEQUENCES

Though, by modern standards, the vaudeville stage in 1913-14 was dimly lit, it was considerably brighter than that seen in the more sombre days of gaslight, limelight, and candles. The object of stage lighting in the vaudeville theatre of the teens was to illuminate the scenery and the performers. It was not generally seen as an important expression of art (though carbon arcs and effects projectors could be used dramatically), and it did not dominate theatrical productions.

Lighting in the vaudeville theatre became increasingly sophisticated. The "tricks" and spectacles it developed seem to have influenced lighting for the legitimate stage. Spotlight effects had been considered the province of variety shows, and vulgarly inappropriate for Shakespearean and other high-toned dramas. Variety entertainments' follow spots, pools of coloured light, and other honky tonk effects were to encroach into the lighting of "respectable" theatrical productions.[19]

There were other consequences. All the tricks and special effects developed may have assisted the demise of the representational scene painter. Realistic designs on drops and flattage often gave way to cycloramas and stark, more abstract sets. Stage art was becoming more and more the province of the lighting designer.

In 1913, the range of colour, intensity, direction, and control available to the vaudeville stage electrician was very limited by comparison to present day. Still, in many respects, a lighting technician (as opposed to a lighting designer) now has less opportunity to use his creativity and skill than his vaudeville-days predecessor. While the latter could exhibit imagination and daring during a show — albeit dimly and traditionally lit — by energetic and even original manipulation of dimmer board switches, modern pre-set and computerized lighting boards have perhaps reduced the opportunities for ad hoc and creative input by the stage electrician working the show.

An extraordinary historic photograph of the backstage operations and equipment, incorporating stagehands perched in the fly gallery, flats, props, portable side lighting, switchboard, and dimmers.

CHAPTER NINE

THE BUSINESS AND ART OF VAUDEVILLE

The stage houses, lighting, scenery, dressing rooms — all the backstage paraphernalia — were dedicated to the continuing predominance of vaudeville as mass entertainment. Between seven and nine "high-class" vaudeville acts and five moving picture reels were promised in Loew's opening publicity in December 1913. Vaudeville was the premiere attraction: titles of the movies to be shown were not mentioned, and would not be consistently announced until late 1916.

When the complex was built, vaudeville was the most popular form of mass entertainment in North America. Essentially, it comprised in one programme a kaleidoscope of varied 15- or 20-minute live acts of anything considered to be entertaining. "Vaudeville" was aptly defined in Ontario's Theatres and Cinematographs Act in 1917: "an entertainment consisting of songs, dances, gymnastics, mimicry, farces, a short light dramatic piece and other specialties disconnected with each other." [1]

Vaudeville by 1913 was not a hodge-podge of acts which combined haphazardly or which were pulled together by a local agent. It was a mammoth, multi-million dollar business, controlled by monopolistic theatre chains and their booking offices, operating across the continent. The centralized booking offices of theatre chains like Loew's controlled the selection and often the order of acts appearing on a bill. The result was the beginning of the continental standardization of mass entertainment: "Vaudeville was the same kind of show available almost all day long, almost every day of the week, almost everywhere in the country." Its variety, rhythms and centralized distribution would be reproduced later in the mass entertainment of radio and television. [2]

Except for local amateurs occasionally employed, a vaudeville artist or act appearing in Loew's Yonge Street Theatre and Winter Garden would have been contracted to the chain's booking office, and would have been engaged to tour for the various theatres in the chain for a specific period. The act and its agent usually had no control over this routing, in spite of the fact that the performers or the producers of an act had to meet their own travel and accommodation expenses. Usually, Sundays were used for travelling, and Monday mornings for rehearsal. Acts appearing in "continuous" shows might be on stage as many as five times in a 12-hour period, six days and nights a week.

Madeleine Berlo and her Diving Girls, featured at Loew's in 1924, 1925, and 1928.

Weber and Fields, special guests on opening night in the lower theatre, 15 December 1913. A classic comedy team formed in 1877 which combined dialect, physical humour and grotesque costumes, Joe Weber and Lew Fields had reconciled only in 1912 after a 1904 break-up.

Buck and Bubbles, a prodigiously talented song-and-dance team who entertained Loew's audiences the week of 30 April 1928. Later, they were in the Ziegfield Follies, an original stage production of *Porgy and Bess*, and in the movies.

SMALL AND BIG TIME

Variety had classified the varied manifestations of organized vaudeville in 1912: there was "big time," offering two shows daily — one matinee and one show at night — with the highest paid performers and at the highest scale of admission. "Small time" vaudeville houses played three or more shows daily, or two shows nightly, at "popular prices," and often included movies. The standard of the dressing room facilities and the size and competence of its orchestra also reflected a theatre's small- or big-time status.

Small-time was the incubator and proving ground of the tiny proportion of acts which attained the dizzying heights of big-time and vaudeville's promised land — the Palace Theatre in New York. It was in small-time where the performer broke in, honed, and perfected an act, and where skills were developed in timing, entrances and exits, and reading an audience. Small-time had the flexibility and the forgiveness required by a novice, or by an act experimenting with a new routine. If it bombed, the disaster might go almost unnoticed, unlike big-time performers who had nowhere to go but down, and unlike acts whose debacles were unrelentingly exposed later to a live radio and television audience of millions.

Variety in 1912 divided big- and small-time into various sub-categories. The gradations understood were numerous and sophisticated, encompassing small small time, medium small time, big small time, little big time, and medium big time. "Small-time" covered the widest ranges as "it could mean theatres with seats, lodge halls with benches,...Mom and Pop operations...or wagon shows."[3]

Loew's double decker in Toronto did not fit easily into *Variety*'s classifications. While the lower theatre could be categorized as "small time" because of the number of shows offered daily, the Winter Garden was more unorthodox. It presented only one show a day at a higher rate of admission, but, unlike most "big time" theatres, it did not showcase top-ranked and high-salaried performers, and it offered movies.

Loew's management was harshly criticized in the *World* the week after the Winter Garden opened for the low quality of acts presented:

> How the management of the Loew's Winter Garden expect to gain the favour of the theatregoing public and at the same time allow such acts to appear as the majority of those on this week's bill is beyond comprehension. It hardly seems possible that some of the actors and actresses could obtain bookings on even a third-class circuit, let alone being allowed to appear on the stage of a theatre advertising a high-class vaudeville bill.[4]

VAUDEVILLE AND MOVIES

Though some "high-class" vaudeville theatres had originally disdained motion picture entertainment, in Loew's small-time vaudeville theatres, movies were considered an important, reliable, and relatively inexpensive item on the bill. Loew's combination vaudeville — or "family time"— was a hybrid entertainment form. It combined the grandiose, large capacity theatres of the big time with the low admissions and movies of the nickelodeon.

Like previous novelties such as shadowgraphs or magic lanterns, short movies had been easily accommodated in a vaudeville programme. Movies on a vaudeville bill had a great deal of appeal for the circuit. Unlike vaudeville performers, movies did not get drunk, sick, or temperamental, didn't complain

Rose's Royal Midgets, "25 little men and women" who offered an hour-long presentation involving songs, dances, acrobatic stunts, magic, and music at Loew's in 1924.

about conditions of work or belong to a union, and didn't require as much manpower and attention to detail as a stage act. Another advantage was that movies could be shown in the position reserved for the "dumb" or non-speaking act at the beginning and end of the show, so as to minimize the disruption caused by the coming and going of patrons.But long movies on a vaudeville bill meant the reduction of number of live acts. This was incompatible with the programme of a big time theatre, which was known for the uncommon class and the number of its live acts.

A VAUDEVILLE BILL

A vaudeville show usually consisted of "...a light comedy sketch, a short playlet, a monologue and a two-man patter team, miscellaneous animal routines, musical spectacles, ventriloquists, novelties, song and dance acts and acrobatics — carefully timed and arranged and trimmed in theme, tone and style so as to reflect the tastes of the predominantly lower and middle class audiences."[5]

E.F. Albee described the relentless production schedule:

> The dramatic sketch must plant its story and have the action stirring rapidly before the curtain has ceased to rustle; the acrobats must show the best they have and bow off; the singer, the monologist, the dancer, and the animal trainer and every other artist must have his or her act boiled down to the essentials and the appeal must be direct, sudden, and unmistakable. [6]

Lewis Stone, the "well-known upside down dancer," who would have had to set up this apparatus on two stages in the same evening during his engagement at Loew's in 1916.

A playlet or one-act play was a constant feature of a vaudeville show, and was the chief user of the "interior" drops and props available. Playlets were "...mainly in the order of domestic farces and light comedies." Many concerned marital fidelity or the immigrant experience. Others were musical comedies or were serious, gripping and intense, involving romance, tragedy and mystery. These melodramas in digest form — skeletal and formulaic — provided constant work for script writers (and hacks) and actors from the legitimate stage. Most of the legitimate actors appeared in dramatic and dignified sketches. One of these was the accomplished thespian Edward Abeles, who appeared at Loew's in January 1916 in a playlet entitled "Self-defence", in which he was a dumb (but not deaf) Italian boy charged with killing his sister, her husband and her baby.

Patricola and Meyer, billed in 1914 as "The Dancing Fool." This act affixed a publicity card to the wall of a Winter Garden dressing room, a memento which still survives.

Song and dance acts were also staples of vaudeville. Vaudeville singers in pre-radio days were responsible for making many popular songs popular. Singers had to belt out lyrics without the aid of amplification systems and microphones to every corner of a 2,000- seat house. Dance acts of all kinds were crowd favourites, and included demonstrations of current "society" dance crazes like the tango and the shimmy, as well as buck and wing, clog, toe, soft shoe and step dancing, as well as "eccentric" or unusual dance acts.

Whistlers and yodellers, extracts from Grand Opera, and spoon and bottle playing mingled with refrains on the piano, accordion, harp, ukulele, harmonica, xylophone, violin, banjo, bagpipes, and saxophone. An act appearing at Loew's in January 1914 played a cigar box with a single string. In the 20s, jazz and other bands were prevalent on the vaudeville stage and at Loew's. Among them was Mamie Smith and her "Jazz Hounds" who headlined during the week of 9 October 1922. Loew's audiences were probably treated to "I Ain't Gonna Give Nobody None o' This Jelly Roll" and "The Darktown Flapper's Ball" recorded that year by the singer and her band. They might have heard, as well, two

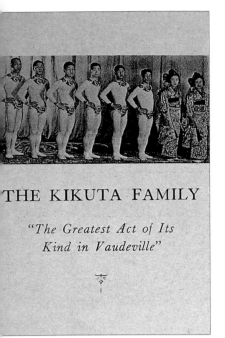

THE KIKUTA FAMILY

*"The Greatest Act of Its
Kind in Vaudeville"*

The Kikuta Family, advertised by
Loew's in Toronto as "Kikuta
Japs" in 1926 and 1927. The
Globe reviewer classed them as
"one of the most skilful of the
acrobatic performances that have
appeared on the vaudeville stage
... rivalling in attraction even the
feature picture play."

influential hits recorded in 1920 by Mamie Smith: "Crazy Blues" and "That Thing Called Love." None of these were named by the *Globe* reviewer, who merely referred blandly to the band's "original syncopated melodies."[7]

Standard vaudeville acts at Loew's and other theatres included magicians, mind readers, ventriloquists, hypnotists, psychics, male and female impersonators, mimics and impressionists, and human imitators of birds, animals, frogs and insects.

Circus acts were perennial favourites. According to Joe Laurie, Jr.,

> The circuses furnished the variety theaters with the 'small stuff' animal acts, like dogs, monkeys, ponies, pigeons, etc., that could play on small stages and get into the small stage doors. When the circus would close, those acts would fill in the winter with vaude dates. The variety houses had no room to keep the animal acts, so the owners would keep their animals in the dressing room during the show, and sleep 'em in a local stable or barn.[8]

Among the trained animals appearing on Loew's stage were seals, ponies, dogs, monkeys, baboons, mules, donkeys, cats, rats, birds, and goats. Many of these acts popularly imitated human behaviour, such as Wanda, the Seal with the Human Brain, Merian's dog carnival: 40 dogs in "a wedding day in dog land," bicycle riding by apes and a bear, or four horses stepping to orchestral dance music. Little Jim and Teddy, wrestling bears capable of dancing and comedy, appeared in 1923 and 1925,respectively. An act which must have been as difficult to train as it was to view from the rear of the balcony was Swayne's Rats and Cats. Reportedly, Swayne's rats, dressed in jockey outfits, would ride around a miniature racetrack on the backs of Swayne's cats. This feat by "Swayne's Rats and Cats" was not described by the *Globe* reviewer, who commented: "these apparent enemies work together amicably, much to the surprise of the audience, and a boxing bout between two of the tabbies is hilariously funny."[9]

Though occasionally the untamed side of the animal kingdom was exploited, as in the bucking bronco on stage on 22 September 1919, usually large and wild animals were not used in Loew's and most other vaudeville shows. Small and domesticated animals were safer and less troublesome, and were more compatible room mates if forced into the dressing room with the trainer, as they sometimes were. A much repeated story concerns a "baby elephant" travelling on the freight elevator to the Winter Garden. One informant remembers this baby elephant offered group rides to children on the Winter Garden stage.

Chinese and Japanese acrobats seem to have been in special demand. Other circus-type acts included jugglers, contortionists, trapeze, tight rope, slack wire, and flying ring specialists, aerialists, some of whom did "teeth" and "neck" stunts, and equilibrists on perch, pedestal, and horizontal bar. Such performers apparently supplied and carried their own equipment, and usually set it up themselves. Other athletic endeavours and stunts found expression in Loew's vaudeville bills with barrel jumpers, tumblers, trampoline experts, gymnasts, "novelty ice skaters" and roller skaters, sharpshooters, trick cyclists, wrestlers, strong men, and lariat and boomerang throwers.

Among acts with special physical skills were hoop rollers and club swingers, "whirling demons," and acts exhibiting treadmill running, muscle posing, and physical culture work. Loew's also presented Madeline Berlo and her diving girls, who, from a trapeze 75 feet [sic!] above the stage, dived into 4 1/2 feet of water, Slayman Ali's Hooloos, "acrobatic wonders and India rubber marvels," and Australian wood choppers, who sliced large logs at lighting speed.

"Baby Sylvia," one of the child
stars who appeared at Loew's
and hosted a free reception for
children, offering Dubarry's
chocolates in the lobby on a
Saturday afternoon in 1924.

The Australian wood choppers, "champs of Canada too," according to Joe Laurie Jr., were classed as an "odd" act, unorthodox in style and presentation. So were Loew's one-legged acrobats, "Resista," a 98-lb. girl who could not be lifted, and "The Great Willard," who could make himself grow by 6 to 8 inches. Vaudeville also exploited "freak acts," which derived from a freak of publicity or a freak event. Most of these did not last for more than a season, and included appearances by people who were newsworthy but often had no specific stage talent. Among these were a pair of Siamese twins, Daisy and Violet Hilton, who were booked in 1925 at $2,500 a week, and "broke all house records" throughout the circuit. Their appearance in the Toronto theatre the week of 19 October was hyped for months in Loew's *Newsette*, and publicity photos of them appear in all three extant issues of that year.

A vaudeville bill might also include such "educational" items as the "scientific demonstration of orange picking by California orange pickers" on 12 November 1917, or Captain Sorcho's submarine show in March 1916, exhibiting in a huge glass tank the work and apparatus of a deep sea diver, and using models to show "submarine operations, the sinking of the Lusitania, and the action of floating mines."[10]

"Stunning models" exhibiting the latest fashions on a vaudeville bill functioned like a shopping catalogue. Other models on a vaudeville stage were scantily clad, posing as "living statuary" or "tableau vivant," an act which was "...often merely an excuse to present attractive models in the nude or near nude..."[11]

Among other vaudeville acts were artists in "allied arts," proficient at rapid painting or crayon drawing, rag, sand, and smoke pictures. Loew's offered boy artists working on "transparent canvas," and clay modelling of "well known men of the present age." The routine finale of the latter type of act, according to Joe Laurie, Jr., was wads of clay being heaved at the bust of a mother-in-law or another unpopular icon. [12]

Humour was an essential component of a vaudeville bill, and was often combined with singing, dancing and novelty. "Tramp," "rube," and "nut" comedians and female comics were in demand. Always present was an abundance of ethnic stereotypes and humour, in sketches and in the routines of stand-up comedians and comedy teams, many in black face. Various acts specialized in crude satire of the Scots, Irish, Germans, Swedes, Italians, and Jews. The Loew's chain must have considered the demand for this type of humour brisk enough to present Senna and Stephens as "a Chinaman and a Coon" the week of 13 June 1921, and "A Coon and a Chink," Racker & Winnifred, the following week. The English "chappie," bemused by American ways, was also the subject of sketch humour on the circuit.

Vaudeville performers came from all ethnic groups, and in all shapes and sizes (including children and midgets), and ranged from the respectable legitimate thespian to circus freaks, and from opera singers to performing rats. Different races mingled in acrobatic, musical and comedy acts, though they were not all accommodated in the same hotels in the different cities. According to E.F. Albee, the variety in vaudeville reflected the constituents of the country and the American way— it appealed to all classes and tastes, represented all nations and races, and embodied "opportunity for everybody, a chance for all." [13]

The performers were as likely to be female as male, and included, for example, the Bennett sisters, "athletic girls wrestling, fencing and boxing." Female performers appeared as comedians, mimics, magicians, acrobats, male impersonators, and animal trainers. Among others at Loew's were Hilda Hawthorne, ventriloquist, with Johnny the singing dummy, Alice Cole, girl tenor, Elly the strongwoman, and the Nicholl sisters, who presented female blackface

The Great Willard, who appeared in 1915 and 1920. Supposedly, he could not only add eight inches to his height, but could extend his arms up to fifteen inches, and could make one leg four inches longer that the other.

The athletic Bennett Sisters, who demonstrated their physical talents at Loew's in 1915.

comedy. In general, female acts consistently received more frequent top billings than male acts, at least in Toronto's vaudeville theatres up to 1914.

Vaudeville bills were usually devised, balanced, and sequenced by the chain's booking office, and not local management. Not only were the acts ordered to provide suitable variety, avoiding consecutive dancing acts or stand-up comedians, but they were arranged to provide the proper tempo and momentum for the show and to coincide with the temper and coming and going of the audience.

This all had to be accomplished within the framework of the stage requirements for each act, and rapid, smooth scene changes. Often, the first act used the full stage, while the second was an "act in one," performed in front of the curtain behind the first entrance during which the scenery for the third act was set up. A full stage act broke the monotony of a series of acts in one. These had been prevalent in the early days of vaudeville. In later years the situation was reversed, and acts in one were needed to relieve the too numerous full-stage performances. An act which opened in one, went to full stage, and closed in one was a treat to book. It incorporated the requisite variety, could follow a full-stage act, and could, in turn, be followed by another full-stage act.

An opening act was traditionally a "dumb act" — acrobats, jugglers, bicycle acts or animals — whose audience and performers did not mind the associated noise and disturbance of patrons filing in. The opening was the lowest item on the billing, a scourge the vaudeville performer sought to escape. The second act and all those following were supposed to be better. A man and woman singing act might follow in this spot to "settle" the audience. In the middle of the bill were the sketches and playlets, "rousing acts," and comedians. The most prestigious location on a vaudeville bill was the next to closing act, a climax that all preceding acts had worked to prepare. Though the closing act was often again a dumb act (as concentration would be disturbed by exiting patrons) it still might be "a big flash, ...an animal act or a costume spectacle, trapeze artists — a showy act to send home audience pleased."[14]

Movies came to play an important role as opening and closing acts in small-time vaudeville theatres. During the first decade of the century, movie newsreels were often shown after the closing act. Later, short comedy films served as the opening "dumb" act. On opening night in the downstairs theatre, moving pictures opened and closed the show, and were not described by reviewers.

OPENING NIGHTS

LOWER THEATRE: 15 DECEMBER 1913

The lower theatre opened on Monday 15 December 1913. The choice of Monday night adhered to the normal weekly travelling and opening schedule for acts touring the chain. The vaudeville bill on opening night was unremarkable at the time and its acts were not named in Loew's advertisements. They promised "Quality *Vaudeville* and Select Photo-Plays Continuous from 9 a.m. to 11 p.m." What was to make the opening special was the New York celebrities in attendance, and the number of Toronto dignitaries who were guests at the opening. Besides theatrical magnates A.L. Erlanger and Lee Shubert and investors George B. Cox and Joseph Rhinock, other New York business associates to arrive with Marcus Loew on a special train were Leon and Gus Fleischmann, the builders of the complex, Thomas Lamb, the architect, and C.F. Zittel, editor of the *New York Evening Journal*, who represented the New York press.

Weber and Fields and Irving Berlin were the New York stars introduced from the stage on opening night. Weber and Fields gave "some of their famous Hebrew act," according to the *World*. The routines of Joe Weber and Lew Fields as "Mike" and "Myer", performed with a Yiddish or German accent, usually involved the tall and bullying Fields gouging the eyes, pummelling, or choking his shorter, rotund partner. The team was associated with Loew in the theatre business. Weber was a theatre owner himself, and Fields had just entered a partnership with Loew to produce a big musical show at New York's Winter Garden, movies of which were to be exhibited in all Loew theatres in greater New York.[15]

The *World* reported, "Another surprise from the box was Irving Berlin, composer of `Alexander's Rag Time Band.' Berlin sang his latest, `The International Rag,' and followed it, owing to determined recalls, with several songs even better." The *Telegram* named some of these renditions, though referred to him as "Mr. A.L. Berliner":

> He sang several of his past hits and one or two new
> preparations which were not only new to Toronto but had
> never been presented on any stage before, "Daddy come home"
> of which there is just one verse and the chorus now completed
> will doubtless soon be humming[?] on the streets judging from
> its reception by the audience last night. These old rag-time
> songs, which have been murdered by successive artists in
> Toronto take on a new and novel charm when they are
> rendered by the author, and Mr. Berliner's presentation of
> "Trala, la, la" brought him back three or four times.[16]

Berlin copyrighted "Daddy Come Home" on 16 December 1913, one day after he introduced it to Toronto.

Favourable and detailed reviews of the opening vaudeville acts were forthcoming, both in the *Telegram* and in the *Toronto World* which went so far as to call the opening night bill one that "could not be bettered on this continent." The *Globe* bubbled that the debut vaudeville bill was "...the most pretentious...ever seen in this city, and probably upon any stage in this country."

The *World* described the sketch on the regular bill by Ryan and Richfield Company, "Mag Haggerty's Father," as "most laughable." To the *Globe*, it was "irresistible," while the *Telegram* considered it "good in spots" though it "would soon get the nerves of onlookers if continued very long."[17] Husband and wife Thomas J. Ryan and Mary Richfield had been performing "Mag Haggerty's Father" since at least 1906. Ryan played an elderly Irish "ex-hod carrier" who had stumbled into a fortune, but remained ignorant of expected deportment, to the chagrin and horror of his socially ambitious daughter. This sketch was set in a hotel in Atlantic City, and was climaxed by Ryan jumping out of a window after a dollar bill.

Singer Sadie Ott was a big hit with reviewers. According to the *World*, she was "...a delight to the great crowd that filled the new theatre. Her songs and singing were catchy and her acting was high-class coquetry." The *Telegram* was even more approving: "She has a personal charm and a refinement rarely seen on the Toronto stage, while her snappy little songs and her clean cut jokes rank her amongst the best of comediennes." In spite of this acclaim, Sadie Ott was not destined to make the big-time, and has faded into obscurity.

For the *Telegram* reviewer, any defects of the main sketch were more than repaid by "The Hunter's Game," by Frank Stafford and Company, though, the reviewer added, it has "often appeared here before." The "company" seems to have been two hunting dogs, and the setting of the sketch apparently shifted abruptly from a woodland scene to a barnyard. As described by the *World*:

Frank Stafford opened his sketch with a pointer waiting for him in a southern wood. At his command the dog crouched while he shot over. A retriever helped the pointer to bring two partridges to the bag. It was pretty work. Then Mr. Stafford whistled as the mocking bird makes music. He also imitated the sounds of barnyard animals and fowls. It was all clever.[18]

Cecile, Eldred and Carr presented some "first class comedy juggling," according to the *Telegram*. The *World* wrote this act up as "a novelty act that was very funny and became sensational when Cecile balanced himself upon one of his forefingers thrust into the neck of a champagne bottle." The "exceedingly graceful dancing" of O'Boyle, according to the *Telegram*, was described in the *World* as "a demonstration of the step dancing of old-time artists." Completing the bill was "clever cycle work" of the Levering troupe of comedy cyclists, and California tenor Frank Morrell, "at his best," according to the *Telegram*. This newspaper did not refer to Knowles and White, nor the "numerous recalls for their singing and dancing" registered by the *World* reviewer.

WINTER GARDEN OPENING: 16 FEBRUARY 1914

The opening of the Winter Garden on Monday, 16 February, promised to "eclipse" that of the lower theatre, which had been to date "the most brilliant" in Toronto. The *World* (and Loew's press release) announced that Mr. Loew was bringing a number of artists from New York solely for the Monday evening's performance. For whatever reason, no special New York guest artists appeared.

Loew's showed its good citizenship by donating profits of the evening to the Riverdale settlement, "an east end philanthropy in which a number of well-known people are interested." This public relations and public-spirited gesture probably attracted the return patronage of the Lieutenant Governor of Ontario and some of the "fashionable people of the city" who were said to have filled the theatre on opening night.

The *Sunday World* described on 15 February 1914 the opening night bill:

Among the features for the coming week will be Roland West "Thru the Skylight," a delightful playlet of fun and adventure. Another Loew headliner, Polly Prim, a dainty maid of melody, whose songs, recitations and impersonations captivated her audience at the American Theatre, New York, last week. Wormwood's animals, a marvelously trained troupe of dog and monkey actors, will also appear. This is a treat for the little ones as well as the grownups, by the best animal trainer in stageland. Sam Ash, a tenor of unusual ability, will sing some of the latest song hits. Gordon & Marx, "jolly joking Germans," are a well known team. G.A. Haya and Co., three Japanese handwriting experts, have a real novelty. Savoy and Brennan in a riotous comedy skit, Mlle. Amoros and Ben Mulvey in "A day in Paris", the Moscrop sisters, clever singers and dancers, and the three Ernests, in their whirlwind "trampoline" or bounding act, will be on the vaudeville program. Photoplays will also be shown.

The comedy team of Savoy and Brennan came to be the most famous of the opening night acts. Bert Savoy, an outrageously swishy drag queen in "a flaming red wig, an oversized curvaceous costume and an enormous picture hat," is considered to have been the most accomplished of the transvestite comics of his day, and his style was allegedly copied by Mae West. Jay Brennan was the straight man of the act. Savoy and Brennan reappeared at Loew's in Toronto, performing "The London Show Girl and the Johnny" in June 1915, when the team was on the threshold of the big time. By 1916 the act was commanding $1,500 a week, and had appeared at the ne plus ultra of vaudeville, the New York Palace. Loew's newspaper advertisement in 1913 failed to list Roland West, Wormwood's animals, or G.A. Haya and Company. Instead these acts were replaced by the sketch "A Day in Ellis Island" by Maurice Samuels & Co., electrical wizards Moffatt-La Reine & Co., and Castellane, whose act was neither described in the ads nor reviewed.

Another special guest on 15 December 1913: Irving Berlin, then twenty-four years old and a veteran of the vaudeville stage. Newspaper accounts noted that on opening night he sang "The International Rag," "Daddy Come Home," and "Trala, La La." It would be surprising if he was allowed to omit "Alexander's Ragtime Band," his monster hit of 1911.

Moffatt La Reine & Co., offered "a series of unusual electrical demonstrations...[and] showed the X-rays in active operation." Fred La Reine toured for twenty eight years with an act in which "...he charged himself with electricity and set torches on fire in different parts of his body." As described by Joe Laurie, Jr., acts featuring electrical wizardry brought "a lot of important looking paraphernalia on stage" which would give out "tremendous sparks, etc."

The sketch on opening night, "A Day in Ellis Island," like so many other acts in vaudeville, explored and exploited the turmoil and comedy engendered by the great wave of European migration to the continent. The comedy-drama was said to encompass catchy musical numbers and witty dialogue in a story of an Italian who sends for his sweetheart and an adopted boy, a gifted violinist. A slightly different version of the sketch was described in *Variety* in 1912:

The opening night playlet in the Winter Garden Theatre, "A Day in Ellis Island".

Maurice Samuels and Co. (4)
"A Day at Ellis Island."
25 mins.; Full Stage. Interior Special.
....The scene is laid in the detention room at Ellis Island. An Italian has been waiting two days for his daughter, and her aunt, to whom he is to be married....When it is found that the aunt has no money she is to be sent back....The daughter is brought forward and she plays a violin solo in the detention room, entertaining the inspector and the Irish attendant who have nothing to do (as only 4,500 immigrants have landed within the past two days)....In going for laughs Samuels has sacrificed the story completely, which may be just as well. [19]

"A Day in Paris" by Mlle. Amoros and Ben Mulvey was a singing and dancing act. The act's publicity (two years later) attested it was a rapid-fire item, during which "the lady is seen in some marvelous acrobatic gyrations." Mlle. Amoros had mastered oriental flip-flops and the "somersaults and butterfly whirls of the Arabs," according to another article. *Variety* in 1916 itemized her dancing costumes: "a cloak of brocaded material edged in blue fox," with a grey satin dress underneath with a short bodice of cerise, together with cerise stockings and slippers and "cerise wings in the hair." She changed into "a cloak of tan plush edged in skunk, with a dress underneath of black and white scroll design."[20]

The overall review in the *Mail and Empire* was generous, referring to acts as "excellent" and "good," and to the repeated encores for Sam Ash's singing. The *World* reviewer was not so kind:

> While charity may cover a multitude of sins, it is no excuse for the quality of the entertainment provided by Mr. Marcus Loew last evening. With possibly one exception the acts were far below the intelligence and the appreciation of Toronto's first families who paid their money. It was not the fault of the people on the stage. They did their best and they worked hard, but they were out of place. A more expensive variety of entertainment will have to be imported before the house registers a hit. The chief item on the bill was Maurice Samuel & Co. in a sketch called "A day at Ellis Island" which has been seen here before. With the exception of Miss Polly Prim, the remainder of the show, to let it down easy, lacked refinement.[21]

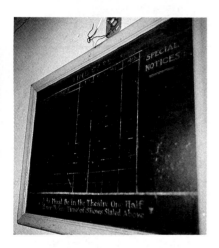

One of two blackboards which graced the dressing room of the complex. This one served as a "time card" and for special notices. An identical abutting blackboard was simply labelled "Roof Garden."

Notwithstanding the review, "A Day at Ellis Island," Fred La Reine's electrical novelties, Polly Prim, and Amoros and Mulvey would continue to appear in Loew's Yonge Street complex during the next decade. No act billing itself "Jolly Joking Germans" could appear in Toronto during the Great War or shortly thereafter. During those years, many German acts were transformed to Swiss.

DOUBLING UP: TWO THEATRES AND ONE SHOW

According to the Winter Garden's opening publicity, there would be "an increased number of acts necessary to make possible a simultaneous performance in theatre and Winter Garden." [sic][22] Presumably, identical rather than simultaneous was meant, and the same show in both theatres was expressly promised throughout much of their operating history. Nonetheless, the *World* testified in an April 1914 feature article on the complex that both theatres presented "one and the same, or practically the same, show…" and that no act worked more than three performances a day. If so, the same show could not have been mounted continuously downstairs and in the Winter Garden, especially during the period when the lower house opened before noon.

The presentation of exactly the same show must have been complicated by the difference in the depths of the two stages and the difficulties of transferring up and down large properties or scenery associated with a particular act. According to the *World*, an act's stage settings and properties for each act were "hoisted or lowered by special elevators at the rear" as required by the time table. The daily transfer of stage settings for every act is unlikely to have taken place, since duplicate stock scenery was provided in the two theatres and the (single) backstage elevator was too small to carry flats and battens. Certain acts, however, used unique scenery or large properties. A large diving tank, for instance, would have been difficult to move and was time-consuming to set up. Two tanks may have been required for the same show to be mounted on both stages, no doubt an excessive expense for the act or the theatre's management.

The names of the acts and the times they appeard on stage were inscribed weekly in chalk on a large framed blackboard in the dressing room corridor. Up to four appearances a day were feasible, according to this board, likely two afternoon and two evening shows. One of the evening shows was in the Winter Garden.

Above: Ventriloquist Edgar Bergen and Co. Though he had already played the Palace in New York, at Loew's in Toronto in 1928 Bergen was billed as a secondary attraction.

Left: Comedy team Bert Savoy and Jay Brennan, who appeared on opening night in the Winter Garden Theatre, 16 February 1914.

Left: Singer Sophie Tucker, photographed about 1914. She headlined at Loew's in March 1915. She and Marcus Loew retained soft spots for each other as they had started off in show business together. She declared she could play his theatres whenever she wanted, even after she had climbed into the "big-money brackets."

Right: George Burns and Gracie Allen, one of vaudeville's best loved and most enduring male and female comedy teams, who performed at Loew's in 1925.

CELEBRITIES

Not many of the performers appearing at Loew's were big-time vaudeville headliners. A few of them are now renowned, though some did not receive special publicity or top billing at the time. One of the first was Sophie Tucker, singing comedienne who performed the week of 1 March 1915. Loew considered Tucker "his good luck charm." Some years previous, she had been engaged to sing between movie reels for 20 shows in a 12-hour period in one of Loew's ten-cent theatres in Harlem.

According to Loew's publicity, Frank Fay, who appeared during the first week of January 1923 was the highest paid single act to appear, and the highest paid ever produced at popular prices. Fay, advertised as "New York's Famous Winter Garden Star, also Famous Screen Artist," was a dapper monologist whose style of insulting humour crested in the mid-twenties when he became master of ceremonies at the Palace.

Milton Berle, "droll talker and singer", appeared with headliner "Jack Wyatt's Scotch Lads and Lassies" in August 1924. The 16-year-old Berle was then working his way back up to the big-time as a solo act, having literally outgrown his partner. His rising star is reflected in his next two engagements at Loew's: In June 1929, he headlined as Master of Ceremonies in "Good to the Last Drop," In January 1930 he was back in "Get Hot," with "12 Berle-ing Hot Dancers".

During May, 1928, Edgar Bergen & Co., ventriloquist, presented his comic newsboy skit, playing second fiddle to headliner Lieutenant Gitz Rice with his North West Mounties, a group of costumed males who sang the compositions of its Nova Scotia-born leader. One of the best known and most enduring vaudeville entertainers, George Burns and Gracie Allen, headlined with their "domestic argument comedy, songs, and dances" in September 1925. The following year they were in the big-time. Another act on its way up was Paul Whiteman's Romance of Rhythm orchestra, which played popular and jazz music on the stage in January 1923.

In the 1920s, celebrity stars of motion pictures appeared in person to boost attendance. These included Doraldine and Viola Dana, whose movies were often shown at Loew's, and an appearance by Zena Keefe, Diana Allen, and Eugene O'Brien. Child stars Dolly Dumplin, Baby Sylvia and Miriam Battista appeared in 1923 and 1924 at several afternoon receptions for children in the lobby where free candy and souvenirs were dispensed.

DOUBLE DECKERS AND "THE EFFICIENCY PRINCIPLE"

The operation of double decker theatres, maximizing the use of real estate, investment dollars and human resources, had great appeal in a period in which time-motion studies, efficiency, and scientific management were seen as the key to modern life. The complicated operating system and timetables in the complex seemed to befit the modern age.

A *Toronto Sunday World* article of 12 April 1914 described the extraordinary operation of the double-decker complex, an "intricate, money-making machine" which, on a busy day, entertained 14,000, or six or seven complete audiences. It exemplified the efficiency principle in show business, and was said to be one of the best examples of an advanced amusement enterprise of this class. According to journalist E.Y. Watson, progress had come to the continuous show, as in one big stride it had more than doubled its possibilities.

The article continued that no part of the show could take a minute more than called for in the schedule in order to appear in both theatres. The system was described admiringly as not unlike that of a big department store and its business arrangements sufficient to make a good many bankers jealous. Daily returns were made to the New York office, which maintained rigid supervision over everything connected with the policy of the house.

However, in spite of the machine-like efficiency and industrialized operation conjured up in this article, from the beginning, the chain at least pretended that it did not have a clear vision of how the double decker complex would be best used. According to a *Star Weekly* article from 22 November 1913, "Two entirely different shows can be put on at the same time, or both theatres can be used for the same show, the one above being taken as an overflow. The upstairs theatre may, and probably will, be used for higher class productions than the one below." This kind of vacillation may have contributed to frequent experiments with the operation of the theatre upstairs, in programming and admission prices.

These novel and hybrid double-decker theatres were built during a period of convulsive changes in the mass entertainment industry, and in a new market across the border for Loew's. Loew's needed to discover what Toronto would bear, how many shows could reasonably be mounted per day in the double-decker complex, and whether the policy of charging a higher admission upstairs for the same show would be a success.

According to the *World* in April 1914, initially the two theatres did tremendous business:

> In the long hall on the ground floor...between 2 and 3 in the
> afternoon and for an hour or more in the evening, there is
> usually a crowd lined up four deep, waiting to be admitted. As
> a few go out a few go in, and for thirteen hours of the day, it
> grinds in the patrons and grinds them out again. The majority
> of the seats are nearly always full.[23]

Loew's succeeded in establishing the Winter Garden as a special, prestige house. It is still remembered as an exotic and romantic venue for courting couples, and became part of a tradition: many soldiers on their way to the trenches of the Great War spent their last evenings in Toronto among its murals and beech leaves. Nevertheless, Loew's continued to grapple with the experimental nature of the double-decker complex, and the evolving logistics of accommodating two theatre audiences on one site and one show on two stages.

ADMISSION PRICES AND HOURS OF OPERATION

The range of admission prices to the lower theatre in December 1913 was between 10 cents and 50 cents, the top price being charged for reserved box seats in the evening. (Between 9 a.m. and noon, there was one admission price — 10 cents. Between 12 and 5, there were three options: 10-cent seats, 15-cent seats, and 25-cent box seats. Between 5 p.m. and 11 p.m., the range of seat prices was increased to four: 10, 15, 25, and 50 cents.)

By the time the Winter Garden opened in February 1914, the downstairs theatre had abandoned the idea of putting on a show at 9 a.m. Its operating hours were 11 a.m. to 11 p.m., with morning and matinee admissions at 10 and 15 cents, and evening prices at 10, 15, and 25 cents. No more 50-cent seats were offered in the lower theatre. Higher prices — 25, 35, and 50 cent seats, all reserved — were the prerogative of the Winter Garden, with its single evening performance of high class vaudeville. The theatre was to be considered high class because it offered only one show a day, not because the show was any different than the one downstairs. The Winter Garden had cheaper admission than Shea's, the high class vaudeville theatre on Victoria Street, which was priced at 25 cents for matinees, and 25, 50 and 75 cents in the evenings. Stock productions at the Princess, Royal Alexandra, and Grand Opera House cost up to $2.00 admission at the time.

A significant experiment followed in February 1915. The Winter Garden was dedicated solely to "high class photo productions" in two daily shows: a matinee at 2.15 for 10 cents and an evening performance at 8.15 for 15 and 25 cents. Continuous shows continued in the downstairs theatre, which was now open at noon and closed at 11 p.m. The noon opening would remain relatively constant. Seven acts of vaudeville commonly appeared on the bill, a reduction from a high of nine and ten offered during the spring of 1914. The all-movie policy upstairs was not a success, and in March 1915 the Winter Garden reverted to vaudeville by popular demand, and to one evening show at 8.15. All seats were reserved at 25 cents.

The Winter Garden was closed for part of 1916. On 27 September, the "Music and Drama" columnist for the *Globe*, wrote,

> Special preparations have been made for the fall opening of the Winter Garden in connection with Loew's Yonge Street Theatre, which will take place at 7.30 o'clock Monday evening next. The curtain will ring up five minutes later.... The policy of the Winter Garden will not interfere with that of the main theatre on the ground floor, which will continue on the same lines as in the past. The Winter Garden will be open in the evenings only, and all seats will be reserved at twenty five and fifteen cents.

A TIMETABLE: THE WEEK OF 12 OCTOBER 1914

One of two surviving timetables for evening shows in the complex is reproduced below. The column on the right is probably the Winter Garden, whose evening show started at 8.15. Each of the eight vaudeville acts was on for fifteen minutes. The same acts appeared in both theatres, though not in the same order. The main disparity is the number of movie reels listed. Four reels were to be shown downstairs, and only two in the Winter Garden, notwithstanding that its top ticket price of 50 cents was double that of the lower theatre.

With the exception of the opening act, the order of the bill in the two theatres varied considerably. Five acts had a forty-five minute interval between performances, but three, including the opening act, had only fifteen minutes.

Programme. Monday, 12 October 1914

Leonard & Alvin [acrobats]	8.00	Reel 3	
Reel 2		Leonard & Alvin	8.30
Harry Rose [comedian]	8.30	Eldred & Carr [acrobatic dancing]	8.45
[J.K.] Emmett & Co.	8.45	Harry Rose	9.00
Reel 3		Eddie Clark [song impersonations]	9.15
Sanoa [Saona] [mimic]	9.15	Reel 2	
Cook & Stevens [ethnic comedy]	9.30	Ogden Quartette [classical music]	9.30
Eldred & Carr	9.45	Emmett & Co.	9.45
Reel 6		Cook & Stevens	10.00
Eddie Clark	10.15	Sanoa	10.15
Ogden Quartette	10.30		
Reel 1			

Throughout the fall it was "open every evening, 7.30, same show as Lower Theatre." Loew's was sufficiently encouraged to initiate upstairs in December 1917 a Saturday matinee performance. The matinee continued for the winter season, but was abandoned thereafter. Until 1921, the Winter Garden remained open six evenings a week, with its 7.30 p.m. single show, the same as the lower theatre, at popular prices.

Publicity in 1920 concentrated on the Winter Garden being "the only theatre in Toronto playing a combination policy of high-class vaudeville and the best of photoplays where patrons can RESERVE their seats at POPULAR PRICES." Winter Garden seats could be reserved as far as two weeks in advance. The scheme of showing movies only in the Winter Garden was resurrected in October 1921, but would last only until 11 February 1922. In this period, prestige movies at premium prices were offered, with all seats reserved, and was inaugurated with *Four Horseman of the Apocalypse* for a 4-week run in two shows a day, at 2.15 and 8.15, at a charge of between 50 cents and $1.00 for matinees and up to $1.50 for evening shows. The ticket prices would decline for subsequent, less bally-hooed movies, until matinee seats were available for 25 and 35 cents, and seats in the evening for 50 cents. Other movies shown were *The Three Musketeers, Way Down East, Little Lord Fauntleroy, Forever, J'accuse,* and *Our Mutual Friend.*

In March 1922 yet another new policy was introduced, which would endure to about 1927, and would keep the Winter Garden mostly dark. The upstairs theatre was open only on Saturday nights and holidays with the same show as the downstairs theatre and for the same admission, though Winter Garden seats were reserved and could be secured in advance. Between weekends, its stage was used as rehearsal space and occasionally was loaned or rented for fund-raising benefits.

LOCAL INFLUENCES AND EVENTS

The reviewer of the opening show in the downstairs theatre in December 1913 acknowledged:

> Perhaps the thing which delighted most persons last night was the diplomatic manner in which the patrons were made to feel that they were in a playhouse, located on Canadian real estate, but managed from New York, and yet full recognition given to the fact that we are not too fond of having Old Glory flaunted in our faces as well as crammed down our throats. The Canadian atmosphere in the new playhouse launched last night is a thing well worthy of cultivation.

A notable exception to this diplomacy and consideration occurred on 18 December 1916, when the comedy skit by Winters and Strauss fell very flat because its climax was not adjusted to Canadian sensibilities. As the reviewer wrote, "After showing a number of girls from different nations, they asserted to wind up the matter that no girls any place could compare with `the American girl in the U.S.A.' They should hardly be surprised that Canadians fail to cheer the sentiment."[24] For the most part, however, Loew's acknowledged that it did business on Canadian soil, and from time to time took a high-minded interest in the life of the city and the nation. The theatre immediately threw its support behind the Great War effort, showing, by the week of 10 August 1914, a film on the mobilization of the British Army. A show presented in the Winter Garden in February 1916, "The Belles of Boo Loo," was a local production for the war effort, a skit on the Women's Home Guard of Toronto. Large recruiting rallies also took place on various Sundays at Loew's. One of them, on 27 May 1917, must have resembled a vaudeville show, with two bands and exhibitions of bayonet fighting and physical drill. One of the last war-related events was a Sunday afternoon lecture by Mrs. Emmeline Pankhurst on "What women have done to help win the war" on 16 September 1918.

A quartette of returned Canadian soldiers, "The Shrapnel Dodgers," appeared the week of 10 September 1917, offering songs and skits. This act apparently toured the United States, and is described by Joe Laurie, Jr. in his book on vaudeville: "they told about their experiences in the war and sang. One had only one eye, the other had a leg and arm off. They were Canadians. They did a real good act, and certainly didn't depend on sympathy, but when they finished there wasn't a dry eye in the house". [25]

Another act which featured Canadian soldiers in October 1918 was "Billet 13," a playlet depicting life behind the front lines in Flanders, written and performed by three "returned heroes": Corporal Jack Slack and Private Neville of the 48th Highlanders, and Private Pickens of the "Little Black Devils" of Winnipeg. The *Globe* reviewer noted that the sketch "...created enthusiasm by its patriotic appeal, but it also received praise for the magnitude of the production, scenic and costume effects, and especially for the merit of its principals...." [26]

On at least two occasions in the mid-twenties, fund-raisers by Zionist organizations were staged in the Winter Garden. In September 1924 Junior Hadassah put on "Springtime," a musical love story consuming three generations of the Wainwright and Brewster families. Louis Rasminsky, later the Governor of the Bank of Canada, is listed in the cast in the "Society Group." The Herzl Zion Club was another beneficiary of the Winter Garden's inactivity on a week night in 1924. These shows were not advertised in Loew's normal weekly publicity.

Jack Slack, George Picken, and James Neville in "Billet 13," produced by Toronto cartoonist Lou Skuce, and directed and staged by Cadet Thomas H. McKnight.

The Winter Garden was also loaned for the filming of scenes of *Satan's Paradise* which was released in 1922 and was only the fifth feature film made in Canada. Directed by producer Blaine Irish and cameraman Roy Tash, it was a drama about professional spiritualists. It was reviewed quite favourably in the *Canadian Moving Picture Digest*, but had limited distribution, and no copy now survives. *Satan's Paradise* did not exhibit the Winter Garden. Interiors were filmed in one of the Winter Garden's interior sets on stage, and the theatre's carbon arc stage lighting assisted the operation.

Loew's embarked on projects which showcased and advertised Toronto talent when the Winter Garden's stage was available for rehearsals 6 nights a week. In 1922 it was the "Toronto Follies," followed in 1923 by "Toronto Frolics" and "The Frolics of 1923." In 1924, two more shows were presented: "Amateur Minstrel Frolics" and the "Amateur Summer Bathing Revue." For whatever reason, local amateur productions were not continued in the complex. But the amateur shows of these years epitomize vaudeville's appeal and accessibility to ordinary folk.

Cast of Loew's Amateur Minstrel Frolic on the stage of the Winter Garden Theatre, photographed during a dress rehearsal. The wife and son of theatre manager Jules Bernstein are the audience.

The "Toronto Follies," a two-hour "whirly girly song and dance revue" with every member a bona-fide resident of Toronto," was mounted in December 1922, and returned for a second week with improved performances. It included songs by Pauline O'Connor, a Harry Lauder imitator, tramp and newsboy singers, a jazz band, and many dance numbers: Oriental, Russian, clog, and barefoot. One of the dancers was Jeanne Piggott (née Cook), who still remembers clearly her participation. She was then 15 years old, and a student at the local Margaret Eaton School of Dancing. Her teacher, she believes, made all the arrangements with

Loew's. Jeanne did not audition for her solo "toe number." when she danced to "Nola", wearing a pink ballet dress and holding a pink parasol. She was paid $15.00 a week, and provided her own dress, ballet slippers, parasol, and make-up. Her recollection of the "Follies" extended to some of the performers who shared the stage: a trio in Scottish regalia who sang Scottish songs; the clog-dancing of a Dutch costumed couple singing "Hansel and Lena", and a moving rendition of "My Buddy" by a fellow in World War I uniform, lit by one spotlight on a dark stage. The vaudeville playlet was called "Little Red Schoolhouse," in which Jeanne's older sister had won a small part as the schoolteacher.

Saturday Night was favourably impressed with the show, and congratulated Loew's management for its freedom from vulgarity and its initiative. Though the performers' lack of training was sometimes apparent, in the reviewer's opinion, a couple of acts ranked several notches higher than the average vaudeville show. More importantly, however, the article noted that crowds were lined up, and that the audience had responded appreciatively. Another Toronto show was bound to follow.

"Toronto Frolics", a "spectacular home-talent song and dance revue," with "shapely and comely maidens" and with singing, dancing, comedy, costumes and scenery headlined the week of 5 February 1923. It was advertised as "not a Toronto Follies rerun." "The Frolics of 1923," the second "Frolics" of that year, was offered in October, with "all home talent" and directed by Victor Hyde of New York. (Hyde was a former vaudeville performer whose act was billed as "Victor Hyde and Sister.")

Loew's mounted "Amateur Minstrel Frolics" the week of 17 March 1924. Again directed by Victor Hyde, it encompassed 49 men and women, all local talent, with Jerry Browne again the interlocutor. It began with a minstrel parade, and continued with five production numbers and 11 specialty or solo numbers. The amateur show must have lasted for at least an hour, but was supplemented by an Anna Nilsson movie and four acts of Loew's vaudeville. (One of these was a female posing and balancing act, the second, comedy songs and talk, and the two remaining acts offered songs.)

The same year, in June 1924, Victor Hyde produced and directed the Loew's "Amateur Summer Bathing Revue," with all local talent, 7 scenes, 15 specialties and 6 production numbers by 10 men and 25 women, including the customary Jerry Browne. To this entertainment was added the movie, *The Code of the Sea*, with Jacqueline Logarn and Rod Laroque, and regular Loew's vaudeville.

The programmes, scenery, costumes, and production personnel of these amateur shows came from New York and probably toured the circuit with the same basic show and sets. Some of the songs and specialty numbers were adapted to the location and to specific local talents. At least two of the key performers, Jerry Browne and Lew Beck, came directly from the United States, and they may have appeared as "locals" and "amateurs" in various cities.

THE MEMOIRS OF A LOCAL AMATEUR

Vivid and detailed accounts of these 1924 revues have been provided by Elsie Bennie (née Scraggs) of Toronto. Then aged 15 but pretending to be older, she and a friend responded to Loew's newspaper advertisement, and successfully auditioned for 2 weeks' employment among the eight dancers in the March Minstrel Frolic. They both returned to auditions in May for the June Bathing Revue, and both easily won places.

In each case, a week's rehearsals took place on the Winter Garden's stage with piano accompaniment. The orchestra assisted the Sunday evening dress rehearsal. Elsie was paid $15 for the week's rehearsal, and $15 the following week

The Toronto *Telegram*'s ballyhoo for the "Our Gang" contest in 1928.

for three performances downstairs and an additional show on Saturday in the Winter Garden. She got to keep her opera hose and dance shoes. She remembers Edna Liggitt as a local star and toe dancer who was paid $25 per week as a soloist in the Minstrel Show. (She was a dancing teacher in Toronto who went ahead in show business to become a Rockette at Radio City Music Hall in New York City.

Elsie recalled a special ship drop essential to a Bathing Revue number, "All Aboard," which would have been either moved or duplicated upstairs for the Winter Garden show. "Legs, legs, legs," was one of the most memorable numbers, and contrived with a stage curtain lowered to the level of the dancers' knees, who were seated on a long bench. The audience could see only 16 legs, kicking and stepping in tune, while Lew Beck sang about "lovely" female legs.

Elsie also remembers vividly one of Loew's vaudeville acts, a juggler (Alexander Patty) who stood on his head at the top of five steps, drank wine, ate a banana, and then descended each step on his head. During the show at Loew's, Patty's child, aged about a year, sat quietly in a carriage in the wings. While Elsie looked on in amazement, after his act Patty wheeled over the stairs he had descended, picked up the child, turned him upside down, and lowered him gently on his head down each step. To Patty, the death of vaudeville must not have seemed imminent.

PUBLICITY STUNTS

Loew's occasionally offered contests to increase attendance and publicity for the theatre: amateur diving contests, prizes for the best school child's essay on Dickens during the movie Our *Mutual Friend*, and three weeks of balloting for the "most popular shop girl in Toronto." The winner by more than 3,000 votes was the 70-year old Mrs. McMillan of New Method Laundry. The stage appearance the previous week of the various candidates had stimulated "wild outbursts of applause." Publicity stunts and contests continued to be featured well into the movie age, and were encouraged and abetted by head office.

One of the splashiest was the "Our Gang" contest in 1928. Loew's joined with the Toronto *Telegram* to mount massive full-page coverage of an "Our Gang" competition. Toronto youngsters between the ages of 3 and 12 who resembled the stars of Hal Roach's popular short comedies were invited to mail application and photographs to the *Telegram*'s "'Our Gang' editor." The six local winners were to gain "the opportunity of a Lifetime...to Become a Real Honest-to-goodness Movie Actor," and would be paid $25. to appear in an "Our Gang" movie filmed in Toronto. It would be directed by Jack Roach, the brother of Hal.

The newspaper summed up the "Our Gang" principals for whom lookalikes were sought: "Farina, of the dusky complexion; Mary Ann Jackson, with the bright eyes and the turned-up nose; Jean Darling, the petite blonde vampire; Joe Cobb, the fat boy; Wheezer, the diminutive youngster to whom everything is a joke; and Harry Spear, the world's freckle champion." Several pages of the *Telegram* were taken up with winsome photographs and characterizations of young contestants. The judging took place on Loew's lower stage between 30 July and 4 August at five evening shows and a Saturday matinee. Winners were determined on the basis of the volume of audience applause.

Each character was assigned a particular day of the week. On the Tuesday, hundreds of small, blonde "Jean Darlings" vied for the role. The auditorium of the lower theatre was "crammed beyond capacity." The *Telegram*'s report of the evening 's preliminaries pulled out all the stops:

Little fluffy pink frocks and dresses of buttercup and
rainbow shades fluttered down a laneway and through a side

entrance, where these diminutive fairies were then transported
to realms above (in this case to Loew's Winter Garden.) Even
up there, the fairy touch was evident. Colored lights winked
and twinked [sic] amongst foliage and shone brightly on the
tiny theatre patrons. There was a splendid "Our Gang" comedy
playing showing "Peter" the Gang dog doing the smartest
tricks so that everyone loved this "bow wow" and wanted him
for their very own.

'Twas thrilling to see the youngsters clap when the real
Jean Darling was flashed on the screen. 'Twas an involuntary
homage that a queen might envy.... Such pretty heads with hair
like spun gold bobbed up and down — some children seem still
to be wearing the halo all surely have when they first enter his
funny old world. Never did [a] roof garden boast such bounte-
ous blossoms [27]

The winner, 8-year old Sybil White, dressed in a black sateen romper with white
collar and cuffs (not a fluffy pink dress), was selected by an audience with a
preference for "blonde little girls in black frocks" and one described as "delight-
fully enthusiastic and discriminating, doing their judging courteously and
kindly." The *Telegram* reporter remarked on Sybil's personality and clever
poise. She had been the second of "900" competitors presented, and had
endured a long wait backstage for the finals. On being named the winner, she was
quoted as saying "I'm so glad. I'm a singer and a dancer and a reciter and I don't
know what else — and now I'm 'Jean Darling' for Toronto."

The newspaper had also disclosed extensive details of the plot and script of
the "Our Gang" movie shot in Toronto in which Sybil and the five other local
winners would appear. It was entitled *Pie Eetin' Contest* and it centred around the
training and participation of Farina in a pie eating contest, abetted by Gang
members who planned to share his $10. purse. This movie was later shown at
Loew's. It was one of 25 coupled to corresponding contests then being made in
"leading cities in the United States and Canada." From these, Hal Roach was
supposed to select his favourite lookalikes, and six lucky children were promised
Hollywood contracts at salaries of $100. a week for three months. (The travel
expenses of their parents or guardians would also be covered.)

Though local stars of the lookalike contest and *Pie Eetin' Contest* did not go on
to great fame and fortune as movie stars, most of them probably remembered this
interlude in their childhoods as one which not only provided minor celebrity
status and enviable contact with the glamour and magic of Hollywood, but also
supplied them with money, free pie, and enormous fun.

THE WINTER GARDEN CLOSES, OPENS, AND CLOSES

During the 20s, Loew's did not apply itself to the rational operation of two
theatres on one site. Though the upper theatre captured the heart of virtually all
who reported visiting it, the corporation was content to have it dark six days a
week. This increased to seven days a week for a period before February 1927.
"Roof Reopened, February 12, 1927" was inscribed on the inside of the switch box
door in its projection booth. Loew's published that the Winter Garden was open
on Saturday afternoons and for the same Saturday evening performance as that
offered in the downstairs theatre. Five or six vaudeville acts were in the offing,
with no reserved seats.

The reopening was not a success. No mention of the Winter Garden is seen
in Loew's newspaper ads after 19 March 1927, until the May 1928 fire in the lower

theatre caused the Winter Garden to be reopened. The Winter Garden was quickly readied to fill the breach during the fire renovation. An advertisement in the *Star* within hours of the flames being doused proclaimed the opening of the Winter Garden at 12 noon on 4 May for the regular show and the normal continuous policy of Loew's Theatre. Manager Jules Bernstein was quoted that fire damage might preclude the use of the downstairs theatre "for a few days." Notwithstanding, the theatre was closed for renovations and repairs until 18 June.

On 12 May the *Star Weekly* wrote: "...the general public seems quite satisfied to use the `roof' theatre, while work goes on in the lower house." After the renovation and reopening of the lower theatre, the Winter Garden closed again, without fanfare. Its last regular vaudeville and movie show was presented on Saturday,16 June 1928. No more tickets would be sold to Winter Garden shows for more than sixty years.

THE DEATH OF VAUDEVILLE

The lower theatre was wired for sound in April 1929. Vaudeville continued to be offered for a while longer — until October 1930. It was not at all obvious that vaudeville would not endure and that talking pictures would. Further, stage-hands and musicians were unionized and could not be dismissed summarily; neither could vaudeville artists with signed contracts. But sound movies meant the Winter Garden was fated to remain closed. Its projection booth and projectors were silent, and it could no longer mount the programme offered downstairs, either in an emergency or at any other time.

In 1929 The International Alliance of Theatrical and Stage Employees in Canada was not panicky over the prospect of sound movies. As the second Vice President of the 11th District discoursed at the 1929 convention:

> There is no cause for the stage employee to be stampeded
> because of the apparent success of the sound pictures. Talking
> Pictures will never supplement [sic] the legitimate
> drama....Synchronized music will not stand, it may for a time,
> but the demand for musicians will come again, they will go
> back in the theatre and they will have employment, this will
> adjust itself.[28]

On 25 September 1930, Loew's ad trumpeted, "Watch for Announcement that is the Most Important in Toronto Theatre History." The following day, Torontonians learned that Loew's Yonge Street Theatre would cease to function as a theatre. It would become a cinema, and begin an all-movie policy on 3 October. Its shows would thereafter change on Fridays.

To end 17 years of combination vaudeville in the lower theatre, the last programme consisted of a skit, "The Man from Miami," with Franklyn Ardell & Co., with songs and wisecracks by Dave Vine, comedienne Primrose Simon, and steppers Sam Swan and Ben Lewis. The Floyd Sisters and Gautier's Toy Shop completed the bill. The stage went dark and the backstage dressing rooms were vacated for the last time. The all-movie policy was inaugurated on 3 October with *Our Blushing Brides*, starring Joan Crawford, an actress that theatre manager Jules Bernstein happened to find particularly loathsome.

Not only stage employees and vaudeville performers were affected by the swan song of live acts. So were numerous businesses which derived income from travelling performers: booking offices and agents, railroad companies, scenic studios and other makers of theatrical commodities, and even local boarding houses, restaurants and laundries.

It is not axiomatic that talking movies caused the death of vaudeville, though they certainly were responsible for the demise of numerous theatre orchestras and theatre organs. Its death had not been sudden. Vaudeville had perhaps committed slow suicide by its endless repetition of the same acts and stale routines, by the monopolistic "black lists" and rigid contracts of the big chains, and by its brightest stars pricing themselves out of the mass entertainment market. And by the late 20s, much of vaudeville's songs, comedy routines, and melodramas could be heard for free on radio instead. Other factors contributing to the decline of vaudeville included the closing of the theatres during the influenza epidemic of 1918, the economic recession following the end of World War I, and the new popularity of revues and unit shows.

The advent of the microphone had an enormous impact by transforming the style of the variety performer. In 1913, vaudeville performers projected their voices to the rear of the balcony without any technical assistance. The microphone killed the traditional vaudeville sketch by its restriction of movement and gesture. It caused singers and actors to repress and tone down some of the brashness and noisy vitality which had characterized vaudeville, though a few, like singer Ethel Merman, continued to project as loudly as ever. Vaudeville was also diminished by the hugeness of the 20s movie palace. Most of these "presentation houses" propagated the stage spectacle as the entertainment standard, as their vast sizes overwhelmed the run-of-the-mill vaudeville act.

And vaudeville may not have died an entirely natural death. It would not be surprising if the owners of theatre chains danced on its grave: in one fell swoop, most of their unionized employees — musicians and stage hands— were eliminated. Only projectionists prevailed.

CHAPTER TEN

OPERATING THE COMPLEX: THE STAFF

According to a *Toronto World* article in 1914, the double-decker complex was staffed by relays of 134 people, exclusive of performing artists. This number included two full orchestras and two stage crews. Though the number given was probably considerably inflated, this roster must have included a management office staff of four or five, and two shifts of some of the remaining staff, as the complex operated at this time from 11 a.m. to 11 p.m. Employees likely comprised four cashiers (for four box offices), six to eight people who served as doormen, ticket takers, elevator operators, and check room attendant, two corps of about 10 ushers, a cleaning and maintenance staff of about 15, four projectionists, perhaps two eight- or ten-piece orchestras and two stage crews numbering five or six men.

In keeping with a Loew's tradition, many on the staff remained for decades. One of these was manager (later managing director) Jules Bernstein, who arrived just before the Winter Garden opened in 1914, and retired thirty years later.

Crowds in front of Loew's Yonge Street Theatre in 1929.

THE MANAGER

Jules Bernstein, manager of the Toronto complex from 1914 to 1944. He retired to Los Angeles, where he died in 1955.

Born in 1885 in Utica, New York, Julius (or Jules) Bernstein had risen from usher to manager of Loew's Delancey Street Theatre in New York City. He was no doubt attracted to Loew's by his older brother, David, who had joined Marcus Loew as a bookkeeper in his nickelodeon days in 1905. David's financial wizardry yielded for him a directorship by 1910 and the position of treasurer and vice-president of Loew's by 1912.

Jules settled quickly in Toronto, marrying Torontonian Frances McKnight in 1915. He was written up in Loew's head office magazine in 1923:

> Up in Canada we first find Julius Bernstein in Toronto, who has been there so long his customers all know him. Julius is so used to whale meat and afternoon tea (after the custom) that he haunts the docks and tea rooms on his infrequent trips to New York (1, I think in the last eight years). Everyone in the office who has been to Toronto has looked up Julius and found him to be among the princes of royalty country.[1]

In September 1927, with fanfare and farewell gifts, he departed to a promotion as district manager at Loew's head office. But he relinquished the position and resumed his old post in Toronto only a few months later, as he disliked being on the road and separated from his wife and son.

A newspaper item on his impending departure in 1927 praised him as "one of the outstanding house managers in the theatrical business. Efficient and genial, his business relationships here have been most cordial, and his contacts with the public have won an enviable confidence." The writer added,

---

While a thorough-going showman, Mr. Bernstein has never had a picture of himself made for publication, and in connection with theatre publicity, he has not allowed his name to be used, believing that the name of his theatre was paramount, and that the service given was its own advertisement. He proceeds...with the good wishes of a host of personal friends...including the newspaper offices, who have never known him to ask a favour, but who received from him innumerable courtesies. [2]

In contrast to certain "big time" managers, Bernstein did not have much say in the programming of his theatres. He may, however, have devised the order of the vaudeville acts when they alternated in the lower theatre and Winter Garden, since the double-deckers were anomalies on the circuit. If Edward Renton's account of the functions of a vaudeville theatre manager is accurate, Bernstein would have received in advance the "plot" for each act, which included publicity material and its dressing room, scenery, property and lighting requirements. This might engender a meeting for him with the stage manager and electrician.[3] Bernstein may have attended the Monday morning rehearsal of the acts in order to counsel on material which might be offensive as well as amusing to Toronto audiences. (Toronto censors also habitually attended this rehearsal.) According to a 1924 article on the business of vaudeville, it was the custom for the manager to sit in the audience for the Monday afternoon debut of a bill, and send a complete report on his own and the audience's reaction to home office.[4] Still, at least in later years, Bernstein did not make a practice of sitting through every movie and act presented in the theatre, and was not enchanted with movies or show business personalities.

A sample of a theatre manager's report on a vaudeville bill. (This one is by Lawrence Solman, manager of the Royal Alexandra Theatre.) A report like this one was invaluable to the booking office of the circuit and to other theatres receiving the tour.

Though Bernstein cultivated and maintained relationships which benefited the theatre's business, he was not a great "joiner." He was, however, a Mason and a life member of the Palestine Lodge, and a life member of the Canadian Picture Pioneers. Bernstein was an "old-style" theatre manager, conservative, careful, and civil. He did not like familiarity, flashiness, nor untidiness of any kind, and did not relish self-promotion. He wore a dark double-breasted suit to work, and

Bernstein's successor, Jack Clarke, and his assistants in the manager's office in 1946.

was at the theatre from about 11 a.m. until midnight, six days a week, with a two-hour break at home for dinner. On Sunday afternoons he habitually laid out the newspaper ads for the following week, a task he enjoyed. Part of his time was taken up reporting to head office on the business of the theatre. The staff, the theatre's public relations, and major local decisions were his responsibility. These remained intact in the cinema era. Though he had no say in determining which movies were booked, Bernstein and succeeding Loew's managers in Toronto were afforded initiative on publicity "tricks" and special local promotion. These were aided and abetted by the suggestions and promptings of Loew's head office.

Jack Clarke, who succeeded Bernstein as manager, had joined Loew's as assistant manager in 1927. He was similarly conservative and formal. His was not a New York or showbiz background: he had worked as a bank clerk and as a pharmacist in Chesley, Ontario. Following a Loew's tradition of long service, Clarke remained at the theatre for 37 years.

FRONT OF HOUSE STAFF: MALE AND FEMALE

Among the staff at various periods were an auditor and a treasurer, a secretary and telephone receptionist. Among those in contact with the public were non-unionized staff, ushers, box office, check room, elevator and (later) candy counter attendants.

In 1914, Loew's staffed three box offices and faced the complications of handling reserved seating in the Winter Garden. Initially, box office staff might have been males. In his 1918 book, Renton assumed that a vaudeville theatre's ticket seller or "treasurer" was a male who should be "a quick thinker, a quiet-voiced and gentlemanly salesman...[with] patience, diplomacy, and tact..." . He added, "If the ticket-seller is a woman, she should be attractive but not too pretty, unless she is one of those rare exceptions who does not unduly value her good looks. Peroxide blondes have no use for other women, and too much attraction for young men."[5] Renton suggested ordinary clothes for the ticket seller: "dinner dress" at night, and light-weight alpaca or lined coats in the summer.

Loew's doormen in Toronto in 1946.

A cartoon from the 40s depicting the life of front-of-house theatre personnel.

During the 20s, an all-female box office staff allowed to wear their own clothes was reported — whether those who might be considered "too pretty" were hired is not known. During the 40s, it was the custom for some Loew's cashiers to be dressed in modest uniforms.

No "footman" is likely to have stood on the sidewalk to open car doors and to otherwise assist patrons trickling in and out of Loew's continuous show in the teens and 20s. This category of theatre employee, however, was gaining currency in 1918, according to Renton: "In these days of automobiles and a general tendency toward 'dressing up' the front of the house, many of the leading theatres in larger cities have added a footman to the staff. Usually this employee doubles in some other capacity during the hours when he is not on duty as a footman."[6] Indeed, some movie palaces later garbed these front-line employees in magnificent regalia, wreathed in gold braid.

Renton's book recommended relatively elaborate frock coats with standing collars and peaked caps as uniforms for the theatre's doormen, charged with taking tickets in the lobby. In the 20s and later, Loew's doormen wore more understated double breasted uniform jackets and peaked caps. They were invariably male, and tended to be among the theatre's most mature employees.

Ushers and "usherettes" were Loew's most youthful employees. In 1914, Loew's employed female ushers, the first large theatre in Toronto to engage in this practice. At least one scandalized citizen complained to the Mayor of Toronto, who referred the matter to the City Architect. He replied on 20 May 1914:

> In reference to women ushers would [sic] say that it has become a general practice in New York City to have women act in that capacity, and I haven't heard any adverse reports on the practice. However, it seems to me to be out of my province to pass on that question. [7]

The employment of women ushers in Toronto theatres was commented upon in October 1918 in *Moving Picture World*: "A number of Toronto theatres have had women ushers for a number of years and they have been found quite suitable for the purpose."

In 1918 Edward Renton considered a corps of young married women between 20 and 28 years old to be the best ushers, as boys were too inclined to be boys. He thought any males employed as ushers should be between 17 and 20. They were not to be allowed to chew gum, smoke, laugh, play, or seat themselves in the auditorium while on duty. [8] Renton did not describe or allude to the elaborate military-type rituals and formations for ushers which later diverted movie palace patrons. Snappy uniforms for male ushers also became a movie palace trademark. The New York Regent, the original movie palace, was said in 1913 to have an "army of clean-cut attendants" who wore their uniforms in "the true military style," with "no hands in the pockets, no dudish cuffs on the trousers, no coats open to show either a flashy necktie or a dirty shirt." This theatre, under "Roxy" Rothapfel's management, even uniformed its projectionists (in white duck coats buttoned to the neck). [9]

According to Renton, girl ushers' uniforms were made in a great variety of styles, "...from the simple house dress to the more elaborate costume, such as different National dresses." More conventionally, they constituted a black dress, perhaps with the additions of white collars and cuffs, white frilled cap and French apron. This description conforms with the "maid's" uniform reported for Loew's female ushers in the 20s, who wore ordinary elbow-length black cotton dresses with detachable white collars and cuffs, and a white apron but no cap.

Vera Teewiss (née Johnstone) clearly remembers this uniform she wore as a female usher at Loew's for about a year in 1925-26. No male ushers were employed at the time. She was nineteen years old, and earned between $10. and $12. a week for a long shift starting at about noon and ending at 10 p.m. or later, with a couple of hours off in between. Because patrons came and went at any time in the darkened auditorium, constant vigilance with flashlights was required. Behaviour codes were strictly enforced: Vera recalls that a member of the squad was fired for smoking in the women's toilet room. Her own employment ended abruptly when, with the rest of the corps of female ushers, she was laid off. The rationale provided was that a corps of male ushers was to be hired who would be strong enough to help with the outside display signs.

Among the males who replaced Vera and her colleagues in December 1926 was Wally Ward. He recollected that thirteen female ushers had just been laid off in favour of a male crew of thirteen. Some of these female ushers were soon brought back to part-time work ushering in the Winter Garden after it was opened two nights a week in 1927. On those evenings the male ushers remained in the lower theatre, with females in attendance above.

A suitably tall and imposing head usher at Loew's in Toronto, photographed in 1946.

Loew's candy counter attendants in 1946, a position that did not exist in the complex during its first decade.

The new corps of male ushers, between 18 and 21 years old, received elaborate new uniforms, the most impressive Ward has ever seen. They looked like military officers, with short grey jackets with high tunic collars and bright red and gold trim. The uniform trousers were grey with a red stripe and gold edge. Ushers also sported dashing red velvet vests, but no gloves or headgear.

Ward was appointed head usher soon after he was hired, and relinquished the uniform for a tuxedo with a wing collar and a black tie. He acknowledged that he was thereby more formally dressed than manager Bernstein and assistant manager John McManus, who wore ordinary dark suits. Ward was flattered by being singled out for promotion, and was seduced by the information that both McManus and Bernstein had begun their careers as head ushers. Ward was then 20 years old, and earned $1 a week more as head usher than the standard $16.00 per week usher's salary. He also had the perquisite of a private dressing room. For this, he worked an extra 1 1/2 hours per day, or 9 hours per week. He had to accept responsibility for unreported burned out bulbs in public areas and the misdeeds of ushers, including proscribed gum chewing and careless hanging up of uniforms. He also checked on reports of defective chocolate dispensers, and supervised their refilling from the stock kept in the check room.

The ushers paraded in formation through the lobby and foyer once a day to open the house. Unlike some other ushers of the period, however, they did not perform military drills and fancy manoeuvres, and did not engage in elaborate hand signal codes. In 1927, their shifts began either at 11.30 a.m. or 1.30 p.m. and lasted, respectively, until the beginning or end of the feature. Loew's ushers were obliged to monitor sexually aggressive male patrons. According to Ward, male patrons noticed changing their seats more than once were to be shown to the manager's office. Ushers were also charged with discouraging men from placing their arms around the backs of seats occupied by women.

An attendant in the check room of the lower theatre was female and wore the same black-and-white maid's uniform as that worn by female ushers. (The Winter Garden coat check seems to have been self-serve.) During World War I, this job became more arduous: lugging so many heavy military coats threatened the health of one check room attendant. A later replacement (in the 1920s) was Lillian McKnight, the sister-in-law of Jules Bernstein.

Females might also have been initially employed as cleaning staff, though later at Loew's' "Downtown" this became a male preserve. The exception was the ladies' maid or matron who dressed like a nurse but who kept the ladies' rooms clean and well provided. Edward Renton in his 1918 manual advocated a female cleaning staff. "Porters," on the other hand, were male. A porter was a cleaner and a general handy man, who knew how to make minor repairs, wield a paint brush, and maintain fire prevention equipment.

The cleaners in both theatres wielded a Spencer Turbine central vacuum cleaning system. This was not a novelty in theatres in 1913. It was not a luxury, either, as the system saved money by prolonging the life of carpets and seats, and facilitated cleaning behind radiators and other places difficult of access.

The theatre's night watchman might also be assigned cleaning duties, and he was relieved in the mornings by porters and cleaners. Renton advised that the watchman should be sober, reliable, industrious, and middle-aged. Isaac Thompson, the night watchman whose alertness saved the theatre during the fire of 1928, was still employed in 1941, when he was reduced to Sunday watchman. He is remembered with a white terrier dog who served as a companion and for rat catching and sounding alarms during the solitary nights in the darkened theatre.

Another employee whose services over almost 50 years were crucial to the well-being of the complex was stationary engineer Alfred Maxwell (Mac) Allaway. He had worked for the Otis Fensom elevator company before joining Loew's in 1919. (Perhaps he had been part of the crew which had installed the third passenger elevator in the complex in 1918.) His familiarity with elevator machinery made him a particularly valuable employee. Allaway kept the elevators and almost everything else in the building in repair, and dealt with all mechanical emergencies outside the stages and projection booths. No one else knew every nook and cranny of the building and its machinery as he did.

Members of Loew's cleaning and maintenance staff in 1946. Note that half of them are wearing ties. Two are holding the hose for the central vacuum system, installed when the theatre was built in 1913. On the far left is Patsy Jones, an Italian immigrant who was the popular and loyal head cleaner for many years.

Routinely, he tended and maintained the coal boilers and ventilating machinery in the stage basement and (usually once a week) he changed the letters on the Yonge Street marquee. During the 20s and 30s, Allaway worked a full day, from morning till night, six days a week. After a dinner break, he donned a suit and returned to the theatre for an evening shift which lasted until 11 p.m. Addressed by the manager's son and officers of the theatre complex as "Mr. Allaway," he was at the top of the pecking order of its maintenance staff, none of whom was unionized.

MUSICIANS

Among unionized employees in the complex were its musicians. They were hired by and were responsible to the orchestra leader, though the manager had ultimate authority. The leader or musical director was supposed to establish artistic rapport with visiting acts. Sometimes, he needed to be almost clairvoyant to meet their needs. According to a 20s memoir,

> The leader was a master of accommodating the numerous changes in tune and tempo which the average act required, whether it was a vocalist, soft shoe dance routine, dramatic sketch, magician, trained animals, comedy turn — or the between-the-acts "chaser" which closed each act, followed by a segue to the opening music for the next act. The leader was a busy man, and he was sometimes the first violinist, conducting with his bow.[10]

Frederick Denning, aged 23 and a native Torontonian, was the musical director on opening night in the lower theatre. He remained for over 11 years, until his sudden death from appendicitis surgery in July 1925. He was replaced by James Lindsay. Earlier, the complex had employed another musical director who went on to become an important figure in the Toronto entertainment world: Jack Arthur was conductor of the Winter Garden orchestra in 1915, likely during the six-week period when the upper theatre offered all-movie shows instead of the vaudeville-and-movie programme downstairs. He was also reported to have "alternated conducting duties with Denning downstairs and in the Winter Garden." [11] (Arthur went on to produce and direct stage shows at numerous Toronto theatres as well as the annual grandstand shows at the Canadian National Exhibition).Two orchestras may have been employed in the complex in the 'teens, likely one on a part-time basis and the other full-time.

Because some acts did not bring their own music and required the orchestra to come up with something suitable, Renton considered that there was "...no field of musical endeavour requiring quite so much versatility, all-around ability, patience and general musical knowledge as that of the vaudeville orchestra." [12] In addition to accompanying various acts and the silent movie, a vaudeville orchestra played overtures of classical and popular numbers.

At Loew's, the leader conducted an orchestra of between eight and ten musicians. Marg Johnstone, a daughter of stationary engineer "Mac" Allaway, readily remembers the ten-piece tuxedoed orchestra

A.M .("Mac") Allaway, Loew's stationary engineer, who maintained the heating and ventilating equipment for nearly fifty years. He retired in 1966.

Kathleen ("Kay") Stokes, organist from 1923 to 1930, now better remembered by thousands of Canadians coast-to-coast as a member of "The Happy Gang," a top-rated daily radio programme broadcast from 1937 to 1959.

Frederick Denning, musical director of Loew's Winter Garden orchestra from 1913 to 1925.

at Loew's in the late 20s, including the instruments they played: piano, cello, clarinet, trombone, bass, violin, second violin, organ, and drums. Edward Renton offered a sliding scale for vaudeville orchestras. Five-piece orchestras had a violin, piano, cornet, trombone, and trap drums "with a complete assortment of effects, chimes, xylophone, tympani, etc." A six-piece orchestra had the addition of a clarinet, and seven, a bass viol. An eight-piece orchestra called for a flute, nine, a second violin, and ten, "an organ for volume, tone and strength."[13] In vaudeville the drummer was very important, as "...he accentuated the falls and crashes of the comedians and played long rolls for the aerialists' sensational slides."[14]

In the lower theatre, until 1919, musicians relaxed and prepared in a basement band room. The Winter Garden had no parallel quarters and its musicians presumably made their way down by the backstage elevator to the same band room. When the Warren organ was installed in the lower theatre in 1919, the band room was sacrificed for organ chambers. In 1928, when the Wurlitzer organ replaced the incinerated 1919 instrument, a band room and separate leader's room were designed. The nine-year absence must have been felt.

Loew's orchestra had two female members in the 20s: violinist Ruby Ramsay (later Rouse), and organist Kathleen Stokes. When hired by Loew's, Stokes was twenty years old, and a licentiate from the University of Toronto School of Music. From about 1923, she played the Warren organs in the lower theatre and the Winter Garden, and remembered later being transported from one theatre to the other by freight elevator. She did not work exclusively for Loew's, giving recitals in all of Toronto's major movie and vaudeville houses in the 20s. She claimed Loew's Yonge Street was her favourite, no doubt because of its Mighty Wurlitzer which continued to be used for overtures, intermissions, short recitals, and "God Save the King" after the orchestra was laid off in the sound movie era. [15] No one played this Wurlitzer after its cable was severed with an axe in about 1935 to end an alleged dispute between the musicians' union and the theatre's management.

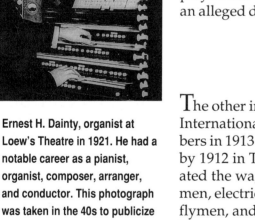

Ernest H. Dainty, organist at Loew's Theatre in 1921. He had a notable career as a pianist, organist, composer, arranger, and conductor. This photograph was taken in the 40s to publicize one of many radio broadcasts of his organ recitals.

STAGE CREW

The other important union working in the complex was the Toronto local of the International Union of Theatrical Stage Employees, which numbered 89 members in 1913 and had won an "absolutely closed shop by 1912 in Toronto".[16] The local of the union negotiated the wages of its members: carpenters, property men, electricians, motion picture machine operators, flymen, and "extra" men. It also regulated the number of stage hands required to be on the crew of a vaudeville theatre. The number depended on the number of acts presented. In general, during the 'teens, the standard requirement was that a house with one act of vaudeville had to employ one man, two to four acts needed three men, four to five acts required five men, and more than five acts necessitated six or more men. These stage hands might be joined backstage by road men, as the international laid down regulations in 1914 which stipulated that

Stagehands or "flymen" at work, aloft and unobserved, on a fly gallery above the stage. They are being pulled off their feet in the process of hauling the ropes (or lines) attached to an item of suspended scenery.

acts travelling with more than a certain quantity of scenery and equipment had to be accompanied by one or more union hands. Usually, according to local IATSE regulations, stage employees reported to the stage 30 minutes before the overture. Their regular employment, paid by the performance or by the week, ended when the last scene was struck. All other work, including rolling drops and putting out scenery, demanded an additional hourly stipend, while work on Sundays called for a rate of time and a half.

When both stages were alive, a stage electrician for each of two switchboards must have been employed. The switchboard operator was required to remember, recognize and interpret cues, and to manipulate dexterously switches with both hands as well as with his elbows, knees, and feet, when warranted. He was probably assisted by another stage hand who moved and worked the carbon arc spotlights and other light instruments in the wings. IATSE had struggled successfully with the electricians' union for dominion over the stage electrician. It also strove to establish his exclusive domain over the switchboard (and no other chores) by recommending that its operator be compelled to remain within 10 feet of it during a public performance. [17]

Bert (or Elrick B.) Rippon is listed in assessment rolls as an electrician in the complex in 1915. His service at Loew's seems to have encompassed almost the entire vaudeville period and several years after, and he was one of the few stage employees to survive the onslaught of sound movies and the death of vaudeville. During the 1930s, he was stationed backstage, where his duties mostly consisted of opening and closing the curtains. His presence may also have served as a safety precaution in case of fire.

A passport photo of Charles W. Scott, Loew's stage manager from 1913 to 1929.

The stage manager was responsible for the backstage crew, and he also needed to be expert on the handling of scenery and lighting. He was the most important local contact with the vaudeville performer. Moreover, "not only must he have a perfect system of stage operation already established, but his mind must be alert for every emergency — he must know what to do in a moment of delay or mishap, what order to give, what electric switch to turn, what drop to raise or lower."[18] Loew's must have benefited from the long experience of stage manager Charles W. Scott, whose employment encompassed almost the entire vaudeville period in the complex. A "Cockney" immigrant to Canada, Scott previously had been employed at the Royal Alexandra Theatre. At Loew's, he worked the standard six days a week, leaving his house at 10 a.m., wearing a black bowler hat, and a jacket and tie. He usually came home for dinner and a good rest between 4 and 7 p.m., then returned to the theatre complex until nearly 11 p.m. His grandson remembers that Scott's Mondays were extremely hectic. He was so busy with new acts, any new scenery, and rehearsals that he did not come home for his break and dinner on that day. His niece, Marjory Wesley, had the task of taking him his macaroni-and-cheese supper at his post. For a week after the 1928 fire in the lower theatre, Scott's relatives recall that he was hardly ever at home, as he was fully absorbed with the inspection and inventory of damaged and ruined scenery.

Another important authority backstage was the property manager. One named Samuel Meredith is listed by assessors only in 1917 and 1918. He would have been responsible for providing and administering all the stage properties in the complex. In 1918, Edward Renton described the property man's prerequisites grandiloquently: "He must be a bit of a carpenter, something of an artist, a great deal of a diplomat, and he must be on the job from the rising of the sun to considerably after the setting thereof..." He might be required to supply "anything from an Egyptian mummy to a three week-old child, upon a moment's notice." [19] He might be required to create sound effects for acts, and to play small walk-on parts on stage. Another important but more prosaic duty of the property man was to send out and receive laundry for the travelling vaudeville artists.

Five or six stage hands were regularly employed at Loew's, perhaps with the addition of one or two more employed on a part-time basis. (By comparison, in good seasons, the crew of the Royal Alexandra and the Princess each numbered 12.) Extra stage hands or road men might sometimes be hired for special acts and occasions.

Out of consideration to women artists on the bill, Renton advised a clean-shaven and gentlemanly stage crew, who neither smoked, gambled, nor were tempted to congregate in the theatre alley or in a saloon in the 20-minute interval an act was on stage [20] (although the Winter Garden's location must have deterred its stage crew from such wanderings). Renton did not disregard noting appropriate behaviour for a flyman. Because he might be aloft and unobserved while acts were on stage, he should not take advantage by sleeping, smoking, or indulging in literary pursuits of the "Diamond Dick" or "Nick Carter" variety. If he had nothing to do, he was to remain near the speaking tube where he could observe the signal light and hear the buzzer activated by the stage electrician or stage manager. The flyman was also responsible for sweeping out the gallery and keeping it free of tangled lines. [21]

Backstage, the communication and cue system in the complex depended on speaking tubes, located on stage left and stage right, in the projection booths, in the orchestra pits, and likely in the fly galleries. An intercom telephone could also be used which linked the stages with the manager's office and box office. Buzzers connected dressing rooms with the stage manager. Another important item in the information chain was a small window in the ground floor of the dressing room corridor looking over the lower stage. Someone standing there could observe an act working "in one" on stage, stage hands setting up scenery behind, the electrician at the switchboard, comings and goings in the dressing room corridor and stairway, and anyone arriving at the stage door.

PROJECTIONISTS

Four male projectionists who worked in pairs were employed for much of the history of the complex. Three of them — William Taylor, Charles Hallett, and Earl Winslow were each employed for over thirty years. Their lengthy service is not surprising, as loyalty and trustworthiness were requisites in their isolated and largely unsupervised jobs. Projectionists were depended upon to be on time, and always present and alert beside their machines, and to understand how to maintain them. Originally, they worked with hazardous nitrate film, and in hot and stuffy projection booths not equipped with toilets or running water.

Even without spotlight responsibilities during the vaudeville years, the entertainment in the complex still relied heavily upon these men. According to former manager Jack Clarke, a singular task facing projectionists in this double-decker operation was to slow down the movie when vaudeville acts in the other theatre were behind schedule. Sometimes the film would "...practically be in slow motion." Clarke added that often, to save time, the projectionist in the Winter Garden would lower the film out the window to the projectionist in the lower theatre's booth directly below. [22]

Projectionists had been regulated by the Province since 1909. In that year, the "machine operator" was required to have "a thorough knowledge of the machine he operates" and to be at least 18 years old. He was not to allow anyone but a Provincial or Municipal Police officer into the "cabinet" (or projection booth), in which no smoking, lighting of matches, or reading material was allowed. Amendments to the Theatres and Cinematographs Act passed in 1918 usefully extended the list of those allowed into the booth to the manager, the local fire chief, the theatre inspector, and the operator's apprentice, and permitted licenses and regulations as reading matter in the booth. The projectionist was prohibited from cutting or speeding up [though not slowing down] films being screened, and from rewinding or leaving film exposed in the "operating room." [23]

Intercom and speaking tubes near the Winter Garden's dimmer board. This apparatus connected by voice the two stages, and the stage manager or stage electrician with the orchestra leader in the pit and with the projectionists in the booth. (A portion of the gas equipment for the Winter Garden's set of gas footlights is visible at left.)

THE END OF AN ERA

The coming of sound movies and the subsequent disappearance of vaudeville in October 1930 had a massive impact on Loew's personnel — specifically, those that were unionized. Silent movies with live musical accompaniment and vaudeville acts were considerably more labour-intensive and expensive than a programme of talking pictures. This must have contributed to the development and the promotion of the latter by the circuits, many of which, like Loew's, were enmeshed in motion picture production.

The savings effected by discontinuing vaudeville took up one of the two paragraphs outlining the history of the Yonge Street Theatre in a 1967 financial report. It read, "In 1930 the type of entertainment at Loew's Theatre was changed. Vaudeville was discontinued and the orchestra dispensed with, effecting an annual saving of approximately $25,000." [24] Loew's announcement on 26 September that vaudeville would be discontinued stimulated a *Telegram* article on 27 September which reviewed the impact of sound movies on employment in Toronto, "400 lost jobs, one result of theatre changes." Loew's "musicians, stage hands, electricians and mechanics" had augmented the number to about 400 in these unionized trades of those who had recently lost jobs because vaudeville was burned out.

According to this article, about 300 musicians in the city were out of work, and few, if any, had been engaged in radio. Their union and the musicians hoped that the public would campaign for the return of orchestras to movie houses, and that movies entailing incidental live music would be the vogue. As it turned out, these former members of stage crews and theatre orchestras would hope in vain for vaudeville's return.

Charles Scott, Loew's hard-working and loyal stage manager, reportedly noticed a deterioration in the vaudeville shows he installed during the late 20s. He considered them to be bereft of sparkle and new ideas, and he voiced his concern for his future when vaudeville disappeared. He would not be there to witness its final passing at Loew's. He had died at the age of 65 on 1 October 1929 — one year and two days before live stage entertainment gave way to an all-movie programme.

Projectionists in the lower theatre's booth in 1946. From left, they are Earl Winslow, Philip Ristow, Charles Sturgess (who died in the booth), and Charles Hallett. Winslow's tenure dated from the 1913 opening of the downstairs theatre until 1948. Hallett joined the ranks by 1919 and remained at Loew's until 1961. William Taylor, another long-time employee, had just retired.

CHAPTER ELEVEN

THE CINEMA ERA: 1930-1981

The era of sound movies in the lower theatre began rewardingly in 1929, with a 61% increase in net revenues. They prompted renovations which enlarged the lower projection booth, adding a rewind room and a toilet. The abolition of vaudeville in 1930 reduced operating costs significantly, as salaries of stage crews and orchestra and the costs of touring acts were eliminated. Notwithstanding, admission prices at the theatre remained the same, scaling up to 65 cents in the evenings. Indeed, Loew's was afforded more opportunities to rake in box office receipts as the theatre opened for business at 11 a.m., an hour earlier than had been the custom. Six shows a day could be offered without too much wear and tear on personnel or conflict with union regulations.

Another reform engendered in 1930 was that the traditional Monday opening for a new programme was changed to Friday. Weekend audiences now experienced fresh new shows, but they were not forewarned about "duds" by word-of-mouth and reviews of weekday audiences.

In the first few years of the 30s, the movie programme was usually changed weekly. This was perhaps a legacy of the vaudeville period and the traditional travel schedules of touring acts. Loew's still expected its regular patrons to visit the theatre every week. (Of course, a few weeks or months after a movie ended at Loew's or another "first run" house, it would reappear at one of Toronto's numerous second-run movie houses.) A movie "hold over" was relatively rare, though an early sound musical in Technicolour, *Whoopee!* starring Eddie Cantor, played to "capacity houses" during its second week at Loew's in November 1930. Perhaps ironically, the next "hold over," five months later, was a silent movie with a music track. Business was so brisk for Charlie Chaplin's *City Lights* in April 1931 that Loew's box office was "obliged" to open at 9.30 a.m.

A still from *Whoopee!* which may help to explain why it played to capacity houses during its unprecedented holdover week at Loew's in 1930.

A clean-shaven Clark Gable with Norma Shearer in *A Free Soul*, one of three films held over at Loew's in 1931. This movie helped to establish Gable as one of the industry's consummate leading men.

Only three other movies were held over during 1931: *Strangers May Kiss* and *A Free Soul*, both starring the Canadian-born Norma Shearer. *A Free Soul* was brought back for an unheard of third week during the summer. This was a romantic melodrama about a society woman who falls in with gangsters. In it, Shearer was manhandled by one of M-G-M's newest and brightest stars, Clark Gable. *Susan Lenox, Her Fall and Rise* which paired this primal heartthrob with the ultimate screen goddess, Greta Garbo, was held over in December.

Not until the late thirties did 2- and 3-week holdovers for features become fairly standard at Loew's in Toronto. Such scintillating all-star classics as *Grand Hotel* and *Dinner at Eight* did not last longer than two weeks (in 1932 and in 1934, respectively). *House of Rothschild*, an extravagant historical pageant (with George Arliss, Loretta Young and Boris Karloff) persisted for three weeks in 1934, a feat of endurance not matched until the following year, when three weeks of the critically acclaimed block buster *David Copperfield* inaugurated a new "modern" look and feel for the theatre in February 1935 — the first renovation since the death of vaudeville.

FROM VAUDEVILLE THEATRE TO MODERN CINEMA

By that time, the stacked theatres had lost their original purpose, and were no longer expected to do what they were built to do. Their double-decker feature, their decor and their facilities were a handicap and a source of expense. The Winter Garden had not been wired for sound movies and remained dark and silent. Flats and drops gathered dust. Both backstage areas became dead storage instead of being the heart and soul of the theatre. The orchestra pit was covered over. The cable for the Wurlitzer theatre organ had been severed. All the entertainment offered now emanated from the lower projection booth.

Loew's renovation plans sought to accommodate a new kind of patron as well as the new kind of entertainment: a patron unimpressed with scagliola, gilded surfaces, great domes and chandeliers. Twenty years after the theatres opened, when a modern system of heating and air conditioning was overdue, Loew's changed the face of its Yonge Street theatre.

A striking new upright sign, soaring 75 feet above the street, and a new marquee heralded the transformation within and its "cooled to comfort" air conditioning in February 1935. The 1919 lobby at 191 Yonge was deleted except for a remnant which was metamorphosed into a "new" lounge. A store was restored to the remaining corridor at 191 Yonge Street to make more money on the site. [2]

The Winter Garden was abandoned in the renovation. An opening was cut between the mezzanine landing of the grand staircase and the balcony of the lower theatre, to end a mortifying eight-year period when this imposing ascent led the public to a locked door. The lower theatre would be brought up to more modern standards in its light fixtures, seats and washrooms. The auditorium chandelier was probably removed at this time. The basic decorative scheme and features of the original lobby, foyer, and auditorium were retained. A change of colour scheme drew attention to the remodelling. The blue colour scheme (dating from 1928) was replaced with "a rose and gold motif," "gorgeous drapes of red and yellow tones," and new "rich warm carpeting, as soft as down." [3]

DOUBLE BILLS AND SERIES

By 1935, there was no question that sound movies were all the entertainment the public really wanted and they were poured on in programmes of double-features. The first to be offered at Loew's in Toronto, in August of 1935, was *Murder in the Fleet* with Robert Taylor and Jean Parker, and *Calm Yourself* with Robert Young and Madge Evans. Double bills occupied 21 weeks of the theatre's programming in 1939. From the mid-30s to the late 40s, the popularity of this format in first-run theatres across the continent fueled the fires of movie production, and kept studios and their stars busy and prosperous. During the Depres-

The new marquee and store after 1935 renovations.

LOEW'S HOLLYWOOD CONNECTIONS

Loew's audiences were fed a steady diet of Metro-Goldwyn-Mayer films, which were produced by the multi-million dollar subsidiary of Loew's Inc. This producing company was formed in a 1924 amalgamation of Loew's Metro studios with Goldwyn Pictures and Louis B. Mayer's independent production company. (Apparently, the merger was the brainchild of Lee Shubert, a prime influence behind the expansion of Loew's Theatres in 1913.)[1] The biggest and most financially successful studio in Hollywood, M-G-M became renowned for the glamour and class of its productions, its leonine trademark, and its boast that it had under contract more stars than there were in heaven.

M-G-M's principal stars and its publicity mill worked non-stop, churning out a steady stream of movies and stories which were practically guaranteed to bring a return on the investment, even during the depths of the economic depression of the 30s. Names like Norma Shearer, Marie Dressler (two Canadian-born actresses), Greta Garbo, Joan Crawford, Jean Harlow, Clark Gable, Spencer Tracy, John and Lionel Barrymore, the Marx Brothers, and Laurel and Hardy were featured in advertising and marquees and served as magnets at the box office. The studio relied on exhibiting M-G-M movies in more than 200 large first-run theatres controlled by Loew's, and in thousands of affiliated or independent theatres. In the early thirties, most theatres needed a new movie nearly every week.

Loew's Toronto theatre also exhibited numerous films by United Artists. Not coincidentally, the Chairman of this studio (between 1924 and 1935) was Joseph Schenck, whose brother, Nicholas, was President of Loew's and the financial controller of M-G-M after Marcus Loew's death in 1927. The Schenck connection, so decisive in the growth and development of Loew's Corporation, was extended even further when Joseph formed 20th-Century Pictures in 1933 and became Chairman of the Board of Twentieth-Century Fox in 1935.

Anti-trust rulings in U.S. courts between 1946 and 1948 addressed the monopolistic tangle of ownership pervading all phases of the American film industry. The courts ordered the studios to be severed from their chain theatres, though the required divorce was delayed and evaded by M-G-M and Loew's Inc.

A poster advertising for one of M-G-M's greatest hits, *The Wizard of Oz*, a magical and enduring film which had its Canadian premiere at Loew's in Toronto on 14 September 1939.

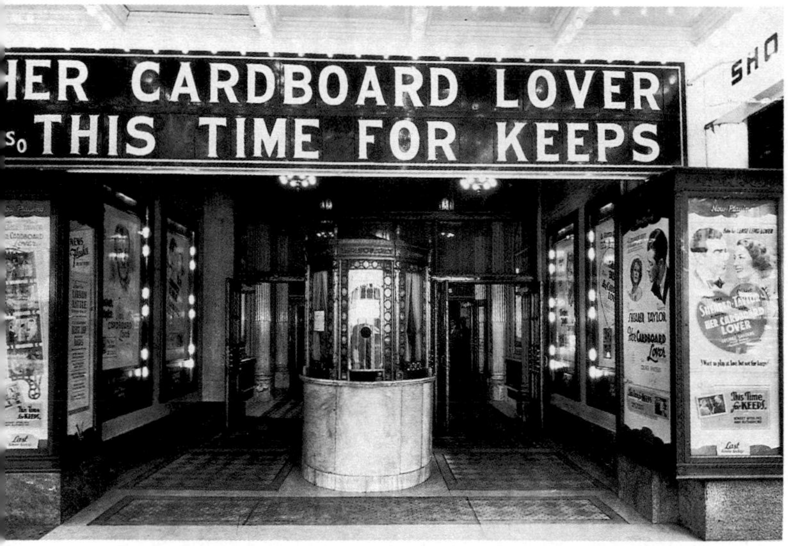

Two movies for the price of one: one of a plethora of double bills shown at Loew's from the mid-thirties to the late forties.

sion, double bills also catered to patrons with idle hours and not much money. Normally, double bills implied "B" movies — films produced in minimum time for minimum money — which were slated to fill the second half of a programme. Though most ballyhooed features with adored leading men and women continued to stand alone, some well-made and significant films like *Algiers*, *The Great Waltz*, and *Stagecoach* were offered at Loew's as half the entertainment programme.

Though by the late 30s single features usually ran for two or more weeks at Loew's, most double features lasted only one week. A double bill was held over for an unprecedented three weeks in July and August of 1940. The main attraction was *The Mortal Storm* with James Stewart, Margaret Sullivan and Robert Young, an anti-Nazi tract about a German family torn apart during the 30s, made before the United States entered World War II. *The Mortal Storm* denounced Nazi ideology but recognized good Germans. This film, described as "the industry's first essay on the Jewish question in Germany," was paired with the less controversial *Out West with the Peppers*, starring Edith Fellowes.[4]

Teenage star Fellowes had made *Five Little Peppers* in 1938 and would make *Five Little Peppers in Trouble* in 1941. These numbered among a spate of low-budget movie sequels produced in the 30s and 40s. Such films promised sure-fire box office return and paid for more ambitious and extravagant films. Among the most popular at Loew's in Toronto and across North America was the homespun Andy Hardy series, 15 films made by M-G-M between 1937 and 1947 which starred Mickey Rooney as Andy, a wholesome and irrepressible teenager living amicably with his all-American family in a small midwestern town.

Among profitable M-G-M series presented at Loew's in the 30s and 40s were five Tarzan movies, starring Johnny Weismuller, five *Thin Man* movies, with William Powell and Myrna Loy as a wisecracking husband-and-wife detective team, a low-budget series starring Ann Sothern about a Brooklyn showgirl named Maisie, and a series of hospital adventures with the young Dr. Kildare and his crusty mentor, Dr. Gillespie.

Double bills and the enduring popularity of M-G-M's stellar attractions and series had helped Loew's to weather the Depression in the black, the only film company that continued to pay dividends and avoid shake-up throughout this bleak period.

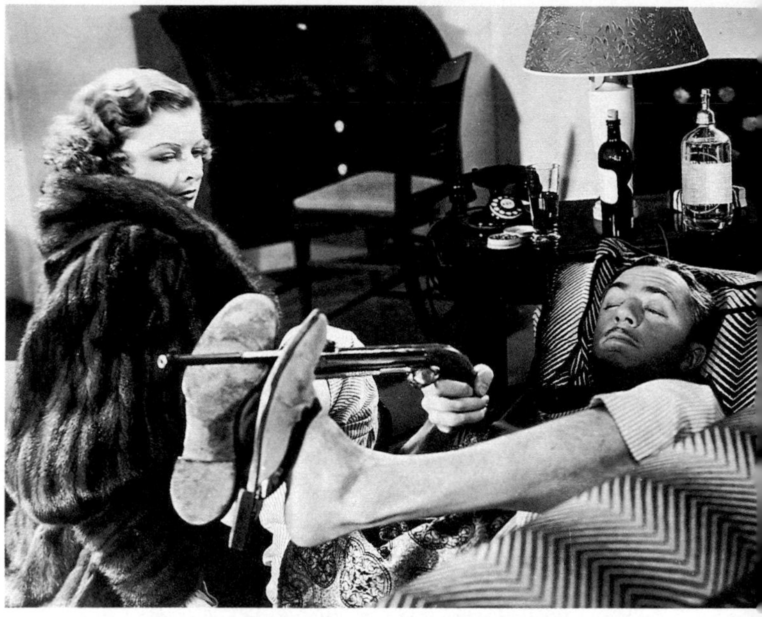

William Powell demonstrates his aim to Mryna Loy in *The Thin Man*, the first of a popular series. This movie lasted only a week at Loew's in 1934, though its successor, *After the Thin Man*, stayed for four in 1937.

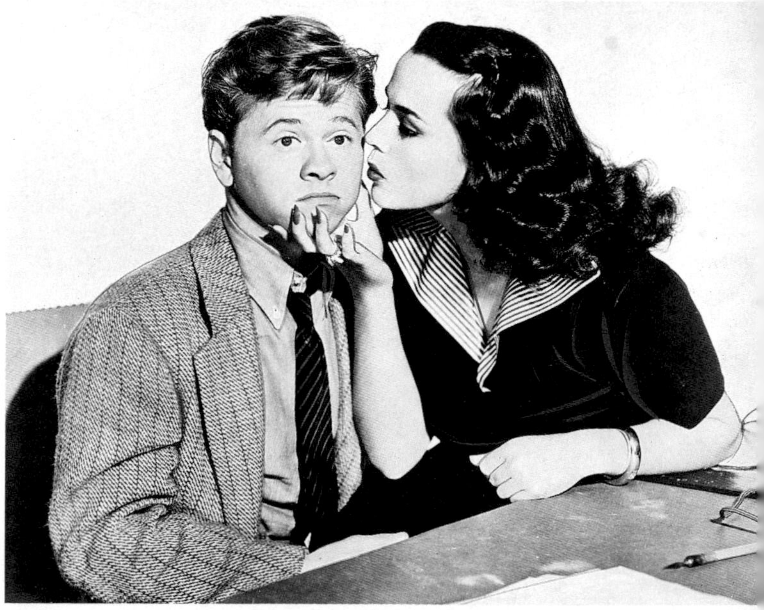

Publicity still for *Life Begins for Andy Hardy* in 1941.

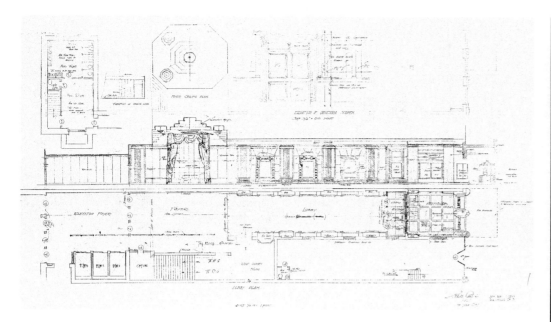

Thomas Lamb's 1933 proposal
(not carried out) for the
renovation of the lobby corridor
of "Loew's Downtown."

Joan Crawford and Clark Gable in
Dance Fools Dance, the first
movie in which he appeared at
Loew's, and one of eight features
he made in 1931. He played a
gangster heavy.

RENOVATION PLANS: THE ROAD NOT TAKEN

In 1919 and 1928, Thomas Lamb had drawn renovation plans for the complex. The 1935 renovation signalled the end of his involvement. His office drew plans in 1933 for the pending modernization, but Loew's opted for a more conservative and cheaper scheme drawn by E.H. Stillman of Loew's Theatres Engineering Division.

Lamb's proposals would have radically altered the lobby, foyer and auditorium and would have left intact much less of his original work. In the lobby, renaissance schemes would have been obliterated in a "moderne" orgy of aluminium, mirrors, and walnut panels. In the auditorium, the opera boxes would have been removed, a venture Loew's did not care to undertake until 1960.

CLARK GABLE AND *GONE WITH THE WIND* AT LOEW'S

No one — not Andy Hardy, Tarzan, or Dr. Kildare — dominated Loew's screen to the extent that the "King" of Hollywood did. For several weeks of most years for a 30-year period, Clark Gable could be viewed there, much larger than life, engaged in daring heroics and romancing some of the most glamourous women in the world.

Gable's 1935 blockbuster, *Mutiny on the Bounty* was only the second movie to be held over for three consecutive weeks in Loew's history, and it augmented his total screen time there to 27 weeks. Added to this was an astonishing 8-week holdover for *San Francisco* in the summer 1936, an extravaganza which featured Gable, Spencer Tracy, Jeanette MacDonald and superb earthquake special effects. It was the biggest money-maker of the year for M-G-M.

All this paled by comparison to the time Gable spent on the screen as Rhett Butler. *Gone with the Wind* had its Canadian premiere at Loew's in January of 1940. This movie remained at Loew's for eight weeks in 1940, to return for four weeks in 1941, five weeks in 1947, six weeks in 1954, and for two weeks at both Loew's and the Uptown in 1961 (following Gable's death).This 220-minute epic was an industry landmark which allegedly helped to usher in intermissions and consequent refreshment stands in movie theatres.

The length of *Gone with the Wind* also caused complications because a Toronto bylaw required commercial showings to be over by 11:45 p.m. on Saturdays. Even starting at 9 a.m. and cutting the newsreel, the last show continued until after midnight. As Loew's manager reported later, "We can get away with running possibly up until 12:15 a.m. on Saturday nights by putting out all our inside lights at 11:45 p.m. and leaving just enough lights in the lobby for the safety of patrons leaving the theatre. This is the way it was handled when we played the picture the last time and we had no complaints from the Lord's Day Alliance who keep close tabs on the observance of the Sabbath in Canada."[5]

WARTIME ENTERTAINMENT

The next great crisis, World War II, turned out to be profitable for the film industry. All-time attendance records were set between 1941 and 1945. [6] The world-wide threat of fascism and the war also inspired numerous films. Among the few anti-Nazi films shown at Loew's in Toronto before the United States entered the war in December 1941 was Charlie Chaplin's first sound movie *The Great Dictator*. It ridiculed Hitler and Mussolini for a three-week run at the theatre in April and May 1941.

One of the first movies shown at Loew's which portrayed the war in Europe was *To Be Or Not To Be*, exhibited for two weeks as the top half of a double bill in March 1942. This was, however, a farce starring Jack Benny and Carole Lombard as Shakespearian actors caught up in the Nazi invasion of Poland. More solemn flag wavers — *A Yank on the Burma Road*, *Nazi Agent*, and *Joe Smith, American* — followed in short order, though each of these was on the bottom of a double bill, with a comedy on top.

Among the most notable movies at Loew's intended to engage hearts and minds in the war effort was *Mrs. Miniver*, with Greer Garson and Walter Pidgeon, which dramatized stiff upper lips on the idealized British home front. This film swept the Academy Awards; it had its Canadian premiere at Loew's and was held over for 8 weeks, from August to September of 1942. [7] Other war movies

Lassie matches expression with Roddy McDowell in *Lassie Come Home*, the first in the series.

which enjoyed extended runs at Loew's included Noel Coward's *In Which We Serve*, *The White Cliffs of Dover* and, in a frothier vein, *Stage Door Canteen*, an all-star musical cornucopia concocted to entertain the troops. [8]

Still, most of the movies shown at Loew's allowed wartime audiences to forget there was a war on. Among holdovers were *Gaslight*, a gripping thriller with Charles Boyer and Ingrid Bergman, Judy Garland's peppy and nostalgic *Meet Me in St. Louis*, and *Lassie Come Home*, the first in a series, which introduced two new stars to appreciative movie goers: the 11-year-old Elizabeth Taylor and a male collie named Pal.

The booming wartime economy and the salutary impact on movie-going habits of war industry shift work prompted plans for another major renovation of the complex — this one pertaining to the abandoned Winter Garden theatre. In 1944 Loew's hoped to remodel it into a modern cinema, and to reopen this wasted space which continued to be steam heated.

The remodelling plans evidenced Loew's interest in standardization within the chain. Toronto architects Kaplan and Sprachman were instructed to copy a recently remodelled Loew's theatre located in Toledo, Ohio. This theatre, named the Valentine, was originally built in 1895 and had been acquired by the Loew's circuit in 1918. It was not the upper theatre in a double decker complex and did not originally resemble the Winter Garden. Loew's simply admired its 1942 "Chinese modern" (or perhaps "1940s aquarium") look which had been created by the Chicago architectural firm of Rapp and Rapp.

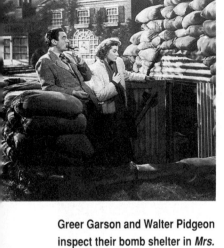

Greer Garson and Walter Pidgeon inspect their bomb shelter in *Mrs. Miniver*, the biggest war-time movie at Loew's, held over for eight weeks. Though originally planned as a low-budget public service movie unlikely to make money, it grossed $6 million and encouraged the production of numerous war pictures.

Two views of the Valentine Theatre in Toledo, Ohio, the prototype for plans in 1944 to remodel and transform Toronto's Winter Garden Theatre.

Luckily (in retrospect), war-time restrictions hampered the progress of the project, as the Department of Munitions and Supply in Ottawa refused to issue a permit because of the shortage of labour. By the time all approvals had been won, the economic conditions and war-time work schedules which had inspired the renovation plans had changed.

THE POST WAR DECADE

Loew's tried to lease the Winter Garden thereafter, and had it listed, to no avail, with a real estate company. This fanciful and romantic theatre was saved from the renovation horrors contemplated, but it was reduced to storage for washroom paper products, popcorn, and candy.

By the end of the war, concessions were entrenched in the theatre's foyer. While its earliest known candy bar was a piece of moveable furniture which dispensed popcorn in sealed bags, by the late 40s an electrified colossus had arrived. It contained a popcorn warmer, an ice cream freezer, and a chilled soft drink dispenser. A swirling illuminated "marquee" promised "candy, drinks, ice cream" in glittering letters. The eating habits, numbers and configuration of the movie-going public were all changing. Regular movie attendance for patrons over 21 dropped drastically, and in 1947 the fortunes of M-G-M and the industry headed for a downturn. In 1948 the studio landed firmly in the red — to the tune of $6.5 million.

There were fewer blockbusters and successful series at Loew's in Toronto in the early postwar period. One of the longest holdovers was the second return engagement of *Gone with the Wind*. The business of Loew's and other Yonge Street theatres was affected by the construction of the north-south subway line underneath and the City's order in 1949 to remove their marquees and upright signs.[9] When all the digging and repaving ended, Loew's new marquee and upright signalled a new era, one requiring aggressive salesmanship.

The new upright planned was 60 feet high and a carnival of ruby red, green, and yellow. It spelled out LOEW'S in flashing red neon and in twinkling lamps. The sequence devised for these letters, and for the upright's green borders, ruby and green base, and ruby, green and gold crown was spectacular:

Spell [Loew's] in neon

" " " lamps all lamps

Twinkling

All off

All on

Head and Bottom to run up & down

Border on and off

In the second floor room over the theatre's lobby, posters are painted for *The Outlaw* in 1946. Jane Russell was described as "the yumma yumma girl" in the theatre's newspaper advertising for this movie.

In March 1947 the theatre is draped with flags and crowds line up for the Canadian premiere of *The Beginning or the End* at Loew's, a semi-documentary about the making of the atomic bomb.

A new behemoth of a marquee studded with bulbs and stylized neon letters loomed over the sidewalk, and a new "modern" and 1950s face was implanted on the theatre's Yonge Street entrance. Loew's needed to seize the attention of passers-by and could no longer take for granted the regular movie-going habits of its customary patrons, many of whom were now nestled far away in suburbia. The design of the new entrance and box office were also becoming a standard around the circuit. Homogeneity was thought to contribute to efficiency. The head office in New York could issue maintenance manuals, could order supplies and replacement features centrally, and would not have to recall as many variations between their theatres. During this campaign in 1952, the exterior vestibule and store front were covered with marble, plate glass and metal. The outside box office was removed, and a new box office was located in a bubble at the south side of the entrance. The entrance and airlock doors and transoms were replaced by curtains of plate glass, and modernization crept into the inner lobby.

A new marquee, box office and store front in 1952. Faced with competition from television, Loew's can no longer take for granted that people will come to the theatre for their screen entertainment.

COMPETITION FROM THE SMALL SCREEN

A downtown cinema had to compete with a newborn monster — television. Sales of television sets in Ontario more than quadrupled in 1951, a factor which may have influenced a reported decline that year in the net profits of Marcus Loew's Theatres Ltd. [10] During that year the most successful movies screened at Loew's were technicolored musicals. *The Great Caruso* with Mario Lanza and Ann Blyth lasted seven weeks, as did *An American in Paris*, with Gene Kelly and Leslie Caron. Other popular movies held over for four weeks or more included *King Solomon's Mines*, an adventure-travelogue starring Stewart Granger and Deborah Kerr, and *Go for Broke* with Van Johnson, which commemorated the heroism of Japanese-American soldiers during World War II.

Two of 1952's biggest money-makers starred the darkly handsome Robert Taylor. *Quo Vadis?* was a mega-spectacle featuring Romans, Christians and lions which M-G-M's publicity averred added "something of permanent value to the cultural treasure house of mankind." Its nine-week run began in February with admission prices scaled up to $1.50. Top prices of $1.20 were charged for *Ivanhoe*, Taylor's next derring-do costume drama which ran for four weeks in November.

In spite of all the singing, dancing, costumes, thrills and swashbuckle on the movie screen, television remained a real threat to box office revenues. This must have been apparent in September 1952, when station CBLT in Toronto announced a schedule of feature-length movies three nights a week. To add insult to injury, the Canadian Broadcasting Corporation was contemplating the broadcast of Sunday movies on television, though theatres in Ontario were not allowed to open on the Sabbath.

Promoting *Melba* on legs in 1952. This movie lasted only a week.

3-D AND WIDE SCREENS

Hollywood responded to television by scrambling to find some technology which would transform the movie-going experience — to turn it into something that could only be found in a theatre. The industry tried embracing 3-D or stereoscopic movies to entice patrons away from the comforts of home and television.

In April 1953, Loew's tendered the Canadian premiere of the first 3-D feature, *Bwana Devil* starring Robert Stack, which promised, unappealingly, "A lion in your lap." This movie arrived with a three-page bulletin to projectionists detailing the complicated procedures and paraphernalia required to create this sensation. The list of projection equipment read:

(a) A replacement polarized surface high intensity sound screen

(b) A suitable interlock to couple the two projectors so that same can run in synchronism.

(c) 2 sets of 24" magazines complete

(d) 4 - 23" spare film reels

(e) A set of polarized filters

(f) Sufficient studio projector indexing test film to provide 2 - 8 foot loops for checking projector synchronism.

(g) 3-D film rewinder. [11]

Only two other 3-D features followed at Loew's in this period: *Arena*, a rodeo drama with Gig Young, and *I, the Jury* with Biff Elliott. The latter received exceptional fanfare: the hardboiled and cowlicked star visited Toronto and horned in on the motorcade parade and reception at City Hall of the International Convention of Fire Chiefs. The following day, the first 100 patrons for Mickey Spillane's "first white-hot movie in 3-dimensions" received copies of *I, the Jury*, autographed by Biff Elliott.

Still, the public was not impressed, and each of these 3-D films lasted only one week. The theatre's management must have sighed with relief at 3-D's early demise, not only because of the practical horrors of running two projectors simultaneously but also of issuing and collecting requisite polaroid spectacles. [12] Audiences were offered respite from wearing these unflattering cardboard glasses and from headaches engendered by out-of-synch projectors, and they probably welcomed the cessation of movies which hurled things towards them at every opportunity. (3-D would be revived in the theatre in the 70s in two soft core porno films.)

Costumed ushers tote a nine-piece walking billboard promoting *Alexander the Great* in CinemaScope.

Another unavailing bulwark simultaneously constructed by the industry in the 50s against on-rushing television was the wide screen movie. Wide screens were not only intended to make puny home screens seem ludicrously inadequate, but once again to handcuff theatre chains to studios and to freeze out the independents in the industry. When a chain installed a studio's patented and expensive wide-screen system, it encouraged the continuance of monopolistic practices and retied an umbilicus between studio and chain which had supposedly been severed by anti-trust rulings.

"CinemaScope" with stereophonic sound was installed at Loew's in March of 1954. This process, owned by 20th-Century Fox and licensed to M-G-M in 1953, involved the use of special "anamorphic" lenses on projector and movie camera. Like a curved mirror, the lens on the camera squeezed onto the film a picture twice as wide as normal. Conversely, the projector's lens threw onto the screen a magnified image in the proportion of 3x7 instead of the traditional 3x4.

Among the new wide movies held over at Loew's were a number of adventure movies and musical pageants. *Knights of the Round Table*, with Robert Taylor and Ava Gardner was the first of these, to be followed by *Rose Marie*, a

third remake starring Howard Keel and Ann Blyth, and *The Student Prince*, again with Ann Blyth.

Popular "women's pictures" at Loew's in 1955 included biopics about ambitious and talented women singers whose careers tellingly ended in disaster: five weeks of *Love Me or Leave Me*, (with Doris Day and James Cagney) recounting the tragic demise of 20s torch singer Ruth Etting, was followed immediately by five weeks of *Interrupted Melody* (starring Glenn Ford and Eleanor Parker) which portrayed opera singer Marjorie Lawrence succumbing to polio. In the same vein, *I'll Cry Tomorrow,* starring Susan Hayward, dealt with the alcohol-inspired ruination of Lilian Roth. (It played for three weeks at Loew's in 1956.)

Comedy remained an important genre in the CinemaScope era. Two popular movies at Loew's based on Broadway plays dealt humorously with Americans confronting the quaint mores of older cultures. Set in Japan and starring Marlon Brando and Glenn Ford, *Teahouse of the August Moon* was held over for eight weeks in 1957. Nine weeks in 1958 were devoted to *The Reluctant Debutante*, a play about an American teenager in Britain, filmed with Sandra Dee, Rex Harrison and Kay Kendall.

These were eclipsed by the ten-week run in 1959 of a milestone film comedy, *Some Like It Hot*, starring Marilyn Monroe, Jack Lemmon and Tony Curtis. Comedies — like *Operation Petticoat*, *Don't Go Near the Water*, *Come September*, and *Please Don't Eat the Daisies* — enjoyed particularly long runs at Loew's. Few "films noires" were screened, and hard-hitting and provocative movies like *Blackboard Jungle*, *Bad Day at Black Rock*, *The Last Hunt*, and *The Defiant Ones* did not last longer than two weeks. Certain domestic melodramas had long runs of six to eight weeks: *Not as a Stranger*, *Some Came Running*, *Separate Tables*, and *Butterfield 8*. A few thrillers had comparable longevity: *Witness for the Prosecution*, and *North by Northwest*.

The fad for wide movies urged on the widening of proscenium openings in older theatres like Loew's. Some prognosticators of future trends had anticipated enthusiasm for extra-wide "Cinerama" movies which employed three synchronized projectors and an even wider, curved screen. A promotional film had been introduced in New York 1952 and was greeted with public excitement, but the enterprise was stalled by financial and technical difficulties. The film, *This is Cinerama*, a two-hour travelogue which began with an impressive roller coaster ride, was installed (to mixed reviews) in Toronto's University Theatre in 1957. The first story film in Cinerama, *How the West was Won*, was not made until 1962, in a period when a new and much more turbulent order reigned at Loew's and M-G-M.

Neither this nor any other Cinerama movie was shown at Loew's in Toronto. The problems and money-losing propensity of this expensive and cumbersome process were never worked out, but the chimera seems to have inspired the most sweeping renovations of the lower theatre in 1960-61.

THE SIXTIES

The lower auditorium was dramatically altered by having its boxes, proscenium arch and columns removed to accommodate a Cinerama screen (though one was never actually installed). The auditorium seating was reduced to a total of 1641. The balcony front and part of its soffit were pared down and denuded of ornament to accommodate new balcony flood lights and "to obtain better sight lines" from the rear of the orchestra. The new colour scheme of the auditorium ceiling was "sand, beige and aquamarine (just a touch)." The grand staircase disappeared from public view behind a new partition wall and ceiling, and lobby and foyer doors were eliminated in three locations.

Draperies were an important component of the redecoration, but served to hide concrete blocks and demolished features instead of adding glamour and suspense. Post-renovation views showing the stage and sidewall arches shrouded with draperies have an almost funereal air. The movies and the theatre certainly weren't what they used to be.

The Winter Garden had barely escaped "Chinese modern" and remained undisturbed. Its seats and organ were sold off. It was an obsolete theatre, an anachronism which only managed to survive because the theatre below it made money and it was not worth the while of the owners to demolish it. The downstairs theatre had been significantly transformed. A vaudeville-and-movie patron transported from the 'teens or twenties into the modernized auditorium would not have recognized the place. That the theatre was not completely gutted is probably testimony to reluctance to spend money and forgo profits during a long and expensive renovation or rebuilding period. Features which had been among the most important in the original theatre were now liabilities.

Its stage and backstage were virtually useless, retained only because they were not in the way, and just in case there was money to be made occasionally by mounting a live show. The orchestra pit and organ were similarly defunct. The proscenium arch and dome chandelier had been removed because they caught reflected light and inhibited the installation of a modern screen. Acoustics, raked seating, and sight lines suiting live theatre and small screens had little relevance to a wide-screen sound movie presentation. Washrooms which had been adequate for continuous show audiences were maddeningly overcrowded during intermissions. The theatre's large seating capacity made it expensive to heat and clean, and made small audiences feel self-conscious and uncomfortable. The theatre's decor, originally a source of elation and fantasy, had also become a liability, expensive to maintain, and evidence of an embarrassing and unprogressive unwillingness to embrace the modern age.

The lobby corridor to Yonge Street with two sets of doors eliminated. The elevators are still visible (they continued to be used for candy and popcorn storage) but the grand staircase has just disappeared behind a partition wall.

In the 60s, M-G-M was not the studio it used to be, either. It issued only 19 releases in 1960, and didn't have even one big hit in 1961. It was clearly losing its grasp on public taste, and its enormous mass audiences were now addicted to watching television instead of going out to the movies. The iron clutches and unrelenting wills of primordial studio head Louis B. Mayer and President Schenck had been dislodged, and the rest of the old conservative guard who had worked with Marcus Loew was disappearing. The new regime and diminished profits spawned frequent internecine warfare and shareholder revolt, deflecting the struggle to adapt to youthful audiences and to unpredictability spawned by the loosening bonds of censorship. [13]

Loew's theatres were required to cater with a new product to new audiences, new schedules, and new standards of public taste. Loew's in Toronto screened a swelling number of "adult" and "restricted" movies, virtually unknown in the innocent, glory years of M-G-M. Loew's had always shown movies with sophisticated or adult themes, but these were not legally off-limits to youthful members of a family. (Restricted movies — all of which would be now innocuous television fare — shown at Loew's in

View towards the proscenium arch of the modernized auditorium, with drapery hiding the removal of opera boxes, proscenium columns and proscenium arch.

1961 were *It Started with a Kiss*, with Glenn Ford and Debbie Reynolds, *Goodbye Again*, with Ingrid Bergman and Yves Montand, and *Town without Pity* with Kirk Douglas).

Nonetheless, extended runs of a few musicals — *The Unsinkable Molly Brown* and *How to Succeed in Business Without Really Trying* — continued to minister to the family trade, as did assorted thrillers and comedies like Doris Day and James Bond movies. Not much had changed since the bad old days of monopolies in the industry: most movies shown at Loew's were M-G-M and United Artists releases.

SECOND-RUN MOVIES AND THE YONGE STREET "STRIP"

But the theatre was slowly losing its prestige as a first-run house. In the 60s, such supercolossal new movies from M-G-M as *Mutiny on the Bounty*, *Dr. Zhivago* and *2001: A Space Odyssey* did not enjoy first runs there. Instead, it screened double bills of revivals and reruns, just like any other neighbourhood cinema: *Seven Brides for Seven Brothers* was shown with *Father of the Bride*; *An American in Paris* with *Brigadoon*. Second-run double bills included James Bond movies, other films featuring the same star (Melina Mercouri in *Topkapi* and *Never on Sunday*), and violent films (*Dirty Dozen* paired with *Point Blank*).

In August 1969 came the announcement that 20th-Century Theatres was buying both the "Uptown" and "Downtown" Loew Theatres. The sale was part of a divestment frenzy under a new Loew regime headed by airline and hotel magnate Kirk Kerkorian and former television executive James T. Aubrey Jr. They got rid of theatres in Australia and India, M-G-M's studio in Britain, the M-G-M Record Company, and its overseas music publishers. The corporation's lucrative and less risky hotel and gambling interests took precedence.

In Toronto, Loew's "Downtown" escaped the fate of the Uptown Theatre, which would soon to be divided into 5 cinemas. The new ownership would be most notably manifested in a change of name. 20th-Century eased into this by reverting briefly to 1913. "Loew's YONGE Street" Theatre was advertised in January 1970, and "The Yonge" the following month. The choice of the new name not only called upon a 57-year tradition, but, more importantly, it saved money. Because YONGE used the same number of letters as LOEWS, the existing upright sign could continue to be used. Patrons were urged to "Think Yonge!" by attending the double bill inaugurating the new name, a "special encore engagement" of *The Graduate* — a 1968 film — paired with *The Producers*, released in 1967.

20th-Century had promised no change of policy for the lower theatre. Nevertheless, as the surrounding Yonge Street area developed a reputation as a teenage hangout and a tough neighbourhood, fewer long runs, even fewer first runs, and more variety of studio product was in evidence at The Yonge, along with more and more sex, sadism and horror. Double bills in 1972 and 1973 coupled *The Lustful Vicar* with *The Amorous Headmaster* and *Maid in Sweden* with *Her Bed a Battlefield. Children Shouldn't Play with Dead Things* was offered with *And Now the Screaming Starts; Raw Meat* with *Cry Out In Terror.* The Yonge ushers were sometimes dressed as ghouls to promote these offerings, which came so thick and fast in 1974 that the theatre's manager queried the line-up: "Horror programs are fine, but so many all in a row? If this keeps up we'll have to put our ushers in monster costumes all the time, instead of uniforms." [15]

The movie screen at the Yonge was also awash with blood baths and kung fu fighting: the manager reflected ruefully on the experience of *Five Fingers of Death*, "...Business was much better than usual and much better than we deserved....The theatre took a worse beating than usual, but with this kind of business, it was worth it." [16] Violence and soft porn were sometimes double billed: *Swinging Barmaids* and *Contract Killers* in October 1975 was followed by *Super Manchu* and *Fraulein Without a Uniform*, and by *Crazy Killers* and *Hot and Naked.*

The stage and backstage came alive twice in 1974: for a Martial Arts Demonstration attached to an action-packed double bill, and for *Cin-A-Rock*, a live show which was "a complete flop" and which had to close after three days "...after much rationalizing from all connected with it." Stepping into the breach, *Creeping Flesh* and *My Son the Vampire* were far more successful in attracting audiences, in spite of not being advertised. "At least," reported the manager optimistically, "our stage is now ready for future productions." [17]

Another glimmer of promise came with another name change in March 1978. The new name, The Elgin, was meant to dispel unfavourable associations. Conveniently, ELGIN also had five letters, and three of them used in the "Yonge" upright sign— the E,G, and N — could be recycled. Vowing an "elegant new look" and "a totally new policy of fine first-run films," the Elgin opened with the "all new family fun feature," *Here Come the Tigers.* It soon slipped into the recent patterns of second-run movies. At Christmas time and in summer holidays,

Puppet on a Chain, which had its North American premiere at the Yonge cinema.

A scene from C.B.C. TV's the Whiteoaks of Jalna filmed in the Winter Garden in 1971.

SPECIAL EVENTS AND PREMIERES DURING THE 60S AND 70S

Very occasionally, something special still happened at the complex. In the lower theatre, "Mr. Universe," David Draper, made a personal appearance in the lower theatre in June 1967 in conjunction with *Don't Make Waves*, an adult beach movie in which he had a small role and Kirk Douglas did the same in connection with the gala Canadian premiere of *Scalawag* in October 1973.

The theatre advertised its selection as the site of various "World" and "North American" premieres, among them *The Champagne Murders, Alfred the Great, Puppet on a Chain* and *Flick It!... It's All There.*

Unknown to the general public, the Winter Garden came to life at least four times in the 60s and 70s. In connection with the World Premiere of *Theatre of Blood* with Vincent Price and Diana Rigg, the upper theatre was used for a post midnight show party at which "Bloody Vincents and "Poodle Pudding" were served. Some enthusiastic guests arrived in a hearse.

On other occasions, it hosted camera crews and actors. In 1963-4 it was the setting for *Roses in December*, an independent Canadian feature by Graham Gordon (never released). Its story revolved around a couple who reopen the old theatre. [14] In 1971 an episode of the CBC's *Whiteoaks of Jalna* was filmed there, the Winter Garden being tricked out with tables and chairs to resemble a cabaret, popular with Canadian soldiers on their way to the trenches of World War I. It was a site for criminal chasing in a Telly Savalas made-for-TV movie, *The Girl Who Cried Murder* in July of 1973.

Fantasia and *Once Upon a Mouse* would again attract children to a theatre whose more typical stock in trade was *Bruce Lee Fights Back from the Grave* coupled with *Kung Fu Massacre*, or *Love Under 17* with *Sensuous Dolls*.

The theatre's large capacity and fine projection facilities earned it a brief reprieve in September 1979 in a two-week booking of the Festival of Festivals (the Toronto equivalent of Cannes). For the first time in many years, the theatre screened some of the best new movies, and hosted prominent critics, and Government and entertainment industry celebrities. Though not widely realized at the time, this event was a turning point in the history of the complex.

Second-run double bills resumed at the Festival's close. The theatre ended its career as a movie house two years later, in 1981. The last movies offered were three single features: two 3-D movies, *Comin' at Ya!* and *Dynasty*, and *What the Swedish Butler Saw*. Then, on 14 November it was closed ignominiously because of outstanding work orders.

Significant plans for its rebirth were already in the works. The Province of Ontario bought the complex in December. The battered Elgin, a Cinderella of a theatre forced into a regime of rough treatment, would be gloriously transformed, and the silent and deserted Winter Garden, a Sleeping Beauty, would awaken.

145

CHAPTER TWELVE

REBIRTH

Within the mandate of the Ontario Ministry of Culture and Communications is the enrichment and stimulation of the Province's cultural life. To these ends, it provides grants, awards, and incentives to theatre companies, both directly and through its arm's-length funding agency, The Ontario Arts Council. The Ministry provides support for both the profit sector and the not-for-profit sector of the theatre industry in the province, when they are community-based and promote excellence.

The purchase of the Elgin and Winter Garden theatres in 1981 was initiated by the Ministry to serve a thriving theatre community hampered by a severe shortage of purpose-built and economically viable performance space. In 1981, Toronto was the third largest producer of English-speaking theatre in the world (after New York and London). It boasted nearly 150 professional and amateur theatre companies, but the city suffered from a notable dearth of mid-sized theatres (seating between 800 and 1,600) into which a long-running success could be established or transferred.

Within Toronto's inventory were dinner theatres, cabarets, recital halls, and numerous small theatres imaginatively established in such existing buildings as a bakery, a church, an electronics factory, a machine shop, a fire hall, a recreation centre and a morgue. The 1907 Royal Alexandra was the only mid-sized commercial theatre in the city. At the time it was a "road house," solidly booked with foreign tours mounted by Broadway or West End producers. (The O'Keefe Centre, a multi-purpose civic auditorium seating 3,200 which opened in 1960, was also fully engaged with foreign road shows, opera and ballet.)

The scarcity of available theatre space in Toronto had incited two 1978 feasibility studies funded by the Ministry. Both of these studies recommended that the Elgin and Winter Garden be restored for live use, and were an impetus to the Government's acquisition. The purchase and restoration of two existing downtown theatres was a far less expensive proposition than the planning and

The lobby corridor, restored in 1984 to give patrons an appreciation of and taste for the completed restoration project.

View of the Elgin auditorium in 1984, about to be readied for the Canadian production of CATS.

In 1987, a basement is excavated under the lobby corridor, and the grand staircase is suspended in the air. Sheets of plywood cover and protect the restored finishes of the lobby corridor above.

construction of two new first-class theatres of comparable seating capacities. The estimated cost of one such new theatre was between $50 and $75 million, not including land acquisition. By comparison, the Elgin and Winter Garden theatres were a bargain, and would also further important historic preservation goals of the Ministry.

As previously mentioned, another spur to the rebirth of the theatres occurred in the Elgin in September 1979, during the Festival of Festivals. Culture and Recreation Minister Reuben Baetz referred in his gala address to the long twilight sleep of the "lost" Winter Garden theatre waiting to be reawakened above, and to the possibility of establishing the Elgin as the permanent base of the Festival of Festivals. These somewhat impromptu remarks generated agreeable press and public excitement.

Within days of the order to close the Elgin on 14 November 1981, Baetz announced that the Government of Ontario would buy and restore the building. The Ontario Heritage Foundation, dedicated to the preservation of the Province's historical, architectural and natural heritage, was the logical beneficiary.

Because the Ministry was obliged to find a means of making the project self-financing, a development agreement with a private operator was signed in December 1981. This failed in 1983, for a variety of reasons. Ministry officials and Ontario Heritage Foundation Board members nonetheless persevered in pursuing the Elgin and Winter Garden project. Its stated goal was "...to restore and revitalize this vintage theatre facility into a economically viable heritage, cultural and economic resource for the live performing arts industry in Canada and the people of Ontario, and to provide new opportunities and incentives for the growth and development of an indigenous commercial theatre industry in Ontario."

Concurrently, the process which resulted in the designation of the complex as a National Historic Site was underway. (In June 1982 the Minister of the Environment, on the advice of the Historic Sites and Monuments Board of Canada, declared that the Winter Garden was of national historic importance. The same designation for the Elgin followed later.) These declarations served to confirm the historical and architectural importance of the building and added impetus to the Province's plans. They would also pave the way for a later cost-sharing agreement.

The support of the public sector professionals and public sector funding ensured that the building would be restored to international standards, befitting its status as a national historic site. At the same time, this unique heritage building was to be a functioning monument, a formidable cultural and economic resource which could stand as a model for future development. As such, it was essential that the theatres be run by experienced and independent theatre operators, with the means and commitment to enable these essential economic and cultural objectives to be realized.

A giant leap forward came in 1984. The Canadian producers of Andrew Lloyd Weber's CATS negotiated a license with the Foundation to present in the Elgin a long run of this show, with a Canadian cast. To this end, the theatre was "retrofitted," brought up to code, and the auditorium was painted black. This merely added another easily removable coat to layers of paint which already covered original colour schemes and finishes.

In time for the CATS opening in March 1985, the Foundation had restored the original finishes of the lobby corridor, with the intention of giving patrons a taste and enthusiasm for the completed restoration. Consultant David Hannivan trained a team hired through the Youth Corps Employment Programme to apply gilding, repair scagliola and marbleize surfaces of the colonnaded entrance from Yonge Street. For the first time in decades, the theatre's patrons were welcomed by a sumptuous vista of richly glazed gilding and high-quality scagliola work. The restored lobby corridor was so stunning that some believed that the restoration was finished, and reported that the Elgin was already a "beautiful" theatre.

The Elgin adapted quite well to its new purposes. The 1960 removal of its boxes and proscenium arch meant that the enormous, sprawling CATS set could be accommodated with minimum disruption in the surviving historic building. The CATS orchestra was stationed in the second story loft above the lobby. Its music was mixed in a computerized sound board and carried through 22 speakers scattered through the auditorium. Orchestra members viewed the show on video monitors, and were allowed the luxury of dressing casually. Their conductor, in turn, cued and conducted the cast using video monitors mounted on the set and the balcony face.

CATS proved the viability of theatre, ending gloomy predictions that patrons could not be enticed at top prices to this site. In its two-year run, this musical spectacle grossed $40 million and entertained over one million people. Canadian theatre professionals had new opportunities for employment and broadened their skills and experience. Merchants on Yonge Street reported its salutary

One of the three historic elevators, equipped with new machinery, is reinserted into its shaft.

impact on pedestrian traffic and commerce, and more tourist dollars were attracted to the city and the province. (The economic impact of CATS at the Elgin was conservatively estimated at $96 million, or 2.4 times the amount spent on the theatre tickets.)

CATS highlighted three main problems with the building (all remedied in the subsequent renovation). Sight lines from the rear of the balcony were poor, there was a paucity of intermission and toilet room space for the public, and insufficient dressing room, lounge, assembly and storage space backstage. These deficiencies were no reflection on Thomas Lamb's abilities as a theatre architect. After all, he had designed the theatre for continuous vaudeville shows, without intermissions or refreshment sales, with only the minimum facilities required for the public and for the few dozen performers on the vaudeville bill. The balcony had been raked for movie shows, not for the CATS stage which was thrust into the auditorium.

Thus, the Elgin faced extraordinarily tricky demands for which it had not been designed — intermissions and bar sales, a cast and crew numbering over 100, a massive 3-dimensional set, and a show lit by a multitude of lighting instruments which spilled into the auditorium and extended right to the top of the proscenium. On the whole, the theatre performed gallantly, and the vast majority of patrons and performers thoroughly enjoyed the CATS experience.

It closed in March 1987. A two-and-a-half year construction and restoration period ensued which

CATS opens in the Elgin in March 1985, and closes two years later, having grossed $40 million and entertained over one million people.

Above: The Winter Garden's 75th birthday party, held across the street at the Eaton Centre, on 15 February 1989. Torontonians connected with its history cut the cake: Marg Johnstone and Maxine Allaway, daughters of long-time stationary engineer "Mac" Allaway (far left and second from right), Elsie Bennie, performer in two amateur shows at Loew's in 1924 (second from left), Jeanne Piggott (far right) who danced in one of Loew's amateur shows in 1922, Wally Ward, the head usher in 1927 (rear), Emma Levine (centre), who played the piano and danced in *Springtime*, a Junior Hadassah benefit show in the Winter Garden in 1924; and Walter Stockdale (third from right), who regilded part of the dome of the lower theatre in 1913 and painted railings and window frames in the Winter Garden.

Above: In 1987 Milton Berle revisits the theatre in which he had three engagements as a vaudevillian.

Right: H.R.H. Prince Edward is given a tour by Project Manager Janis Barlow and Ontario Heritage Foundation Chairman Richard Alway.

SELLING AND FINANCING THE PROJECT

The building cost $4.5 million, a sum derived from Lottario funds. The City of Toronto permitted, as its substantial contribution to the project, the sale and transfer of density rights for the site, an arrangement which would garner $7 million for the Province. (Since $3 million from the sale and transfer of density rights was returned to the Province's general account, the building's actual cost in public funds was $1.5 million, leaving $4 million to help fund the restoration.) The $29 million project has been funded by a variety of sources. The Province and the Federal Government have contributed $12.2 million under the terms of the Economic and Regional Development Agreement (ERDA) and its subsidiary Canada/Ontario Cultural Development Agreement. The Historic Sites and Monuments Board of Canada's designation made possible a later cost-sharing agreement with the Canadian Parks Service, one which provided $490,000 to defray restoration costs in 1988-9. The Toronto Historical Board contributed $5000 towards the restoration. One million was contributed by the commercial operator, in accordance with the terms of the licence agreement.

In an ongoing campaign, $7 million is anticipated from private and corporate donations. A portion of this revenue was raised by a "seat sale." Elgin and Winter Garden seats were endowed by donors, who were entitled to an engraved brass plaque on the arms of their seats, a tax receipt and a fine art poster.

In order to raise funds from private sources, the project needed to be in the public eye. Every opportunity was taken to obtain press coverage, from such occasions as the Winter Garden's 75th birthday party, leaf removal and harvesting operations, and a visit by ex-vaudevillian Milton Berle. An elaborate and superbly crafted model of the finished project, displayed at such sites as the Eaton Centre, the Canadian National Exhibition and the Toronto Public Library, assisted in winning attention for and believers in the project. So did the numerous volunteers who manned the display and offered slide presentations at historical societies, senior citizens' residences, church and community groups, and service clubs. Volunteers also saved money by their donations of manual labour — stringing beads for restored chandeliers and harvesting and painting beech branches.

saw bulldozers and backhoes performing in the auditorium and stage house. They excavated a new basement under the auditorium and lobby to yield administrative offices, new washrooms and a lounge. (The latter is accessible from Victoria Street and can be rented for private functions.) The renovation has included much needed new mechanical and electrical systems, and new roofing. Five floors of cascading lounges with escalators were built over the lobby corridor. Recessed behind the original second storey parapet, they allow the restored historic façade to dominate the pedestrian vista. Similarly, a new eight-storey backstage addition serves both theatres without invading the intricate interrelationship of the original stage houses. It is acoustically and structurally a separate entity.

Some of the original vaudeville scenery in the complex is used to decorate the new lobby additions.

Major problems reported during CATS have been remedied. The balconies in the auditoria have been restepped to yield improved sightlines for live performance. New additions have attached nearly 7000 square metres to the complex. They incorporate abundant public lounges and toilets, administrative offices, and loading, assembly and rehearsal spaces, along with crew, prop, wardrobe and green rooms, carpenter's rooms, dressing rooms, and quick change rooms. The complex's multi-purpose orientation is evidenced in two rehearsal halls which can function as sound studios or as reception rooms. The additions improve substantially the public, production and administration effectiveness — thus the commercial viability — of the theatre complex, and have been integrated in a manner sympathetic to the original architecture.

As much as possible, the historic theatres have been left intact, including two archaic Winter Garden toilet rooms, virtually unchanged since 1914. These unusual relics will be available for display only. One dressing room has been restored and refurnished to the original period, and the Winter Garden's dimmer board has been retained in a backstage display. The historic passenger elevators in the complex have been refurbished and restored to use.

Some new elements have been introduced into historic spaces to conform with current requirements. These include first aid rooms, wheelchair positions and a hearing-impaired system, concession bars, an enlarged orchestra pit and an acoustical enhancement system in the Elgin, and a stage-level VIP/green room in the Winter Garden. Every effort has been made to avoid permanently disfiguring the auditoria with modern lighting instruments and their supports. Solutions found include the installation of moveable battens and trusses, and carving out as unobtrusively as possible panels in unornamented areas of the Elgin's dome.

New washrooms are located in the mezzanine corridor of the Elgin, reopened to a cross over for the first time in decades. To facilitate audience traffic, elevator stops have been established on the mezzanine level of the grand staircase and an escalator begins at the level of the second floor loft above the lobby corridor. The loft, formerly used as storage space, is now converted into a modern lounge whose expansive arched windows and balcony overlooking Yonge Street can be enjoyed by theatre patrons. A new stair bridge links this lounge and the lobbies above with the grand staircase.

Following a request for proposals in 1987 and a rigorous selection process, The Ontario Heritage Foundation announced in April 1988 that WGC Facility Management Corporation would manage and operate the Elgin and Winter Garden complex. Principals in this company are Marlene Smith and Ernie Rubenstein. They have been in partnership for nearly 20 years, producing and co-

Marlene Smith and Ernie Rubenstein of WGC Facility Management.

producing commercially successful theatre in Toronto, and have presented and encouraged original Canadian plays and musicals like *What's a Nice Country Like You Doing in a State Like This*, and *Tonight at 8:30...9 o'Clock in Newfoundland*. Smith and Rubenstein gained intimate knowledgè of the building during the 2-year run of their production of CATS and they had come to treasure its unique heritage. They welcomed the opportunity to bring both stages back to life, showcasing first-class live theatre with a minimum of 60% Canadian content, as specified in the Government's request for proposals.

According to the terms of the agreement, the operators are fully responsible for the operation, maintenance and programming of the two theatres and the costs incurred in carrying out these responsibilities. Fifty cents per ticket sold is allocated to a capital maintenance fund. No alterations or renovations to the building can be undertaken without prior written approval of The Ontario Heritage Foundation. The Province derives a monthly license fee, and a share of net profits, as well as a surcharge of 50 cents per ticket which will establish and contribute to a Theatre Development Fund upon which Canadian theatre producers can draw.

Marlene Smith and Ernie Rubenstein intend to manage and operate in this unique and historic complex in such a manner as to ensure that it is a "beehive of activity." While its self-contained spaces can be appropriately rented, the two theatres and their additions will be largely devoted to world-class commercial productions with appeal to all sections of the community. These will employ Canadian technical staff and performers and will capitalize on the differing ambience and sizes of the two theatres. Smaller, more intimate, and less technical shows are foreseen for the Winter Garden, some of which will use its original vaudeville scenery.

Other plans include offering senior citizens and other specialty groups programming, lunch time theatre, and apprenticeship programmes in the technical and performing arts. Smith and Rubenstein hope to create a whole new audience of theatregoers, along with ever-increasing demand for Canadian theatrical product.

Over 1,400 direct and indirect jobs will have resulted from the construction, restoration and reopening of the theatres, and their continued operation will bring a broad range of economic benefits. The incentives provided to Canadian theatre will have a far-reaching impact on the cultural life of the Province and the country. The complex already stands as a beacon, illuminating and encouraging the revival of other vintage theatres. And, perhaps best of all, all of this will flow from the preservation and restoration of a unique survivor, perhaps the last remaining historic and fully intact double-decker theatres in the world.

ENDNOTES

INTRODUCTION

1 "At Opening of New Theatre," *Daily News*, 16 December 1913, p. 4.
2 *The Canadian Newspaper Directory*, Toronto A. McKim, 1913, p. 82.
3 *The Canada Year Book , 1913* (Ottawa: King's Printer, 1914), p. 93. See also Frederick H. Armstrong, *Toronto: The Place of Meeting* (Burlington, Ontario: Windsor Publications, 1983), p. 135; *Toronto of To-day, To Commemorate the Twelfth International Geological Congress*, (Toronto: Morang, 1913), p. 20.

CHAPTER ONE

1 Robson Black, "The Theatrical Field in Canada, " *The New York Dramatic Mirror*, 8 January 1913, p. 4.
2 *Toronto Sunday World*, 7 December 1913, p. 8.
3 City of Toronto, *Report on a Survey of the Treasury, Assessment, Works, Fire and Property Departments*, prepared by the Civic Survey Committee, New York Bureau of Municipal Research, Nov.-Dec. 1913 (hereafter cited as *Civic Survey*), pp.176-79.
4 The Sheas had operated a Shea's theatre at 91-3 Yonge Street between 1899 and 1910. It was a renovated building which seated about 1500, and had two balconies, minimal washroom and lounge space, and a serious shortage of exits. The Sheas abandoned this theatre in 1910. It was then leased to motion picture interests and renamed the Strand. As Lawrence Solman reported to Lee Shubert in 1923, the Strand had a "really wonderful" location, but was "an old theatre built many years ago as a museum." It had a "terrible gallery," about 12 dressing rooms, and a "fair stage," but was "not fireproof by any means." Solman considered it "a firetrap" which had been "sort of overlooked" by the authorities. Shubert Archive, Solman file 180, Solman to Lee Shubert, 26 May 1923.
5 *Moving Picture World*, (hereafter cited as *MPW*) 29, 3 (15 July 1916), p. 410.
6 "Shea's Hippodrome," *Construction*, 8, 4 (April, 1915) p. 150. See also *Variety*, 34, 8 (24 April 1914) p. 31.
7 *Variety*, 29, 3 (20 December 1912), p. 52.
8 *Variety*, 29, 1 (14 February 1913), p. 5. The Toronto *World* headlined the project and published site plans on 7 February 1913.
9 City of Toronto Archives, RG 5 Series D, Boxes 17-19, Transcript, Judicial Investigation, City Architect's Department, hereafter cited as JICAD, p. 1338. See also "Our Veterans, " *Loew's Ink*, July 1926, p. 1.
10 JICAD, p. 340.
11 Archives of Ontario (hereafter cited as AO), RG 53, Series 41, Vol. 19, Extra Provincial Corporations, Licence Charter Book 19, Marcus Loew's Theatres Limited, p. 139.
12 AO, MU 908, Dinnick Papers, correspondence.
13 R.S. McLaughlin to J. Bernstein, 29 July 1920, Private Collection.
14 Toronto *Sunday World*, 12 April 1914, p. 12.
15 JICAD, p. 1708.
16 Shubert Archive, file 180, J.J. Shubert to Solmon, 15 March 1914.
17 The Winter Garden," *Architecture and Building*, 43, 8 (May 1911), pp. 330-332.
18 Irving W. Cahn, "The Winter Garden," *The Metropolitan Host*, 13, 5 (9 August 1941), p. 6. See *Variety*, 29, 11 (14 February 1913), p. 5. and *Variety*, 61, 11 (7 November 1919), pp. 2, 11.

19 See Shubert Archive, Loew's Inc. file #295, Marcus Loew to J.J. Shubert, 31 Jan 1925; J.J. Shubert to Marcus Loew, 21 October 1919, Loew to J.J., 23 October 1919; Loew's claim that the American Roof used to be called the Winter Garden has not been corroborated. Loew may have been referring to the roof of New York's former Olympia theatre, a building in his possession since 1915. Its roof theatre was called the New York Winter Garden in 1901, but had been renamed the New York Roof Garden by 1902.
20 *Variety*, 34, 13 (29 May 1914), p. 1
21 *Motion Picture News*, 20, 21 (15 November 1919), p. 12.
22 Shubert Archive, file #180, Solman to Shubert, 29 June 1921. The only other comment on Loew's business provided by Solman was made in September 1914: although things did not look too bright for the Royal Alexandra because of the war, "...the cheap houses such as Shea's and Loew's are playing to good business." Solman to J.J., 16 Sept. 1914. This would change as the war continued. In 1918 *Moving Picture World* reported that "Canadian film interests were agreed that the moving picture business had been shot to pieces by influences of the war, war taxes, elections, Government bond issues, storms, conscription and other details." *MPW* , 36, 5 (4 May 1918), p. 684.

CHAPTER TWO

1 *Toronto World*, 12 April 1914, p. 12. *Saturday Night* erroneously referred to the complex as "one of the only two double-decker theatres in existence." 14 February 1914, p. 23.
2 He added, "The upper theatre is called the Winter Garden and is prettily decorated....I had the privilege of meeting Mr. Burnstein [sic] who showed me around the two theatres with evident and pardonable pride. *MPW*, 36, 6 (11 May 1918), p. 860.
3 Ruth Crosby Dimmick, *Our Theatres, To-day and Yesterday* (New York: H.K. Fly, 1913), p. 79.
4 Charles R. Sherlock, "Where Vaudeville Holds the Boards," *Cosmopolitan*, 32 (February 1902), p. 412.
5 Stephen Burge Johnson, *The Roof Gardens of Broadway Theatres, 1883-1942* (Ann Arbor, Michigan: UMI Research Press, 1985), p. 187.
6 *New York Clipper*, 17 September 1892, p. 439.
7 *Ibid.*, 10 and 24 August 1895.
8 *New York Times*, 20 September 1903, p. 22; see Johnson, p. 110.
9 Dimmick, p. 79.
10 From Harry Lines, "The New Amsterdam Aerial Gardens," in New Amsterdam Theatre," *Theatre Historical Society Annual*, 10 (1983), p. 27.
11 "Morris Roof Garden a Sylvan Bower," *New York Times*, 20 July 1909, p. 7.
12 "American Theatre Roof Garden, New York City. Thomas W. Lamb, Architect." *Architects' and Builders' Magazine*, 51, 12 (September 1909), pp. 494-7.
13 *Toronto World*, 7 February 1913, p. 1.
14 *Variety*, 29, 8 (24 January 1913), p. 5
15 *New York Times*, 31 December 1911, Part 8, p.2.
16 Writers Program, Ohio, *Cincinnati: a Guide to the Queen City...* (Cincinnati:Wiesen Hart Press, 1943), p. 284.

17 See Ben M. Hall, "Baltimore's Fabulous Double-Decker," *Marquee*, 2 (April 1970), pp. 2-5. See also Robert K. Headley, Jr. *Exit: A History of the Movies in Baltimore* (University Park, Maryland: The Author, 1974), pp. 58-59, 131.

CHAPTER THREE

1 Personal Communication, Stuart M. Lamb.
2 JICAD, p. 1800. See also *American Institute of Architects' Directory* (New York, 1892, 1895-6); *Key to the Architects of Greater New York* (New York: Forbes, 1900).
3 Philip Hamp, Unpublished Manuscript, "The Architecture of Thomas W. Lamb."
4 "Thomas W. Lamb Dies; Designed the Garden and 300 Theaters," *Herald Tribune*, 27 February 1942. See also Thomas W. Lamb, "Good Old Days to These Better New Days," *Motion Picture News*, Sect. 2 (30 June 1928), p.29.
5 *Architects' and Builders' Magazine*, 42 (June 1910), pp. 3514; See also Thomas W Lamb, p. 29.
6 Personal Communication, Michael R. Miller.
7 See J. Victor Wilson, "Strand Theatre, New York. Mr. Thomas W. Lamb, Architect" *The American Architect*, 106, 2022 (23 September 1914), pp. 183-186; *Architecture and Building*, 46 (6 June 1914), pp. 248-50. Lamb referred to the Strand as "the forerunner" of the large capacity movie palace of the 20s. Lamb, p. 19.
8 Unpublished Report of New York Landmarks Preservation Commission, 16 November 1987, Designation List 196. See also *Architecture and Building*, 45, 3 (March 1913), pp. 106-9.
9 See *Motion Picture News*, 7, 14 (5 April 1913), p. 11; *Ibid.*,8, 22 (6 December 1913), p. 28. See also Ben M. Hall, *The Best Remaining Seat: the Golden Age of the Movie Palace* (New York: Bramhall House, 1961), pp. 30-35.

CHAPTER FOUR

1 Correspondence, *Construction*, 9, 9 (September 1916), p. 308.
2 JICAD, p. 2462.
3 *Ibid.*, 2567. These fire towers in the Victoria Street and "court" (or alley) elevations were made much of in opening publicity.
"In the matter of fire protection it is the most perfect edifice of its kind in Canada...magnificent precautions have been taken against accident in case of panic from any cause. Mr. Lamb is the inventor of the enclosed fire tower, which provides ample facilities for emptying the theatre without obstructing the street. This is a deep shaft absolutely enclosed on the theatre side, but open from the street, extending from the roof to the sidewalk. It contains a wide winding stairway, the steps of which are gradual...and down which the audience can walk four abreast without crowding or jostling. Wide balconies from the various exits lead to this stairway, and both theatres could be emptied in good order in a very brief space of time." *Toronto Star Weekly*, 13 December 1913, p. 33.
4 City of Toronto Archives (hereafter cited as CTA), RG 2, Series A, Board of Control Minute Book 147l, City Clerk to McCallum, 9 May 1913.
5 *Ibid.*, Minute Book, 1556, Report No., 16, 16 May 1913. The 20' dimension of the

"passageway" to Yonge Street is a mystery. The lobby was neither 20' long nor 20' wide. It was 17' 9 1/2" wide for the length of the store (95 feet), and 37'6" wide for the remaining 74 feet of the length of the grand staircase and elevator lobby.
6 *Detroit Saturday Night*, 29 May 1915, p. 12.
7 JICAD, pp. 1322, 1336.
8 JICAD, p. 2468.
9 *Ibid.*, pp., 2468-9. The Victoria Street ticket booth was supposed to serve both theatres and had two windows. The window for the lower auditorium was located a few feet inside the door. The other faced the enclosed stairs from Victoria Street to the roof garden. Lineups to both ticket windows would have been difficult to manage. Patrons would have experienced an abrupt and disconcerting entrance to both theatres, devoid of pleasant introductions provided by lobbies and foyers. One entailed stepping from the street directly into the dimly lit downstairs auditorium, and the other an immediate and lengthy climb to the Winter Garden in a stairwell devoid of distraction and decoration.
10 *Ibid.*, p. l330. Lamb claimed that the section of the Toronto bylaw copied that of New York City, and he could show "a hundred or more built the same way in New York City under the same clause." He further argued, "we have 25 feet of legal exit on Victoria St." He was referring to New York bylaws requiring an exit not less than 25 feet wide in "one front on the street." He was not aware, apparently, that Toronto bylaws made no such stipulation.
11 "Loew's Yonge Street Theatre, Toronto," *Construction* 8, 4 (April 1915), pp. 132-43.
12 Charlotte Kopac Herzog, *The Motion Picture Theatre and Film Exhibition 1896-1932* (London: University Microfilms International, 1980), p. 85.

CHAPTER FIVE

1 R. W. Sexton and B. F. Betts, *American Theatres of Today*, (New York: Vestal, 1977 [Reprint of 1927 edition]), pp. 5, 9. In the core of many large cities, security concerns and trepidations of lone female attendants have lessened the appeal of the free-standing sidewalk ticket booth.
2 Edward Renton, *The Vaudeville Theatre: Building, Operation, Management* (New York: Gotham, 1918), p. 33, see also p. 96.
3 See AO RG3, 66/395, 1st June 1911, passed pursuant to I George V. Cap. 73.
4 Clarence H. Blackall, "The American Theater, III. Foyers and Anterooms." *Brickbuilder*, 17, 2 (February 1908), p. 24.
5 CTA, Toronto Bylaw 6401, April 1913, Section 66(2), p. 197.
6 Blackall, "The American Theater I". *Brickbuilder*, 16, 12 (December 1907), pp. 216-7; II, 17, 1 (January 1908), p. 2; III, 17, 2
7 Clement Scott, "The Playhouses," *Illustrated London News*, 12 December 1891. Clipping file, "Theatres: Concessions", Billy Rose Theatre Collection, Performing Arts Research Center, New York Public Library (hereafter cited as NYPL).
8 *MPW*, 20, 3 (18 April 1914), pp. 436-37.
9 *MPW*, 17, 2 (12 July 1913), p. 260.
10 Renton, p. 274. In any event, Renton thought that theatre owners needed to shun sales of rustling paper bags and chewing gum, and were not to tolerate a candy boy running in the aisles or seating himself in the theatre.
11 *MPW*, 40, 5 (3 May 1919), p. 726.

(February 1908), p. 23. American commercial theatres followed the English example in sacrificing crush room and foyer space to seating capacity. The ample amount of foyer space allocated by Continental theatres seemed extravagant and even wasteful, by comparison. See Mora Dianne Guthrie O'Neill, "A Partial History of the Royal Alexandra Theatre, Toronto, Canada, 1907-1939" Ph.D, Louisiana State University, 1976, p. 54.

12 Sexton and Betts, p. 24.

13 See Herzog, pp. 133-4.

14 Thomas W. Lamb, "Some High Lights in Motion Picture Theater Design," *The Architect and Engineer*, December 1929, pp. 53-54.

15 Quoted in John DiMeglio, *Vaudeville U.S.A.*, (Bowling Green: Bowling Green University Popular Press, 1973), p. 129.

16 CTA, RG 2, Series B 3, Board of Control Correspondence, Pearce to Hocken, 20 May 1914.

17 *Canadian Moving Picture Digest* (hereafter cited as *CMPD*), 23 June 1928, p. 8. See also *Daily Star*, 18 June 1928., p. 16.

CHAPTER SIX

1 Thomas Lamb, *Motion Picture News*, p. 37.

2 "Unique Features of New Toronto Theatres,"*Contract Record*, 21 January 1914, p.89.

3 Lamb, p. 37. Harold Rambusch provided the perspective of the movie palace decorator in a 1927 article in *American Theatres of Today*, Sexton and Betts, pp. 26-7.

4 *Telegram*, 17 February 1914, p. 21; *Toronto Star Weekly*, 14 February 1914, p. 26; *Toronto World*, 15 February 1914, p. 3.

5 *Motion Picture News*, 10, 6 (15 August 1914), p. 31.

6 *Ibid.*, 10, 24 (19 December 1914), p. 140.

7 Harold S. Kaplan, "Acoustics as a Decorative Ally," *Theatre Catalog* (Philadelphia: Jay Emanuel,1941), p. 158.

8 Walter Sobotka, "Hints on Remodeling Obsolete Auditoriums," *Theatre Catalog*, 1945, p. 162.

9 Quoted in Ross Thorne, *Cinemas of Australia via USA* (Sydney: University of Sydney, 1981), p. 24.

10 "Loew's Yonge Street Theatre, Toronto." *Construction* 8, 4 (April 1915), p. 137.

11 *The Builder*, 15 October 1915, p. 275.

12 *Toronto Daily News*, 17 February 1914, p. 13

13 Quoted in Herzog, p. 180.

CHAPTER SEVEN

1 Quoted in O'Neill, p. 54.

2 Gerald Lenton, "The Development and Nature of Vaudeville in Toronto from 1899 to 1915," Ph. D, University of Toronto, 1983, p. 457. Shea's Hippodrome, which opened in April 1914, was the second large vaudeville theatre in Toronto built with a single balcony.

3 William Albert Swasey, "A Few Essentials in Theatre Construction," *The American Architect*, 103, 1935 (22 January 1913), p. 54.

4 Renton, pp. 15.

5 Blackall, II, pp. 3-4.

6 JICAD, p. l326

7 Blackall, II, p. 4.

8 *CMPD*, 23 June 1928, p. 8

9 "New York Loft Building Fire an Object Lesson to Canadian Municipalities," *Construction*, 4, 8 (July 1911), p. 46.

10 *Globe*, 19 June l928, p. 14. See also *Toronto Daily Star*, 19 June 1928, p. 5.

11 *Mail & Empire*, 12 December 1913, p. 13.

12 Civic Survey, p. 186

13 City of Toronto, Central Records, Fire Prevention Branch, Register Book 208, Fire Report 000550.

CHAPTER EIGHT

1 Archival Collections, University of Guelph, X21 Ms A140, Engineer's Notebook, Toledo, Ohio, ca. 1897.

2 Blackall, "The American Theatre, IX. The Stage" *Brickbuilder*,17, 8 (August 1908) p. 164; see also William J. Birkmire, *The Planning and Construction of American Theatres*, (New York: Wiley, 1896), p. 95. The first American playhouse with a flat stage was Booth's Theatre in New York, completed in 1868. See Donald C. Mullin, *The Development of the Playhouse* (Berkley: University of California Press, 1970), p.131.

3 Edwin O. Sachs and Ernest A.E. Woodrow, *Modern Opera Houses and Theatres*. (New York: Benjamin Blom, 1968). Reprint of 1896-98 editions Vol. 3, p. 10 suppl.

4 Arthur S Meloy, *Theatres and Motion Picture Houses* (New York: Architects' Supply, 1916), p. 45.

5 Sophie Tucker with Dorothy Giles, *Some of These Days: The Autobiography of Sophie Tucker* (Garden City, N. Y.: Doubleday, 1945), p. 147.

6 Blackall, XI, "Stage Accessories." *Brickbuilder* 17, 10 (October 1908), pp. 232-3.

7 Tucker, p. 39.

8 C. Lance Brockman, "The Twin City Scenic Studio," in *The Twin City Scenic Collection* (Minneapolis: University of Minnesota, 1987), pp. 90-1.

9 *Lo!*, 15 April 1945, p. 15.

10 *Loew Down*, 1, 8(18 July 1930), p. 3.

11 Brockman, p. 48.

12 Blackall, IX, p. 164.; see also Mullin, p. 131.

13 Sachs and Woodrow, suppl., p. 13

14 Renton, p. 204.

15 *Mail and Empire*, 25 March 1916, p. 14.

16 See Andrew Johnson, "A Calendar of Vaudeville and Film Attractions at the Loew's Yonge Street Theatre and Winter Garden Theatre, 15 December 1913 to 16 June 1928", Unpublished Paper for Canadian Theatre History, University of Toronto, 1982.

17 "Theatre Illumination," *Architecture and Building*, 50, 1(January 1918), p. 4.

18 Lindsay Lambert, personal communication.

19 See Walter René Fuerst and Samuel J. Hume, *XXth Century Stage Decoration* (London: Knopf, 1928), p. 112.

CHAPTER NINE

1 AO, RG3, Orders in Council, No. 42/81, 6 February 1917.

2 Frederick E. Snyder, "American Vaudeville — Theatre in a Package. The Origins of Mass Entertainment," Ph. D., Yale University, 1970. p. 93.

3 Bill Smith, *The Vaudevillians* (NewYork: Macmillan, 1976), p. 7.

4 Toronto *World*, 24 February 1914, p. 4

5 Snyder, pp. 1-2.

6 Albee's statement appeared in the *New York Clipper* in February 1913. Quoted in Snyder, p. 3. See also Charles Stein, ed., *American Vaudeville as Seen by its Contemporaries* (New York: Knopf, 1984), pp. 179-81.

7 *Globe*, 10 October 1922, p.3.

8 Joe Laurie Jr., *Vaudeville from the Honky-Tonks to the Palace*, (Port Washington, N.Y.:Kennikat Press, 1967), p. 155.

9 *Globe*, 7 September 1920.

10 *Saturday Night*, 18 March 1916, p. 6.

11 Lenton, pp. 83-4.

12 Laurie, p. 212.

13 Quoted in Anthony Slide, *The*

Vaudevillians: a Dictionary of Vaudeville Performers (Westport, Ct.: Arlington House, 1981), p. xii.

14 See Snyder, pp. 123-128.

15 *Motion Picture News*, 8, 19(15 November 1913), p. 41.

16 Berlin wrote "The International Rag," the song described as "his latest," while crossing the Atlantic in the summer of 1913 for a London Hippodrome engagement. See Michael Freedland, *Irving Berlin*, (New York: Stein & Day, 1974), p. 43, and H. Wiley Hitchcock and Stanley Sadie, *The New Gore Dictionary of American Music*, Vol. 1, A-D, (New York: Macmillan, 1986), p. 193.

17 "Brilliant Opening at Loew's," *Telegram*, 16 December 1913, p. 21; "Big Audience Heard First Loew Program," *Toronto World*, 16 December 1913, p. 12, "Brilliant Opening for Loew's Theatre," *Globe*, 16 December 1913, p. 8.

18 According to Joe Laurie Jr., "Frank Stafford had a beautiful posing act with his dogs; he also was a fine whistler..." p. 161

19 *Variety*, 25 October 1913, p. 23. Robinson Locke Collection, Envelope 2004, NYPL.

20 Clipping file, Amoros and Mulvey, NYPL.

21 *Toronto World*, 17 February 1914.

22 *Sunday World*, 15 February 1914, p. 4.

23 *Toronto World*, 12 April 1914, p. 12.

24 *Mail and Empire*, 19 December 1916, p. 21.

25 Laurie, p. 221

26 *Globe*, 8 October 1918, p. 6.

27 "Pick Petite Sybil White for Local Jean Darling," *Evening Telegram*, 1 August 1928, p. 6.

28 National Archives (hereafter cited as Na) MG 28 196, Vol. 4, Proceedings of 15th Convention of the 11th District, International Alliance Theatrical Stage Employees and Moving Picture Operators of the United States and Canada, Peterborough, Ontario, June 1929, p.5.

CHAPTER TEN

1 "Terry Turner Turns the Spotlight on Managers from Maine to Memphis," *Loew's Ink*, August 1923.

2 "Honour Departing Manager," *Evening Telegram*, 21 September 1927

3 Renton, p. 198.

4 Marion Spitzer, "The Business of Vaudeville," in Charles Stein, *op cit*. p. 177.

5 Renton, p. 129, p. 137.

6 *Ibid.*, pp. 159-60.

7 AO, RG 4 C-3, #789, fol. 1 , W.W. Pearce to Hocken, 20 May 1914.

8 Renton, pp. 149-51, p. 265, 267.

9 *Motion Picture News*, 8, 22 (6 December 1913), p.28.

10 Stu Green, "Vaudeville: an Appreciation," *Marquee*, 3, 2 (Second Quarter, 1971), p. 16.

11 See *MPW* , 25 November 1916, p. 1206. See also Na, MISA, Bossin collection 80-B-1;, file 49; see also *The Canadian Who's Who*, Vol. 9, 1961-63 (Toronto: Trans Canada Press, 1963), p. 32.

12 Renton, p. 292.

13 Renton, pp. 296-7.

14 John E. DiMeglio, *Vaudeville, U.S.A.* (Bowling Green, Ohio: Bowling Green University Popular Press, 1973), p. 75.

15 See John C. Lindsey, *Turn Out the Stars Before Leaving* (Erin, Ontario: Boston Mills Press, 1983), p.121. In 1921, Ernest H. Dainty was listed by Toronto assessors as Loew's organist. See Kathleen M. Toomey and Stephen C Willis, eds., *Musicians in Canada: a Biobibliographical Finding List* (Ottawa: Canadian Association of Music Libraries, 1981).

16 Na, MG 28 I 96, Vol. 3, IATSE, Proceedings of 20th Convention, July 1912, p. 387.

17 See Na MG 28 I 96, Vol. 3, Combined Convention Proceedings, 1893-1926, p. 587;

Report of IATSE representative to Trade and Labour Congress of Canada to 22nd Convention, July 1915.

18 Western Vaudeville Managers' Association, *Vaudeville Year Book* (Vaudeville Year Book Co., 1914), p. 27.

19 Renton, p. 175

20 *Ibid.*, p. 166.

21 *Ibid* .,pp. 182-4.

22 Peter Harris, "Wanted: a Future for a Theatre with a Past," *Toronto Star*, 23 December 1967, p. 27.

23 RG3, Orders in Council, No. 62/353, Regulations for Moving Picture Machines, passed pursuant to 9 Edward VII (1909) Cap. 87; No. 87/223, Theatres and Cinematographs Act, R.S.O. 1914, Chapter 236; 7 May 1918.

24 *Marcus Loew's Theatres Limited*, The Financial Post Corporation Service, Toronto, rev. Jan. 1967.

CHAPTER ELEVEN

1 See John Douglas Eames, "Fade In," in *MGM: BFI Dossier Number 1* (London: BFI Publishing 1980), p. 6.

2 The store's tenant in 1935 was Helen McCombie's corsetry shop. It was replaced in 1939 by Jane Grey Hat Shop, an enterprise which remained at 191 Yonge until 1955.

3 *Globe*, 14 February 1935, p. 16.

4 See Gary Carey, *All the Stars in Heaven: Louis B. Mayer's M-G-M* (New York: Dutton, 1981), p. 244; Clayton R. Koppes and Gregory D. Black, *Hollywood Goes to War: How Politics, Profits, and Propaganda shaped World War II Movies* (New York: The Free Press, 1987), p. 34.

5 J.H. Clarke to District Manager C.E. Kurtzman, 22 August 1947, Ontario Heritage Foundation Collection.

6 See Paul Michael, ed., *The American Movies Reference Book: The Sound Era*, (Englewood Cliffs, N. J.: Prentice Hall, 1969), p. 14.

7 See Gary Carey, p. 255. A post-war sequel, "The Miniver Story," was much less engaging, and lasted only three weeks at Loew's Toronto theatre in 1950.

8 *Stage Door Canteen*, shown for seven weeks in 1943, was said to establish a new all-time high for a single engagement in Canada, playing to 279,887 people.

9 *CMPD*, August 27 1949, p. 4. Loew's business was expected to be adversely affected by the renovation, and consideration was being given to building a "new entrance" on Victoria Street, an ironic twist to the original and spurious claim that this was the theatre's main entrance.

10 See *CMPD*, 2 June 1951, p. 4. 15 September 1951, p.4. December 8, 1951, p.4.

11 Projector Bulletin, Dominion Sound Equipments Limited, 3-D film"Bwana Devil," Issue # 1, 16 March 1953. Ontario Heritage Foundation Collection. This bulletin is brimming with admonitions about misalignment of projectors and consequent eye strain.

12 See Leslie Halliwell, *The Film-goer's Companion*, (London: Granada Publishing, 1972), p. 950.

13 John Douglas Eames, *The MGM Story, The Complete History of over Fifty Roaring Years* (New York: Crown, 1975), p.296.

14 See *Globe and Mail*, 13 Feb. 1965, p. 13.

15 20th Century Theatres, Weekly Summary Report, Yonge Theatre, Toronto, Week Ending 18 April 1974, Private Collection.

16 *Ibid.*, Week Ending 26 April 1973.

17 *Ibid.*, 21 February 1974.

A NOTE ON SOURCES

ARCHIVES

A brief inventory of the most useful archival collections and periodical sources consulted follows. Complete bibliographical citations can be found in a larger, more detailed manuscript written for the Elgin and Winter Garden project team. A copy is deposited with The Ontario Heritage Foundation in Toronto.

TORONTO

Archives of Ontario
Orders in Council; files on extra provincial corporations; Theatres Branch records: files, photographs, blueprints, correspondence, inspections, licenses.

City of Toronto Archives and Central Records
City Architect's Department: 1914 judicial investigation, building permits, inspection records; minutes and files of City Council, Board of Control and Committee on Works; building bylaws, assessment rolls, city atlases, photograph collection.

Metro Toronto Central Library
Clipping files, architectural drawings and other documents re. Toronto theatres; John Ross Robertson and Toronto collections; Archindont Index to periodical articles on Ontario buildings.

NEW YORK

Billy Rose Theatre Collection, Performing Arts Research Center, New York Public Library
Vast and superbly indexed collection of clippings, photographs, scrapbooks and manuscripts relating to theatres and the entertainment world.

Drawing and Archives Collection of the Avery Architectural & Fine Arts Library, Columbia University
Thomas W. Lamb Collection: job book, large collection of drawings and blueprints, small and miscellaneous collection of photograph albums and specification books, office files.

Shubert Archive
Lawrence Solman and Loew's Inc. files, along with copious documentation on Shubert operations.

Theatre Collection, Museum of the City of New York
Exceptional New York theatre photographs and drawings of New York theatre facades; files on New York theatres and many other theatrical subjects.

CHICAGO

Archives of the Theatre Historical Society of America
Loew's Collection of photographs, architectural drawings and in-house magazines; large and diverse collection of photographs, publications and clipping files relating to theatres and movie palaces.

PERIODICALS

Construction in Canada and *Architecture and Building* and *The American Architect* in the United States were the richest sources of articles and published illustrations relating to early 20th-century theatre buildings in North America. *Marquee, the Journal of the Theatre Historical Society* is the current publication which meets this criteria.

Toronto newspapers and *Saturday Night* provided indispensable articles and details of the daily entertainment in the complex, but very few photographs of the building during the vaudeville period.

Such trade journals as *Variety, The Canadian Moving Picture Digest, The Moving Picture World,* and *The Motion Picture News* were indispensable to my research, as were City Directories, editions of Julius Cahn's *Theatrical Guide,* and the periodical entries in Richard H. Stoddard's *Theatre and Cinema Architecture: A Guide to Information Sources* (Detroit: Gale, 1978).

FURTHER READING

A list of available books and monographs not cited in endnotes follows:

American Theatre Planning Board. *Theatre Check List: A Guide to the Planning and Construction of Proscenium and Open Stage Theatres.* Middletown, Ct.: Wesleyan University Press, 1969.

Baillie, Joan Parkhill. *Look at the Record: An Album of Toronto's Lyric Theatres.* Oakville: Mosaic Press, 1985.

Bordman, Gerald. *The Oxford Companion to American Theatre.* New York: Oxford University Press, 1984.

Bowers, Q. David. *Nickelodeon Theatres and their Music.* Vestal, N.Y.: Vestal Press, 1986.

Burris-Meyer, Harold, and Edward C. Cole. *Theatres and Auditoriums.* New York: Van Nostrand Reinhold, 1964.

Edwards, Murray D. *A Stage in Our Past. English-language Theatre in Eastern Canada from the 1790s to 1914.* Toronto: University of Toronto Press, 1968.

Evans, Chad. *Frontier Theatre.* Victoria: Sono Nis Press, 1983.

Eyles, Allen. *London's West End Cinemas.* Sutton, Surrey: Premier Bioscope, 1984.

Glasstone, Victor. *Victorian and Edwardian Theatres: an Architectural and Social Survey.* Cambridge, Mass.: Harvard University Press, 1975.

Harmon, Robert B. *Perspectives on a Vanishing Series in Architecture - the Movie Palace: a Select Bibliography.* Monticello, Illinois: Vance Bibliographies, 1981.

Hartnoll, Phyllis, ed. *Oxford Companion to the Theatre,* 4th ed. New York: Oxford University Press, 1983.

Henderson, Mary C. *The City and the Theatre: New York Playhouses from Bowling Green to Times Square.* Clifton, N.J.: James T. White, 1973.

Izenour, George. *Theater Design.* New York: McGraw-Hill, 1977.

Junchen, David L. *Encyclopaedia of the American Theatre Organ.* Vol. 1. Pasadena: Showcase, 1985.

Lacloche, Francis. *Architectures de cinémas*, Paris: Editions du Moniteur, 1981.

Landon, John W. *Behold the Mighty Wurlitzer: the History of the Theatre Pipe Organ.* Westport, Ct.: Greenwood Press, 1983.

Lounsbury, Warren C. *Theatre Backstage from A to Z.* Seattle: University of Washington Press, 1967.

Martineau, Jocelyne. *Cinémas et patrimoine à l'affiche.* Québec: Ministère des Affaires culturelles, 1988.

McCallum, Douglas J. *Vancouver's Orpheum: the Life of a Theatre.* Vancouver: Social Planning Dept., 1984.

Morrison, Andrew Craig. *Opera House, Nickel Show and Palace.* Dearborn, Mich.: Greenfield Village and Henry Ford Museum, 1974.

Mullin, Donald C. *Development of the Playhouse..* Berkeley: University of California Press, 1970

National Trust for Historic Preservation. *Great American Movie Theaters.* Washington, D.C.: The Preservation Press, 1987.

Naylor, David. *American Picture Palaces: The Architecture of Fantasy.* New York: Van Nostrand and Reinhold, 1981.

Norman, Charles. *When Vaudeville was King: a Soft Shoe Stroll Down Memory Lane.* Melbourne: Spectrum Publications, 1984.

Rees, Terence. *Theatre Lighting in the Age of Gas.* London: The Society for Theatre Research, 1978.

Russell, Hilary. "All that Glitters: a Memorial to Ottawa's Capitol Theatre and its Predecessors." *Canadian Historic Sites No. 13: Occasional Papers in Archaeology and History.* Ottawa: Parks Canada, 1975.

Samuels, Charles and Louise Samuels. *Once Upon a Stage: the Merry World of Vaudeville.* New York: Dodd Mead, l974.

Sobel, Bernard. *A Pictorial History of Vaudeville.* New York: Citadel Press, 1961.

Thorne, Ross. *Picture Palace Architecture in Australia*, South Melbourne: Sun Books, 1976.

Tidworth, Simon. *Theatres, an Architectural and Cultural History.* New York: Praeger, 1973.

Trapido, Joel et al., eds. *An International Dictionary of Theatre Language.* Westport, Ct.: Greenwood Press, 1985.

Wagner, Anton, ed. *Contemporary Canadian Theatre: New World Visions.* Toronto: Simon and Pierre, 1985.

Wilmeth, Don B. *American and English Popular Entertainment: a Guide to Information Sources.* Vol. 7. Performing Arts Information Guide Series. Detroit: Gale Research Co., 1980.

ACKNOWLEDGEMENTS

This book could not have been written without the assistance and support of numerous people and research institutions. My primary indebtedness is to Janis Barlow, Manager of the Elgin and Winter Garden Theatres Project of The Ontario Heritage Foundation. Her expert and unwavering dedication to the rebirth of the theatre complex and to a comprehensive account of its history has been the driving force of the project and this book.

My appreciation must be expressed to all members of the Project staff (past and present) with whom I have worked closely and cordially. Among them, special recognition is owed to Kevin Harper and Natalie Rewa for outstanding and meticulous research assistance, and to Claire Smerdon, Christine Gutierrez and Marie Bekessy for their extremely capable and generous support. Jim Clarkson initiated the process with Dundurn Press and provided editorial comments. Project consultants Mandel Sprachman and Richard Smerdon shared their time and expertise. I also benefited from numerous consultations with members of the committed crew led by David Hannivan who quickly mastered the restoration of historic finishes as well as the preservation of Winter Garden beech boughs.

Acknowledgement is due to certain libraries and archives whose staff provided invaluable assistance. Along with all those engaged in research in theatre history in Canada, I am indebted to all the librarians of the outstanding Theatre Collection of Metro Toronto Library. Staff maintaining the Archives and Records of the City of Toronto offered unstinting and exceptional service. Karen Teeple, Alan Meisner, Randall Ross and Jim Bitaxi are those singled out for special thanks. Valuable assistance was provided by Judith McErvel of Eaton's Archives.

I was fortunate enough to visit superb collections in the United States, including the incomparable Billy Rose Theatre Collection at the Performing Arts Research Center of the New York Public Library, headed by curator Dorothy Swerdlove. Special thanks are also due to Janet Parks at the Drawing and Archives Collection of the Avery Architectural & Fine Arts Library, Columbia University, to Kathryn Mets of the Theatre Collection of the Museum of the City of New York, to Reagan Fletcher and Maryann Chach of the Shubert Archive, and to Terry Geesken of the Film Stills Collection, The Museum of Modern Art. I am also grateful to Bob Cosenza of the Kobal Collection. At the Archives of the Theatre Historical Society in Chicago, particular tribute is due to all its unpaid volunteers and its Director, William T. Benedict, whose persevering commitment and efficiency are a marvel, notwithstanding that the Archives is now stored in a Church basement and is normally open only one day a week.

My research was also expedited by other archivists and librarians too numerous to list. They work at the Archives of Ontario, the National Archives and National Library of Canada, the Baldwin Room and other collections at Metro Toronto Library, the Libraries and Archives of the University of Toronto, and the Archives of York University and Queen's University.

A large community of theatre scholars and dedicated theatre enthusiasts in Canada and the United States shared time and information with me. Among them, Stephen Burge Johnson was exceptionally generous. Many thanks are also owing to Gerald Lenton, Ross Stuart, Andrew Johnson, Robert Hunter, Heather McCallum, Paul Dilse, John Lindsay, Dane Lanken and David Dymond, and, on the other side of the border, to Michael R. Miller (who I could not have done without), and to Brother Andrew Corsini, Frank Cronican, Craig Morrison, Tom B'hend, Bill Frisk, Mike Young, Stuart Lamb, Daniel Harter and Mary Henderson. Among those who tutored me in their areas of specialized expertise were Jim Leworthy, H. Clealon Blakely, and David Legge (theatre organs), Bill Counter, Lyman Brenneman, Steve Weinrieb and Bruce Whitehead (theatre lighting) and Lance Brockman (theatrical scenery).

I am grateful to members of IATSE local 58 who furnished special insight into their work, and for gracious and informative interviews with Catha Grace Rambusch of Rambusch Studios, New York, and Andrew McCausland of Robert McCausland Ltd. of Toronto. For unforgettable and heart-stopping tours of two other surviving double deckers, I have to thank Theatre Consultant Roger Morgan in New York, along with Benjamin Weng and Tito in Newark.

Several remarkable people contributed documentation and detailed memories of their working involvement in the complex during the vaudeville period. Among them were Elsie Bennie, Wally Ward, the late Roy Tash, Arthur Benson, Jeanne Piggott, Emma Levine, Marg Johnstone, Maxine Allaway, Sybil Mines, Douglas Scott, Margery Wesley, Vera Teewiss and the late Walter Stockdale. Others linked with the history of Loew's to whom I am grateful include G. Leith Mackie, R.R. Cockburn, Pat O'Sullivan, Phyllis Clarke, and Charles Kurtzman. Among helpful people connected with Famous Players Limited were Dudley Dumond, Barrington Brown, Jack Bodam and Fern Marleau.

The Canadian Parks Service was extremely generous in allowing adequate time and other support for my research and writing. For this I am grateful to Max Sutherland and Terry Smythe, and for the help freely contributed by Jean-Pierre Jérôme, Robin Letellier, Peter Sawyer, John Bell, Linda Fardin, Julian Smith, Pat Young, Pat Lockwood, Peter Leroy, Marie Jetten, Roseanne Wilson, Jean Frances Burgess, and Rodney Won. I must acknowledge, as well, my former boss, Elizabeth Wylie, who supported my instinct in 1971 that we needed to visit this unusual theatre complex in Toronto.

It was a great pleasure to deal with everyone at Dundurn Press. The kind and sympathetic interest and treatment unfailingly offered by my editor, Kirk Howard, surpassed all of my expectations, as did the creative and sensitive layout of designer Andy Tong.

Finally, I am thankful for the patience and understanding of my husband, Richard, and my son, Blake, who lived with me through every word and picture.

ACKNOWLEDGEMENT OF PROJECT FUNDING

The Elgin and Winter Garden Theatres are owned by The Ontario Heritage Foundation, an agency of the Ministry of Culture and Communications.

The restoration and preservation of the theatres was made possible by grants from:

-the federal and provincial governments through the Canada-Ontario Cultural Development Agreement

-Environment Canada - Canadian Parks Service

-Ontario Ministry of Culture and Communications

-The Ontario Heritage Foundation

-The City of Toronto through the Toronto Historical Board

And Private Contributions of over $1,000

AT & T Canada Inc.
American Express Canada, Inc.
Apple Canada Inc.
BMW Canada, Inc.
Bell Canada
Bell Cellular Inc.
Birks Family Foundation
Bramalea Limited
Edward Bronfman
Businessland Canada Limited
Ceyx Properties Limited
CKO Radio Incorporated
The Cadillac Fairview Corporation Limited
Vivian & David Campbell & Family
Camrost Development Corporation
The Canada Trust Company
Canadian Imperial Bank of Commerce
Classic Mouldings Inc.
Canadian Tire Corporation, Limited
Comcheq Services Limited
Commonwealth Hospitality Ltd.
Corptech Systems Inc.
Coscan Development Corporation
Fidelity Investments Canada Limited
George A. Kelson Company Limited
Morgan and Bente Firestone
Harding Carpets Limited
Harlequin Enterprises Limited
Hewlett-Packard (Canada) Ltd.
Imperial Oil Limited

Kelly Services, Ltd.
William M. Mercer
Mrs. Paul S. Newell
Page Flooring Enterprises Inc.
Paradigm Electronics Inc.
Remenyi, House of Music
Sandra & Joseph Rotman
The Royal Bank of Canada
Scotiabank
Allan Silber
Skyway Equipment Company Limited
Snyder Furniture Limited
Joseph F. Stauffer Foundation
Lawrence M. Tanenbaum
The Toronto Dominion Bank
Toshiba of Canada Limited
Wardair Canada Inc.
The W. Garfield Weston Foundation

And Seat Endowments:

Acura
Marcy Adelberg
Richard M. H. Alway
Dr. & Mrs. William Appell
Peter J. Armstrong
Helen Arthurs
Ara & Ared Arzuman
Kent Banting
David E. Barlow
Janis Barlow & Ed Bowers
Hartley Barlow
Harry Barrett
Lois Becker
Gary Beechey
Beinhaker/Irwin Associates
Margaret A. Bell
Jeniva Berger
John Berges
Mr. & Mrs. R. Best
Brian G. Boyd
Bradbury Tamblyn & Boorne
Sally and Lawrence Brenzel
Greta Brett-Evans
Heather R. Broadbent
James B. Brotchie
Ralph Brown
Harriet Bunting Weld
K.H. Campbell
Cara Operations Limited
Neil Carragher
Mr. & Mrs. Hiles Carter
John Ceolin
Cherudon Futures Limited
J. Christodoulou
Julie Clark
James Clarkson
G. Clever
Janet Conover

Roberta Corey
John B. Cronyn
Aaron Currie
Helen Davidson
Joyce Devlin
Carmen Dunjko
Keitha M. Dunning
Durham Shoestring Performers
Anna-Stina Edhorn
Allard Edhorn
Elgin & Winter Garden Project Staff
Etobicoke Musical Productions
Gay Evans
Virginia Evans & Anita Taylor
C.B. Farrar
Mike Filey
Marlo A. Finlayson
James Fisher
Sheila Forbes
Robert Foster
M. Shirley Frazer
Lynda Friendly
Reginald Garbutt
Michael Gee
C. Gibbs
R-J Gilbert
Carolyn P. Gill
Edwin A. Goodman
Carol Graham
Grant Construction Company
Gordon C. Gray
Guild Electric Ltd.
George Gutierrez
A.A. Haasz
Vera Hall
David Hannivan & Company
David Harper
Ruth Hartman-Adams
Nona M. Heaslip
Jean Heeley
Helmhorst Investments Limited
Jim Henshaw
Katie and Peter Hermant
Mr. & Mrs. Mike Hirschberg
G.R.B. Hodgson
Richard L. Holbrook
Michael & Bridget Hough
Mark Hukezalie
Hunt Real Estate Limited
Shirley Irvine
Caryle Jakobsen
Calvin V. Johansson
Joan Johnston
Mildred Jose
Nina Kaiden Wright
Lesley Kempson
Janet Komars
Diane Lackie
John R. Latimer
Richard Lau
John B. Lawson

Paul LeBlanc
Howard J. Levine
Mrs. Ian Burns Lind
David G. Loree
Catherine Macdonald
Hartland M. MacDougall
J. Magee
A. Mahon
Dorothy Marriott
Donald S. Marshall
Dorothy Mathieson
Donald J. McCartney
The McConnell-Weaver Group
David McCullough
Stella McDonald
T.C. McHugh
Mark McLean
Donald McLeod
Donald M. McMurchy
Robert H. McNairn
Ina Meares
Media Communication Services Ltd.
Medi-Group Incorporated
Dale & Gordon Moore
J.H. Moore
Richard Moorhouse and Jean Simonton
Moriyama and Teshima Architects
T.V. Mosur
Owen J. Mougenot
Naruth Foundation
Nancy Nevile-Smith
Peggy Ng
Lisa Norrington
#1 Productions Ltd.
Robert Oloman
Bernard Ostry
Page Flooring Enterprises Inc.
Dianne Parnell
Ian Paterson
Margaret Ann Pattison
Ken Pauli
Jean Payne
Freda Pearl
Nancy Pearson
Dennis Perlin
William Petts
William C. Phoenix
Harold M. Povilaitis
Eleanor C.M. Prentis
Prolight Ltd.
Pussycat Purroperties
Robert J. Pyne
Susan E. Reid
Kati Rekai
Mr. & Mrs. Douglas Reynolds
Ed Reynolds
Carol H. Rykert
Marty Schmerz
Rocky Scrivo
Jacqui Shumiatcher

Mr. & Mrs. Monty Simmonds
Six-O-Nine Enterprises Ltd.
Carol Slater
Richard Smerdon
Marlene Smith
Christina P. Smith
Mabel Smith
Margaret J. Snell
Sam Sniderman
Marna & Bernie Snitman
Tom Sparling
Carol Sprachman
Mr. & Mrs. Emanuel Stoiou
Sure Print Ltd.
Douglas Tallon
Tapestry Music Theatre, Toronto
Richard D. Teminski
Theatre Five Willowdale
Joyce & Jack Thompson
Paul Thorner
Charles W. Tisdall
Chris Tossell
Toronto Black Creek Rotary Club
Toronto Real Estate Board
Trudie Town
Alan & Dora Track
Mr. & Mrs. Andrew Trklja
Rita Turner
Peter Turvey
June & Jack Verbeem
Jacob Verkade
James Wardlaw
Frances M. Weir
A.M.V. White
G. Widdifield
Webster Callahan Inc.
Jack R. Williams
Sheila Williams
Douglas C. Woolley
York Heritage Properties
Yorkminstrels
Anna Young

As well as hundreds of project volunteers who have donated thousands of hours on behalf of the project. Time is money and their contribution is greatly appreciated.

ACKNOWLEDGEMENT OF INDIVIDUAL PARTICIPATION IN THE PROJECT

The Elgin and Winter Garden Theatres Restoration Project has its roots in the 1970's in the Ontario Ministry of Culture and Recreation. Many hundreds of individuals, too numerous to list, have contributed to this project over the years both before and after the Provincial Cabinet decision to purchase the building in 1981. The current incumbents of key provincial positions affecting the project are listed below. A very special thanks is due to them, their predecessors, colleagues, assistants, staff and volunteers who had the vision and tenacity to believe in these theatres and work for their magnificent revival.

The Ontario Government:

David R. Peterson, Premier of Ontario
Christine E. Hart, Minister, Culture and Communications
David P. Silcox, Deputy Minister, Culture and Communications
Linda L. Stevens, Assistant Deputy Minister, Culture
Angela Longo, Director, Cultural Agencies and Industries Branch
Linda Loving, Director, Arts Branch

The Ontario Heritage Foundation Elgin and Winter Garden Advisory Committee

Directors
J.H. Moore, Chair
Joan Johnston
John Cronyn
Ted Teshima
Richard M.H. Alway

Staff
Robert Montgomery
Richard Moorhouse
C. Scott Alllington
Janis Barlow

The Elgin and Winter Garden Council:

Christopher Plummer, Honorary Co-Chair
Shelley Peterson, Honorary Co-Chair
Hilary Weston, Chair
Isabel Bassett
Martha G. Blackburn
Carole Bradshaw
Edward M. Bronfman
James R. Bullock
David M. Campbell
C. David Clark
Paul D.J. Clark
Adrienne Clarkson
George B. Cobbe
Marshall A. Cohen
J. Trevor Eyton
Fraser M. Fell
Morgan Firestone
Dr. James Fleck
Robert J. Foster
Dale Gee
Patricia Gray
Allan R. Gregg
Barclay Ann Heisey
Peter A. Herrndorf
Sydney Kessler
Robert Latham

Michael A Levine
Hugh L. Macaulay
Philip C. MacDonnell
Bernard Ostry
Morris A. Perlis
Frances Price
J. David Rae
Heather M. Reisman
Joseph L. Rotman
Benjamin L. Scott
Allan C. Silber
Jack E. Sinclair
Allan Slaight
Benjamin Swirsky
Lawrence M. Tanenbaum
Liz Tory
John Vivash
R. Michael Warren
Ken Yokoo

Seat Sale Committee:

Carole Bradshaw, Chair
Valerie Brown
Linda Camp
Anne M. Delicaet
Eveleen Dollery
Dale Gee
Jeanie Hersenhoren
Inta Kierans
Beverly King
Richard Laprairie
Peggie Lind
Gretchen McDowell
Eileen Newell
Frances Price

Project Staff:

Janis Barlow, Project Manager
Wendy Bisnath-Arjoon, Administrative Assistant
Gary Bovay, Building Security
Deborah Burgoyne, Development Assistant
Kit Carrothers, Marketing Assistant
Jerry Colman, Marketing and Media Manager
Aaron Currie, Assistant Project Manager
Alison de Peralta, Office Administrator
Jennifer Ginder, Development Officer
Christine Gutierrez, Collections Officer
Kevin Harper, Computer/Research Officer
Claire Hopkinson, Development Manager
Arnie Lappin, Marketing Officer
Graeme Shone, Building Security
Claire Smerdon, On-site Auditor
Victoria Steele, Donations-In-Kind Consultant
Thomasina Wallace, Site Assistant

Project Design Consultants

Mandel Sprachman, Architect
David Hannivan & Company, Restoration Consultant
Grant Construction, Construction Management
Richard Smerdon, Theatre Consultant
Robert Tanner, Acoustician
Neil Muncy, Sound Enhancement Consultant
Gordon Dowdell, Structural Consultant
Crossey Engineering, Mechanical and Electrical Consultants
Arts & Communications Counselors, Fund Raising Counsel
Carmen Dunjko, Design Consultants

Project Design Committee

Janis Barlow
Aaron Currie
David Hannivan
Paula Mannone
Richard Moorhouse
Hilary Russell
Mandel Sprachman